AN
ECONOMIC GEOGRAPHY
OF
WEST AFRICA

BELL'S ADVANCED ECONOMIC GEOGRAPHIES

General Editor

PROFESSOR R. O. BUCHANAN
M.A.(N.Z.), B.Sc.(Econ.), Ph.D.(London)
Professor Emeritus, University of London

A. Systematic Studies

AN ECONOMIC GEOGRAPHY OF OIL
Peter R. Odell, B.A., Ph.D.

PLANTATION AGRICULTURE
P. P. Courtenay, B.A., Ph.D.

NEW ENGLAND: A STUDY IN INDUSTRIAL ADJUSTMENT
R. C. Estall, B.Sc.(Econ.), Ph.D.

GREATER LONDON: AN INDUSTRIAL GEOGRAPHY
J. E. Martin, B.Sc.(Econ.), Ph.D.

GEOGRAPHY AND ECONOMICS
Michael Chisholm, M.A.

AGRICULTURAL GEOGRAPHY
Leslie Symons, B.Sc.(Econ.), Ph.D.

REGIONAL ANALYSIS AND ECONOMIC GEOGRAPHY
John N. H. Britton, M.A., Ph.D.

B. Regional Studies

AN ECONOMIC GEOGRAPHY OF EAST AFRICA
A. M. O'Connor, B.A., Ph.D.

AN ECONOMIC GEOGRAPHY OF WEST AFRICA
H. P. White, M.A., & M. B. Gleave, M.A.

YUGOSLAVIA: PATTERNS OF ECONOMIC ACTIVITY
F. E. Ian Hamilton, B.Sc.(Econ.), Ph.D.

AN AGRICULTURAL GEOGRAPHY OF GREAT BRITAIN
J. T. Coppock, M.A., Ph.D.

AN HISTORICAL INTRODUCTION TO THE ECONOMIC GEOGRAPHY
OF GREAT BRITAIN
Wilfred Smith, M.A.

THE BRITISH IRON & STEEL SHEET INDUSTRY SINCE 1840
Kenneth Warren, M.A., Ph.D.

AN
ECONOMIC GEOGRAPHY
OF
WEST AFRICA

H. P. WHITE, M.A.

Reader in Geography,
University of Salford

&

M. B. GLEAVE, M.A.

Senior Lecturer in Geography
University of Salford

LONDON
G. BELL & SONS, LTD
1971

ISBN 07135 1721 2

PRINTED IN GREAT BRITAIN BY NEILL AND COMPANY LTD., EDINBURGH

TO
JEAN and JEAN

Acknowledgements

Many of the ideas in this book were generated by our talks with other Africanists and by our familiarity with their writings. The three to whom we owe a special debt for the inspiration they have given us are Professor R. W. Steel, Dr. W. B. Morgan and Dr. B. W. Hodder. We are also greatly indebted to the late Sidney J. Wells, Professor of Economics at Salford, who read much of the manuscript and gave us much help, especially with Chapter 8.

Our grateful thanks are also due to Miss Margaret Parker and Mrs. Pauline Stuart of the Department of Economics and Geography at Salford for typing the manuscript and to Mr. R. Oliver of the Department for drawing the maps. Without their help the book would never have been completed.

We must also thank Mr. A. C. Bubb, Librarian of the University of Salford, and his staff for their help in obtaining books and data, and the staffs of the West African High Commission and Embassies for their material.

Lastly we must express our sincere thanks for the help and encouragement freely and patiently given by the General Editor, Professor R. O. Buchanan.

Contents

Tables

Maps and Diagrams

Authors' Note

Orthography

Many place-names in francophone West Africa are known by their anglicised spelling (thus: Wagadugu for Ougadougou), by translations (thus: Upper Volta for Haute Volta) or by peculiar hybridisation (thus: Cape Verde for Cap Vert: Portuguese Cabo Verde). But most must be rendered in their French form. For consistency therefore we have rendered *all* place-names in francophone West Africa in their French form, however well they are known by their English (thus: Sénégal for both river and country, Guinée and Côte d'Ivoire), and all in anglophone West Africa in their English form. A word of caution is necessary, a sounded terminal -e is accented in French but not in English. In both Lomé and Benue the terminal -e is sounded.

Currency

Prior to Independence the four Commonwealth countries had a common currency based on the West Africa £1 at parity with Sterling. The French West African currency was based on the *Franc Colonial Français Africain* (franc CFA) at 50 to the New Franc. Liberia uses the US $ and the Portuguese and ex-Spanish territories the Escudo and Peseta respectively.

After Independence all the francophone countries kept to the franc CFA, except Guinée and Mali, while West Cameroun left the Sterling bloc to join in 1962. The Guinée and the Mali franc were left to move independently (eventually downward) and at the time of writing Mali was seeking to rejoin the franc CFA bloc.

The Commonwealth countries introduced separate currencies, some of which moved independently of Sterling. Finally, only the Gambian and Sierra Leone currencies were devalued along with Sterling in 1967. We therefore decided to express all monetary figures in terms of the US $ for ease of comparison.

The Relationship of the Currencies to Sterling on 1st January, 1970

Gambia   — £G1: £1
Sierra Leone — 2 Leone: £1

Ghana	— 2.45 New Cedi: £1
Nigeria	— £N85–14–3: £100
CFA	— 660 francs CFA: £1
Liberia	— $2.40: £1

Mensuration

It was decided to express measurements in metric terms. All tonnages are thus given in metric tons.

CHAPTER 1

Essential Characteristics

West Africa is a clearly defined Region of continental scale. It is about 2,000 miles as the crow flies eastward from Dakar to Lake Chad and 800 miles from Accra northward to the bend of the Niger at Bourem. This is equivalent to an area enclosed by the quadrilateral London—the Caspian Sea–Basra–Barcelona–London, or to the whole of the USA east of the Rockies.

Within such a large area there will obviously be great differences in the physical environment, the economy and the society. West Africa, however, lacks the extreme variety and the complexity of regional differentiation encountered in the area between southern England and the Caspian Sea. It is more homogeneous in its level of economic development, though by no means completely so. Although the whole of West Africa is regarded as being economically underdeveloped, the progress towards a modern market economy in agriculture, industry and commerce does vary widely from place to place. Social homogeneity is less pronounced, though over the last century at least its principal external cultural influences have been Western in general and British and French in particular. These have been a distinct unifying factor, even if a somewhat superficial one. In short, while it is easy to over-emphasise monotony of physical and socio-economic features, it is equally easy to over-emphasise regional differences which are minor if viewed on a world scale.

Westward and southward extends the Atlantic Ocean, clearly separating West Africa from the outside world and in the past a major factor in its isolation from the rest of the world. This is reinforced by the coast, which functions more as a barrier, separating land and sea by screens of surf and mangrove swamp and by lack of natural harbours, than as the zone of contact it is in the North Sea basin or in the Mediterranean.

To the north lies the broad barrier of the Sahara Desert. For so long was it an impediment to circulation that it has become a cultural divide separating Tropical Africa (*l'Afrique Noire* of the French writers) from the Mediterranean lands (*l'Afrique Blanche*). The southern shores of the Mediterranean have more affinity in their landscape, culture and economy with the northern shores than with Tropical Africa. There is a strong case for regarding the Sahara rather than the Mediterranean as the northern limit of Africa. Even today there are only two motorable routes northward from West Africa, the Mauritanian route from St. Louis de Sénégal to Agadir and the Hoggar route from Agadès to Ghardaïa in Algeria.[1]

Only to the east is there a possibility of questioning the limits of West Africa. Gautier[2] regarded the Benue Trough as the boundary. But associated with this structural trough is the series of plateaux descending north eastward from the 4,069 metre volcano of Mount Cameroon to the low lying and swampy basin of Lake Chad.

These plateaux are sparsely peopled and in the southern part at least, inhabited by the Bantu peoples, who are culturally and linguistically distinguishable from those of Guinea and the Sudan. Furthermore, the communications across this barrier are very poor. South of Lake Chad is a good road from Maiduguri in north east Nigeria to Fort Lamy, capital of the Chad Republic. But the only other motorable crossings are in the extreme south, a very bad one across the Bamenda Plateau and one which is still very poor in places from Mamfe to Douala. Prior to 1960, when the British Cameroons were administered by Nigeria, the eastern flanks of Mount Cameroon were drawn into the ambit of Nigeria, but this area, together with the Bamenda Plateau, became in 1962 part of the Federal Republic of Cameroun, unquestionably Central Africa.

Thus West Africa is virtually cut off by land from the outside world, and for passengers or freight West Africa is linked with other parts of the world by sea and air. None of these barriers, however, was complete. The Sahara was crossed regularly and frequently after the domestication of the camel about the seventh century.[3] The desert, too, was outflanked by sea, after the period of Portuguese explorations in the latter half of the fifteenth century.[4] But these barriers were difficult and still are costly to cross. They were the cause of the isolation of West

Africa that is its first notable characteristic, though during the present century this has broken down more and more.

While it was true that there was a considerable mediaeval trade across the desert, gold, slaves and 'morocco' leather moving northward in exchange for salt, weapons and armour, and while Muslim culture followed in the wake of this trade to the Sudan, it is as well to remember that such basic inventions as the wheel and the plough were unknown to the indigenous cultures of West Africa. It was therefore impossible for these latter to make any significant technological advance. In contrast, however, the use of iron was widely though not universally known. It is also well to recall how many of the present day staple foods are exotics. Cassava, maize and rice, all staples of the Guinea Coast, were introduced during or after the sixteenth century.[5]

This isolation from external influences is matched by internal isolation, and this in spite of monotonously level relief and lack of mountain barriers. It is the result of a combination of sheer distance and lack of navigable rivers with extensive forest and woodland, and the widespread occurance of *trypanosomiasis*, transmitted by the tsetse fly, which precluded the use of draught or riding animals. Only in the Sudan could horses or camels be used, though lack of the wheel prevented the use of vehicles. It is not without significance that the most extensive and most highly centralised pre-European states, Old Ghana, Songhai, Mali and Bornu were in the Sudan.

Even today, with an ever extending road network and expanding vehicle fleet, this internal isolation still persists. In some areas, such as western Nigeria, southern Ghana and south eastern Côte d'Ivoire, the road net is relatively close meshed and the traffic flow heavy. But in other areas the road net is rudimentary and circulation limited. Even where road nets are developed, they are internal and do not extend over international or even provincial boundaries. In 1960 there were only three motorable roads across the 650 mile (1,165 kilometre) western frontier of Nigeria and only 8 roads across the 1,200 miles (1,930 kilometres) of Ghana's land frontiers. In addition, trunk roads and railways tend to run north and south rather than east and west, or more correctly from the seaports inland. This is partly because, until recently, most of the cash cropping was for

export. It is also the consequence of the distribution of climate
and vegetation. As outlined in Chapter 2, as a very general rule
the length of the wet season and the amount of rainfall fall off
northward from the Gulf of Guinea until the desert is reached.
Since rainfall is the chief climatic influence on the regional
distribution of vegetation, the latter has an east-west zonation.
For our purposes we may recognise four broad zones, Forest,
Guinea Savana, Sudan and Sahel. Because agriculture is the
principal economic activity, farming methods and production
are similarly zoned. Thus any internal exchange tends to flow
along the same axes as the flow of exports and imports.

Paradoxically, the attainment of political independence
between 1957 and 1960 by ten states has tended to increase
isolation by strengthening the existing frontiers. Independence
in general and the fragmentation of the Federation of French
West Africa in particular have led to the erection of customs
barriers and immigration control where none existed before.
On occasion frontiers have been closed for long periods, as those
between Sénégal and Mali and between Ghana and Togo.
While it is true, as Prescott[6] has shown, that these frontiers have
little or no meaning from the viewpoint of local circulation, and
while smuggling is on a large scale, they have affected large-
scale movement along the trunk roads, which can be easily
controlled.

Isolation, both internal and external, is therefore the first
essential characteristic of West Africa. The breaking down of
this isolation is the essential pre-requisite of economic development. But this involves heavy cost, especially where there are
the physical barriers such as coastlines and forest to be overcome
Secondly, the impossibility of providing the whole of West
Africa with a transport system of uniform quality and universal
extent has been a basic cause of differential economic development between and within the various countries. Thirdly, it has
put a premium on development of the interior. For high transport
costs effectively reduce the revenue from exports and increase
the price of imports. A higher proportion of the price received
on world markets of export crops from the Sudan is absorbed by
transport costs than that of exports from the Forest. Conversely,
higher transport costs raise the price of essential imports such as
petroleum, metal goods and cement in the interior compared

with the coast. For example, the relative retail prices of motor spirit in March 1961 were 100 at Lagos, 125 at Kano and 145 at Maiduguri.

A second characteristic of equal importance is the essential severity of the physical environment, a concept developed in Chapter 2. It is sufficient here to mention the general poverty of the soils. With few exceptions, their organic content and nutrient status are low. But because the breakdown of humic material is rapid, as is the consequent leaching of the soluable nutrients thus released, maintenance of fertility is difficult and upgrading almost impossible. Soils liable to laterisation are common and vast areas have been sterilized by a thick lateritic crust. Again, rapid alternation of waterlogging and complete drying out is common.

Soil degradation and associated erosion is an ever present danger. This is mainly the result of the destruction of the vegetation cover, more easily removed than restored. Thus monoculture of maize in the hinterland of Accra has led in a single generation to complete loss of fertility and the reduction of high forest to sterile grassland, while the Udi Plateau of Eastern Nigeria has become a classic area of gulley erosion.

The rate of evaporation is so high that unless there is constant rainfall, soil moisture soon falls below the level necessary to sustain plant growth. Soon after the end of the wet season, therefore, plant growth ceases, and with it agricultural activity. Consequently, over much of West Africa economic activity is at too low an ebb for too much of the year. There is another serious consequence. Because of lack of skill in storage, food is running low when the next rains begin. Physical energy is thus reduced just when maximum effort is needed to prepare the land and plant the crops. This is the so-called 'hunger season' denied by some writers,[7] but nevertheless real. The climate is also conducive to the proliferation of pathogens and the insect vectors, by which so many are transmitted. Unless controlled by costly measures, which must be extensively applied to have any lasting effect, they result in mental and physical debilitation among the people and the lowering of yields from crops and animals. Human beings are probably worst affected by filarial diseases such as hookworm, bilharzia and onchocerciasis, but malaria is endemic and sleeping sickness widespread, though

B

not on the same scale as in East Africa. Animal diseases, especially trypanosomiasis, prevent the keeping of cattle and horses almost everywhere in the Forest and Guinea Savana, while rinderpest is everywhere serious. Thus the diet lacks protein and milk (especially serious when babies are weaned), the supply of organic manure is short, and there are no animals for draft purposes. Plant diseases such as swollen shoot, which affects cocoa, maize-rust, and the rosette disease of groundnuts, reduce yields and on occasions threaten to deprive whole areas of their staple crop.

On the whole therefore the ecological balance is very fragile. Hunter[8] has shown how in Northern Ghana continued cultivation caused exhaustion of the riverain lands and their abandonment in favour of the watersheds. In consequence insect vectors could flourish uncontrolled in their uncleared natural habitats, and so the rivers, which must be visited regularly by man and beast, became a potent source of infection. The balance, however, is usually maintained if population densities are sparse and the economy is purely a subsistence one. But it is liable to severe disturbance with economic development and population growth. The difficulty and cost of restoring and maintaining this balance must be included in reckoning the cost of development.

The third major characteristic is the low overall density of the population and its uneven distribution. This very large region had only just over 96 million people in 1966. The exact number is almost impossible to calculate, because of the unreliability of many censuses and the different dates on which they were held. There is thus an approximate density of 35 per square mile (13·5 per square kilometre), very low by the standards of many monsoon lands, but nevertheless West Africa is on the whole more densely peopled than is Tropical Africa in general.

Such an average figure has, of course, little meaning. It conceals contrasts in rural population densities as those of Iboland, South Eastern Côte d'Ivoire, and the Kano Close Settled Zone, where figures may locally reach or exceed 500 per square mile (195 per square kilometre) on the one hand, and wide areas such as the Middle Belt of Nigeria, the Forest of South Western Côte d'Ivoire and Western Gonja in Ghana, where densities rarely exceed 5 per square mile

(2 per square kilometre). However, it must be remembered that in the absence of high yielding, continuously cropped and irrigated agricultural land any density figure exceeding 250 per square mile (100 per square kilometre) is exceptional. The Eastern Provinces of Nigeria as a whole have a density of only about 120 persons per square mile (46 per square kilometre) and Southern Ghana of about 75 persons per square mile (30 per square kilometre).

A distinguishing feature is the contrast between areas with relatively high population densities and contiguous areas of very low density. To some extent the population can be said to be arranged zonally, following those of climate and vegetation. Thus in general the coastlands and the Forest are the most densely peopled, the Guinea Savana sparsely inhabited, while densities in the Sudan are generally higher than those of the Guinea Savana, but lower than the Forest. Finally the density of population in the Sahel is very low indeed.

The true picture, however, is not so simple. Even in the Forest there are some areas of very sparse population, notably the south west of Côte d'Ivoire and of Ghana and the East Cross River Basin of Eastern Nigeria. On the other hand, in Côte d'Ivoire the Baoulé Salient of the Guinea Savana is more densely peopled than either the Forest to the south or the Sudan to the north. Again, the Sudan of Dahomey is very sparsely inhabited compared with the Kano Close Settled Zone. It is thus better to envisage the rural population of West Africa as being concentrated into 'islands', separated by wide areas of low population density, an idea first put forward by Hance.[9] In general most of the larger and more important 'islands' are to be found along the coast and in the Forest. With the exception of Bouaké (in the Baoulé Salient) there are few of importance in the Guinea Savana, while there are some very important ones in the Sudan and none in the Sahel.

The population is predominantly rural. Even in the indigenous Yoruba town the majority of the inhabitants are farmers. Urbanisation, though proceeding with increasing rapidity, especially in the coastlands and Forest, has not yet affected the majority of the population in any region. It is almost entirely a phenomenon of the colonial and post-colonial periods. Except in parts of the Sudan and in Yoruba-land (Western Nigeria), true indigenous towns are a rarity, while in Iboland (Eastern Nigeria) they are completely absent. There is an increasing gulf in the income levels and consumption patterns of town and country, but the highly sophisticated market provided by the larger towns such as Abidjan and Lagos is as yet very limited.

On the other hand, a fundamental feature of the rural population is its mobility. Migration, short distance and long distance, seasonal, semi-permanent and permanent, is a widespread characteristic. There is a considerable movement from rural areas of population pressure to areas where labour is in keen demand, to the towns, the mines, the plantations and the cocoa belts. This readiness to move in search of self-betterment is a contributory factor in the possibilities of economic and social advance.

In this and other ways the structure of the indigenous society is not without consequences on economic development. The almost classless society, the close ties of the Extended Family and the vesting of land ownership in even larger groups such as the Clan, all delay technological and economic development, being especially inhibiting to the accumulation of capital. Economic development and the breakdown of the indigenous society are inevitable concomitants, however much the latter has been regretted, and whatever the social difficulties that result.

While this predominantly rural population is undergoing social and economic change, extremely rapid in some areas, very slow in others, the economy is still largely subsistence based. A varying proportion, over 90 per cent in some areas, of the output from farming, herding, collecting and hunting is consumed by the family producing it. A subsistence-based economy is characterised by its slow rate of change, though it is never completely static, because of its low level of technology and of capital equipment. Even in a subsistence economy that lacks monetary exchange, however, some forms of capital accumulation are possible.[10]

In the classic African subsistence economy there is plenty of land for every cultivator in the community; it is therefore valueless. Every cultivator, however, has a right to as much land as he can cultivate, and this depends on the size of his family. Wives are therefore a valuable economic resource and may be looked on as capital. In addition the cultivator has a few simple tools, hoes, cutlasses (machetes) and fish-nets. Trees may also be regarded as capital. Customary law preserves harvest rights to the person planting trees, even when these are on fallow land which has reverted to the tribe or clan. Members of these large groups also enjoy rights of collection from wild trees as well as hunting and fishing rights.

Obviously a subsistence economy was everywhere the original basis, though some form of exchange would have evolved at an early date. It is, however, possible to distinguish a number of successive stages of economic development which overlaid the subsistence basis as a sort of palimpsest, for in some measure all the stages still survive. While the most appropriate names for the stages are political terms, it is as well to remember that the economic and political stages were not co-terminal. Quickening economic development was as much a feature of later Colonial times as of the Independence era.

The subsistence stage can be called the *Indigenous Economy*, the second stage the *Proto-Colonial*, which spans the period 1450 to 1885. While there were considerable developments of Trans-Saharan trade during the mediaeval period and up to the eighteenth century, which were part of a general flowering of civilisation in the Sudan,[11] general economic development cannot be said to begin until the present century and then as a consequence of European penetration. The first permanent European trading stations were set up on Gorée Island (off Dakar) in 1445 and at Elmina (Ghana) in 1482. But though numerous 'factories' were set up all along the coast by at least half a dozen European nations, their influence remained very limited for four centuries. It was not until the second half of the nineteenth century that increased activity by explorers and traders led to the partition of West Africa in the period after the Berlin Agreement (1885) chiefly by France and Great Britain. There were, however, some German areas, eliminated in 1914–18. Portuguese and Spanish influence was even more limited, while from the first (1847) Liberia was nominally independent.

The third stage, the *Colonial Period* began with the Berlin Agreement of 1885 and lasted until 1945. Partition of West Africa among the colonial powers led to the imposition of civil order and of an administration, the way thus being cleared for economic development. The principal form this took was the encouragement of export cropping by peasant farmers. Plantations were actively discouraged in the British territories. But though they were allowed and even encouraged by the other powers, their development was patchy and limited. The flow of export crops and of imported trade goods was eased and extended by railway construction from 1885 onwards and by the rapid spread of lorry haulage after World War I. At first therefore the main capital investment was in transport. To a lesser extent it went into mining and lumbering, activities which themselves led to further transport development. The other principal objective of investment was in commercial enterprises such as the distribution of import goods and the buying of export crops.

The inter-war years saw great expansion in cash cropping and some development in industries processing crops, minerals and timber for export. The depression years of the 1930s were a considerable setback, especially in capital works, but exports enjoyed considerable preference in the respective metropolitan countries.

The fourth stage, called here the *Independence Era*, though most countries did not become independent until 1956–60, began in the years immediately after 1945 when the pace of development quickened, both the cause and the consequence of vastly increased capital investment. This came in the form of government aid from the metropolitan countries and, after independence, from the UN Agencies and from other countries; of the ploughing back of profits by established trading firms; and of private foreign capital, though the extent to which this was encouraged varied from country to country and from regime to regime. Much capital was invested in creating an infra-structure of ports, roads and railways, electric power and water supplies. There was also investment in manufacturing industry of all kinds but particularly of the simpler consumer goods. Minerals were also further developed, exploration for oil and the exploitation of iron ore particularly. Indigenous capital went mainly into road transport, into houses for rent in the larger towns, and into small workshop industries and retail businesses.

In all these activities employment and output rose rapidly. But though agricultural production increased, it was more through increased population and some modification of peasant production than through the application of capital and technology. Compared with the others, the agricultural sector tended to stagnate. Though employing the majority of the active population, it remains basically unaffected by investment and innovation, in spite of constant governmental efforts to remedy the situation.

The objects of governments, colonial and independent, since 1945 may be summed up, as far as the economy is concerned, as being to increase exports to gain foreign currency for capital goods, for materials such as cement and petroleum which are vital to economic expansion, and for the social sector, notably education and health. They are also concerned to maintain a flow of aid funds and foreign capital to supplement overseas earnings. All this in an effort to reach the point of 'take-off', when economic growth will be self-sustaining.[12]

This development, has however, been very uneven, varying from country to country and from region to region within each country. The main growth points have been the larger coastal cities. Dakar, Abidjan, Accra and Lagos have reached a size and an employment structure in commerce, service industries and even manufacturing that put them into the world class of major cities. The smaller centres of the coast and Forest may be less economically advanced, but are much more so than those of the interior, and everywhere there is a gulf between town and country.

The rural areas, however, vary greatly among themselves. In terms of infra-structure, numbers of motor vehicles, development of small market towns and growth of purchasing power, the south eastern Côte d'Ivoire and the cocoa belts are as economically advanced as any rural area of Tropical Africa. But other parts of the Forest, such as the East Cross River Basin and that of Côte d'Ivoire west of the Bandama River, have scarcely begun to be developed, except perhaps for timber exploitation. On the whole, the Sudan has not evolved as far as have the coast and the Forest in its economic and social development. But here, too, there is a considerable regional differentiation within the zone. The Guinea Savana and Sahel Zones are scarcely affected by modern development. But these zones illustrate plainly the fact that economic progress inland tends to be concentrated into corridors along the trunk lines of communication, for there is to be found what little development has taken place.

As a general rule, countries with a higher proportion of their area within the Forest, which includes the greatest concentration of natural resources, are the most advanced. These are notably Côte d'Ivoire and Ghana. In 1962 the latter's *per capita* income of $179 was the highest of all West African states. For Côte d'Ivoire the figure was $89. Otherwise, only Nigeria exceeded $50 per head, while the landlocked countries of Mali and Haute Volta achieved only $37 and $39 per head respectively.[13] Land-locked countries, largely because of the burden of transport costs, are at a disadvantage compared with coastal countries with equally limited resources of cultivable land and exportable crops. Obviously, too, countries with a large proportion of desert and Sahel, notably Niger, have even more limited opportunities.

On the whole, while economic development is as rapid as in most tropical areas, *per capita* figures for gross national product and for overseas trade remain very low by world standards, though high by African. To this difficulty may be added political fragmentation. Only Nigeria with some 45 million has a population which is large by world standards. Of all the other countries only Ghana has a population in excess of 5 million. Thus purchasing power and potential markets within each country, with the possible exceptions of Ghana and Côte d'Ivoire, are very limited. This inhibits the establishment of large scale manufacturing industry, at least on a competitive basis.

The pattern of overseas trade and of the supply of capital, while varying from country to country, in general provides a contrast between the English and French speaking countries. Generally, with the exception of the 'left' governments of Guinée and Mali, the latters' ties with France are very much closer, even after independence, than those of the former with the United Kingdom. Traditionally, the links of Liberia have been closest with the USA, while those of the Portuguese colonies of Guinea and São Thomé and the former Spanish island of Fernando Po (which became independent in 1968 as part of Equatorial Guinea) have been virtually solely with their respective metropolitan countries.

It must be concluded that in spite of the spectacular developments since 1945, much of the indigeneous economy remains more or less modified, but essentially unimpaired. The overwhelming majority of the active population, even in Ghana, Côte d'Ivoire and Western Nigeria, is engaged in agriculture, while the majority of their output is for subsistence. This means that the influences of the physical environment affect the economy more than is usual. The links between the two are examined in the next chapter.

REFERENCES

1 In 1960 the Tanezrouft route (Gao–Colomb Béchar) was the only route in use, but by 1970 the Hoggar route had regained its former importance. The best account of modern routes is: Thomas, B. E., '*Trade routes of Algeria and The Sahara*'. *Univ. of California publications in Geog.*, 1957, or '*Modern Trans-Saharan Routes*'. *Geog. Review*, 42, 1952, pp. 267–282

2 Gautier, E. F., *L'Afrique Noire Occidentale*, Paris 1935, pp. 11–15

3 Bovill, E. W., *The Golden Trade of the Moors*, London, 1958 (rev. 1968), Chap. 3

4 The best collection of accounts of early voyages is by Astley, T., *A new general collection of Voyages and Travels*, London, 1745. *See* also Blake, J. W., *Europeans in West Africa 1450–1560*, London, Hackluyt Society, 1942

5 Mauny, R., '*Notes historiques autour des principales plantes cultivées de l'Afrique Occidentale*'—*Bull. d'IFAN*, 15, 1953, pp. 684–730

6 Prescott, J. R. V., *The geography of frontiers and boundaries*, London, 1965, p. 63

7 Miracle, M. P., '*Seasonal hunger: a vague concept and an unexplored problem*'. *Nigerian Inst. Soc. & Econ. Research Conference proc.*, 1958, pp. 36–44

8 Hunter, J. M., '*River blindness in Nangodi, Northern Ghana*', *Geog. Rev.*, 56, 1966, pp. 398–416

9 Hance, W., *African Economic Development*, New York, 1958, p. 5. *The Geography of Modern Africa*, New York, 1958, *passim*

10 For the theory of subsistence economies see Clark, C. & Haswell, M., *The Economics of subsistence agriculture*, London, 1964

11 Bovill, E. W., *op cit.*, Chaps. 7–10

12 Rostow, W. W., *The Stages of Economic Growth*, Cambridge, 1960

13 Hodder, B. W., *Economic Development in the Tropics*, London, 1968, p. 2

CHAPTER 2

The Consequences of the Physical Environment

Because the majority of the people are engaged in agriculture and because for the most part farming is practised at a low technological level, the economy is affected closely and directly by the physical environment. Its consequences must therefore be carefully considered, even in a book on economic geography.

CLIMATE

Over the whole of West Africa the climate is tropical by Koppen's definition, nowhere having a mean monthly temperature of less than 18° C. In the Forest and the coastlands it is only on one or two nights in the year that the thermometer falls as low as 15° C.

Temperatures are uniformly high and there is very little seasonal variation. Along the coast the January mean is about 27°, and at Freetown the annual variation is only 1.0°, at Accra 1.7° and at Lagos 2.1°. Northward the variation increases, but is never significant. At Kano it is 3.9° and at Gao 9.5°. Everywhere the diurnal variation is greater than the seasonal (Table 2.1). With clearer skies the January range is also greater everywhere than the July. In Accra the mean diurnal range in January is 7.7°, but in Gao this rises to 16.1°. In July the diurnal ranges are 5.1° and 13°2. respectively.[1]

These constant high temperatures obviously have consequences on the vegetation, and therefore upon the agriculture. They also affect the nature and distribution of pathogens. It has, too, been said that night is the winter of the tropics and this has economic and particularly social consequences. Life in villages and towns is to a great extent lived out of doors.

In Yorubaland the night markets are a feature of both economy and society. Clothing is more a luxury than a necessity, but one on which a high proportion of many people's income is spent, for clothing is an important 'status symbol'. Conversely, houses need not be designed to keep heat in, and a smaller proportion of incomes needs to go into housing, fuel and protective foods than in temperate lands. Finally, it should be noted that the rapid decomposition of organic matter in

TABLE 2.1
MEAN TEMPERATURES—DEGREES CENTIGRADE

| | MEAN MONTHLY TEMPS. | | | MEAN DAILY MAX. AND MIN. TEMPS. | | | | | |
| | Jan. | July | Range | *January* | | | *July* | | |
				max.	min.	range	max.	min.	range
Freetown	26·7	25·7	1·0	29·4	24·0	5·4	28·3	23·2	5·1
Accra	27·0	25·3	1·7	30·8	23·1	7·7	27·6	22·5	5·1
Lagos	26·7	24·5	2·1	32·5	21·0	11·5	27·9	21·1	6·8
Kano	22·8	26·7	3·9	29·8	13·4	15·4	30·7	21·7	9·7
Gao	22·7	32·2	9·5	30·8	14·7	16·1	38·8	25·6	13·2

constant high temperature may well be one of the chief reasons why there can be unconfined spread of towns and cities without main drainage or more than the most rudimentary forms of sanitation.

It also means, however, that there is enough warmth (and light) for vegetation to grow all the year round. The limiting factor is the rainfall. Seeds will germinate and plants grow all the while there is sufficient moisture in the soil. With high temperatures and low humidities growth ceases with the onset of the dry season, which is thus a period of rest. The dry season therefore is the equivalent of the cold season in temperate lands, and in the farming calendar the season for preparation for new crops and for non-agricultural activities. A very long dry season will thus mean a long period of under-employment of resources. However, just as in North West Europe the growing season can be extended by applying artificial heat, in West Africa it can be done by irrigation, which is less costly. But with some exceptions, irrigation plays little part in the indigenous economy.

So the distribution of rainfall through the year is of equal importance to the amount. 100 cms. distributed in significant amounts through eight months of the year produces a different vegetation, different crops and different farming methods from another area where the same rainfall total is confined to four months. The distribution and severity of the wet and dry seasons is related to the two air masses directly affecting West Africa. Tropical Maritime air originates in the South Atlantic and is hot, humid and normally unstable. Tropical Continental air originates over the Sahara and is hot, very dry and very stable.

The junction of the two masses is the Inter-Tropical Front. At the surface its position fluctuates daily but is clearly defined and is mapped daily.[2] It tends to move southward to reach the Gulf of Guinea coast, which it may affect for a few days in late December or early January. It then retreats northward to the latitude of the Niger Bend in July. Thus the further north, the shorter the period during which a place is affected by Tropical Maritime air and therefore the shorter the wet season.

Garnier[3] lists four fundamental differences between the two masses:

	Tropical Maritime	Tropical Continental
1. Vapour pressure:	Over 20 millibars	Consistently under 20 millibars
2. Saturation deficit:	Under 10 millibars	Always over 15 millibars and often over 20
3. Relative humidity:	Over 65 per cent.	Never over 65 per cent. for five days or more
4. Diurnal temperature range:	10° or less. Temperatures never below 16°.	11° or more. Night temperatures often below 16°.

In June, 1956, one of the authors experienced a complete change from Saharan to Equatorial conditions in half an hour as the ITF passed over Dakar. A similar swift transition is recorded offshore by ships which keep meteorological records.

At any time of the year, therefore, the various weather types are aligned in east-west zones, though the position of each zone will vary according to the time of year. H. O. Walker distinguished five such zones, and his classification may be followed.[4]

ZONE A. This is the zone of Tropical Continental Air, the condition universally known as the *harmattan*. Very stable and very dry air drifts from the north and north east with very light winds. The skies are cloudless, but there is often a dust haze. The days are hot, temperatures of 35° or more in the Forest and over 38° inland, but the nights are cool. The low humidities cause discomfort by drying the mucous membranes of nose, throat and eyes.

ZONE B. Immediately to the south of the Inter-Tropical Front is a zone of clearer weather with warmer nights but hotter days. There is plenty of bright sunshine but on one to five days a month there may be a convectional thunderstorm.

ZONE C. This is the zone of high humidities and unstable air, traversed from east to west by 'disturbance lines'. These are up to two hundred miles long and their approach is heralded by a line of black cumulo-nimbus clouds towering to 6,000 or 9,000 metres. This passes overhead accompanied by squalls of 60 m.p.h. (96 kms.) but of short duration. They are not dangerous as are tropical revolving storms, of which there have been only a few instances in West Africa. A few minutes later there follows a torrential downpour, accompanied by continuous lightning, which frequently affects power-lines and electrical installations. The wind soon dies down and after about half an hour the rain eases to a drizzle, which may last a further hour. Since a disturbance line may bring 5 to 8 cms. of rain (intensities of up to 23 cms. per hour have been momentarily recorded at Accra) and at certain seasons the passage of a disturbance line is a daily occurrence. 25 to 50 cms. a month may fall at any one place.

ZONE D. In this zone humidities are high and there is an almost continuous cloud cover. Daytime temperatures are relatively cool, rarely exceeding 30°. Rainy days are the rule, and while there may be convectional storms, the rainfall tends to be prolonged and less intense. In Freetown however up to 38 cms. have been recorded in 24 hours. This is usually called 'monsoon' rain. This zone is limited to the coasts and the Forest Zone.

ZONE E. Reaches West Africa only during July and August and then only the regions within about a hundred miles of the Guinea coast. Although the air is very humid, it is also stable and so brings a distinct break in the rains, accounting for the second dry season experienced by places with an equatorial as opposed to a tropical regime. Because of the cloud cover, days are cooler, 27–30°, and nights warm, 21–24°. But insolation is still high and plant growth is vigorous if the soil is moist.

In general it can be said that on the south coast and up to 150 miles inland there are two wet seasons, the second being of shorter duration and lesser intensity. The short break in the rains gets less reliable and disappears altogether, giving way to a zone with a single rainy season. Northward this gradually gets shorter and less intense until the Sahel/Sahara border is reached and an occasional shower is all that remains. The growing season thus varies from 11 months in south west Ghana, and even more in the Niger Delta, to one month in the Niger Bend.

There are some variations in this pattern. First, the north-south alignment of the coast, backed by high plateaux, north of Cape Palmas prolongs the monsoonal influence as far as the République de Guinée. Secondly, there is an anomolous dry zone along the coast between Accra and the Nigerian border. The rainfall at Accra averages only 72.6 cms. and at Lomé 78.7 cms. Thirdly, the coastal rainfall in Southern Nigeria rises significantly eastward until at Debunscha on the slopes of Mount Cameroon an annual mean of 762 cms. is recorded.

The general absence of physiographic barriers reinforces this east-west zonation of climate. Since climatic influences are the principal ones affecting distribution of vegetation, at least in the large, the vegetation will display a corresponding east-west zonation. Climate and vegetation obviously are the main controls over agriculture, the basic activity. Climate is thus the best single basis for regional differentiation, certainly much more so than physiography, but it is not a complete one.

Population, for instance, does not show this same marked pattern, nor does economic activity.[5]

There remain three general points on the influence of rainfall. In the first place, the rain falls largely in the form of downpours from disturbance lines, convectional storms or particularly heavy monsoonal rain. It thus encourages the leaching of plant nutrients and can lead to extensive sheet and gully erosion. Secondly, it can be very variable and, as is usual, variability increases with declining totals. In the period 1921–50 the annual mean at Accra was 73.43 cms. but the absolute range lay between 27·5 cms. and 115·0 cms. In 13 of the 30 years it was below 70 cms. and in 12 years above 70 cms. December, the dryest month, had a mean of 2·64 cms. and a range of 0·0 to 13·4 cms. June is the wettest, the mean 17·7 cms. and the range 0·2 to 60·86 cms. This results in wide seasonal fluctuations in crop yields of both annual and tree crops. While locally some crops may fail completely, a variety of subsistence crops is normally grown and there are no recorded cases of serious and widespread famine. In the Forest the farmer is not dependent on a single food crop ripening at any one time of year. In the Sudan there is greater dependence on the grain harvest, but total failure of the whole wet season is mercifully rare and local.

Thirdly, the influence of rainfall on the distribution of vegetation and on crop growth is not a direct one. Of more importance is the effectiveness of the rainfall. As we have seen, this is partly a function of its distribution through the year. But it is also the result of the balance between moisture added to the soil, mainly by precipitation but also by flooding or by irrigation, and the moisture lost by evaporation and by transpiration.

'Potential evapotranspiration' is the amount of moisture lost in this way, expressed in centimetres. The rate varies surprisingly little with the various vegetation types, even between forest and a pure stand of maize. Short grass cover on experimental plots is as good a guide as any. But it depends a great deal on the amount of radiation, surface temperature, atmospheric humidity and wind speed. Obviously potential evapotranspiration is much greater in the Sudan, subjected to harmattan conditions for much of the year, than it is on the Guinea Coast, where humid Tropical Maritime conditions pertain for all but a few days in the year. Garnier has shown that in Tropical Maritime conditions potential evapotranspiration from a grass surface is 7·5 cms. per month. This is a measure of the rainfall requirement each month to ensure plant growth.

In all but the very wettest areas, the potential evapotranspiration over the year exceeds the rainfall. The growing season therefore tends to end as soon as precipitation falls below the rate of moisture loss. Even in South West Ghana/South East Côte d'Ivoire and in the Niger Delta there is a deficit over one or two months. Elsewhere precipitation is in excess only during the wet season, when moisture accumulates in the soil and there is runoff as well.

Garnier recognises three zones in the area between 3° and 7°E (the western part of Nigeria) and between the coast and 15°N.

Zone 1. Coast to 8°N. 12 months atmospherically humid, that is, mean monthly temperature over 20°, mean vapour pressure over 20 millibars, mean relative humidity over 65 per cent., 9 months over 7·5 cms. of rainfall.

Zone 2. 8° to 11°N. 6 months atmospherically humid and 6 months over 7·5 cms. of rainfall.

Zone 3. North of 11°N. Less than 6 months of humidity and of 7·5 cms. of rainfall monthly. Mean minimum temperatures less than 16° and mean diurnal range over 11°. Mean annual rainfall less than 100 cms.

SOILS

For a number of reasons soil and vegetation in West Africa must be regarded as parts of a single complex. The reserve of nutrients is not only in the soil, but also in the vegetation associated with it. In the Forest the reserve may in fact be principally in the latter and the most luxuriant vegetation may be growing on soils which by themselves are deficient in nutrients. To make a complete clearance of Forest vegetation for agriculture may therefore bring difficulties. These may be increased by allowing bare soil to be exposed for longer than brief periods.

Climate is the overriding influence upon soil formation.[6]

In Northern Ghana the soils of the Voltaian sandstones are similar to those of the Pre-Cambrian granites of Western Gonja. But the climate is similar and consequently the vegetation is a similar kind of savana. On the other hand, soils developed on the Cretaceous and Tertiary clays, sands and gravels of various coastal structural basins, which occur under a wide variety of climates, vary equally widely. The *terre de barre* soils of Lower Dahomey and Togo, formed under 100–125 cms. of rainfall, are reasonably fertile, whereas the Benin Sands, developed under a rainfall in excess of 250 cms., are almost sterile.

While climate and vegetation may be the principal agents in the development of soils on the continental scale, however, geology and geomorphology have an overriding influence on a local scale. The geology is especially important where soils are relatively young. In the *terre de barre* of Togo and Dahomey and in the Accra and Trans-Volta Plains of Ghana, soil types are directly related to geological outcrops.[7] The formation of lateritic hardpans is often related to the distribution of certain erosion surfaces.[8]

The principal factors in soil formation were brought out by C. F. Charter in his soil classification developed in Ghana.[9] He recognised four soil orders, each based on the two chief influences upon their formation, (i) Climophytic Earths (climate and vegetation), (ii) Topoclimatic Earths (mountainous relief and climate), (iii) Topohydric Earths (relief and drainage) and (iv) Lithocronic Earths (Geology and age). In West Africa the first Order is the most common, the others being of local importance only.

When making a study of soils in a particular area, it is normally convenient to use the 'catena' concept developed by Milne in East Africa[10]. Over the monotonously rolling surface of much of West Africa, the soils of the interfluves, mid-slopes and valley floors will be quite different, but this triple combination may be repeated over a wide area and characterise it as an agricultural region. Agricultural region X is characterised by a combination of soil types, $A+B+C$. The boundary with region Y is crossed when at least two elements are replaced by different soil types, thus giving combinations of $A+D+E$ or $F+D+C$.

C

The constant high temperatures and long periods of humidity speed up bacterial decomposition of humic matter, thus rapidly releasing nutrients, which are liable to be leached out of the upper horizons of the soils by the heavy rainfall. Bacterial activity doubles with each five degree Centigrade rise in soil temperature. Ploughing speeds the process still further, and land thus treated shows at first an apparent increase in fertility, but nutrient levels then decline very steeply.

In general therefore the humic content of the soils is low, but very much more so in the Savana. In the Forest there is a constant leaf fall, and the continuous cover slows up bacterial activity. In the Savana, not only are there fewer trees, but leaf fall stops during the long dry season. In addition the soil is deprived of much organic material through annual burning. But the level of the humic content is not only important as a source of direct supply of nutrients. Of all the components of the soil complex, humus has the greatest ability to 'hold' plant nutrients and to prevent them from dissolving in the groundwater. On the other hand the holding power of kaolinitic clay is very low. Unfortunately tropical weathering results in kaolin being a large proportion of the clay minerals.

It has been found that there is a slow build-up of nitrogen in the soil during the dry season, rapidly rising with the onset of the rains and then falling to a low level with leaching and rapid plant growth. Planting is done with the first rains so that germinating crops do not suffer a nitrogen deficiency, and of course there are two annual peaks in the nitrogen level in the south with its two rainfall maxima in the year. In general phosphorous is deficient, the supply from mineral decomposition is limited and the reserves quickly leached. The main supply comes from decomposition of humus, and phosphorous and to a lesser extent nitrogen and potassium are the key elements in our understanding of the traditional systems of land rotation, for they are the elements whose deficiency shows up first, and it is the shortage of these elements that is responsible for 'exhausted' or 'worked out' soil.[11]

The replacement of nutrients lost through leaching and harvest therefore presents problems. The supply of manure is limited by lack of animals. The use of green manure has been widely canvassed by research workers, especially in Western Nigeria and Casamance (Sénégal). When green crops are ploughed in, however, there is a temporary decline in available nutrients and reduction in fertility just when the need is greatest. The application of artificial fertilisers offers the best opportunity, but they must be used with care and are very liable to be lost through leaching. Their cost is a great drawback in a predominantly subsistence economy, but there have been good results from their use on the groundnut crop of Northern Nigeria (see page 123). For the agriculturalist in West Africa it is difficult even to maintain the rather low levels of fertility; it is almost impossible to raise them, and especially to create a crumb structure in the soil.

Another widespread climatic consequence is that rapid seasonal alternation of waterlogging and drying out in combination with high temperatures may lead in certain soils to the silica being rendered solvent and leached out. This increases the clay fraction and therefore the proportions of the sesquioxides of iron and aluminium. When such soils are exposed to air by the removal of the vegetative cover they may develop a crust or hardpan of what is in effect iron ore, which may be several feet thick. Such soils are called *ferralitic* and, where the hardpan is present, *lateritic*. Laterites are common in the Savana Zones and fossil laterites are occasionally found in the Forest Zone. Obviously a thick crust will entirely inhibit agriculture.

Another climatic factor is the intensity of the rainfall. This together with the fragile or non-existent soil structure means that soil erosion, both gulley and sheet, is a potential threat. There is little erosion in the Forest, where vegetative cover, natural, fallow or crops, is normally complete, but wherever the cover is thinned out by over-cultivation or low rainfall, there is evidence of erosion. Very serious gulleying is a marked feature of the Udi Plateau in Eastern Nigeria, especially along its scarp edge in the region of Enugu.[12] It is also a serious threat in Northern Ghana[13] The intense rainfall also may lead to compacting the surface of the soil, if vegetative cover is thin. This increases runoff, so that soil-moisture replacement is lost, and liability to erosion is increased.

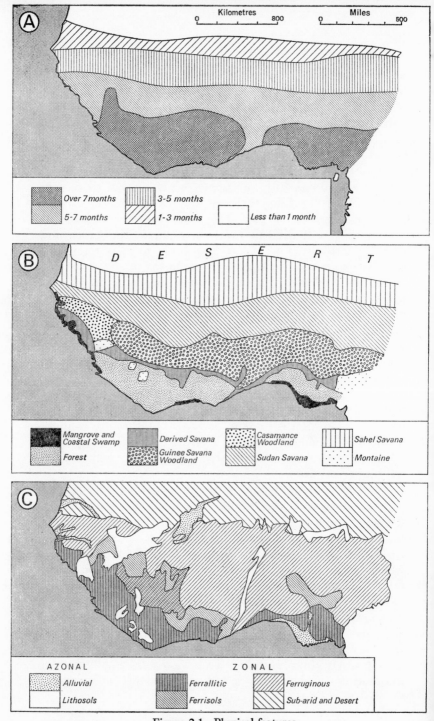

Figure 2.1. Physical features

(A) Number of months with an average rainfall in excess of 10 cms. (after Harrison Church).
(B) Vegetation zones (after Keay).   (C) Principal soil types (after Pullan).

Survey work on the distributional aspects of soil types has been patchy. Much work has been done in the Forest Zone, especially in the principal areas of cash cropping, the cocoa belt of Ghana and Western Nigeria and South East Côte d'Ivoire, and of food cropping, in Lower Dahomey and Southern Togo. But the literature on the soils of the Guinea Savana and the Sudan is scanty, though the French have done much survey work in the groundnut areas of Casamence, and Richard Toll in Sénégal. The position is best summed up by Pullan.[14]

With only local exceptions the Forest soils are climophytic Most are old and are developed on highly weathered parent material, which cannot supply mineral bases at a sufficient rate to replace those lost by leaching or harvest. Occasionally, as on the Birrimian outcrop of southern Ghana, the parent material is partially weathered and rich in bases, so new supply balances losses. In general, however, Nye and Greenland consider the forest soils of Ghana to be reasonably fertile. The same would apply to those of Côte d'Ivoire and Western Nigeria, but those of Eastern Nigeria are much poorer, because of the higher rainfall.

Some Forest soils are ferrallitic, but the continuous plant cover prevents the formation of lateritic crusts, though occasionally there may be outcrops of fossil laterites. Soils of valley bottoms and swamps which are seasonally waterlogged have a considerable accumulation of organic material and are frequently very acid. If the swamps dry out seasonally this may lead to toxic concentrations of salts brought to the surface by efflorescence. Such soils lead to the presence of savana patches in areas of high forest in South West Ghana and South East Côte d'Ivoire. Finally, we must note the saline soils of the mangrove swamps of the Rivières du Sud (Sierra Leone and Guinée) and the Niger Delta.

Most of the literature does not distinguish between the soils of the Guinea Savana and of the Sudan. Pullen, however, differentiates between two important groups of cultivable soils, (i) ferruginous and (ii) reddish brown and brown. The ferruginous are typical of the Guinea Savana, the latter of the Sudan. The Savana soils, as already indicated, are in the main much poorer than those of the Forest, and it takes longer to restore their fertility after cultivation. In the main the soils are also climophytic. There are also extensive lateritic areas. Seasonally-flooded bottom lands also have their own characteristic soils.

In contrast the soils of the coastal savanas of the Accra-Dahomey dry zone are for the most part lithochronic. Much younger, they vary considerably with the rock outcrop. Some of these are montmorillanite clays, which give rise to intractable clay soils, plastic when wet and brick-hard when dry, and low in organic matter in spite of their dark colour, known as *poto-poto* soils.[15]

Generalisations about soils can easily be misleading. In the first place, however, it can be said there is an intimate connection between soil and vegetation as far as the nutrient status of the former is concerned. Secondly, soils are normally not of great fertility, while maintenance of the natural level under continuous cultivation is difficult. Most soils are deficient in plant nutrients. Finally, husbandry must be carefully adjusted to the essential environmental fragility. If it is not, soil deterioration is rapid.

VEGETATION[16]

In any consideration of West African vegetation it must be clearly borne in mind that extensive modifications have been made by Man almost everywhere. Because there are few visible field boundaries in the form of hedges, banks or walls; because the irregular cultivation patches are surrounded by bush fallow in all stages of regeneration; and because 'wild' trees stand, often in profusion, among cultivation and fallows, it might be inferred that Man's influence on the vegetation is less than in other parts of the world. But with the simplest of equipment, no more than 'cutlass' (*machete*), hoe and fire, he has modified to some extent virtually the whole of West Africa. True 'virgin' forest or natural woodland or savana are rare, if they exist at all.

It must therefore be understood that while the division of West Africa into vegetation regions is based on natural vegetation, areas of true natural vegetation must be regarded as very limited. Nevertheless, these regions are important in the study of the agricultural economy, for they reflect the range of crop-possibilities within each region and therefore the types of agriculture and the development potential. Equally, however, it must be understood that when we talk of the Forest Zone, the whole or even the larger part of the zone is not literally Forest, in the sense that the tree canopy is unbroken. Areas of true Forest are restricted, and every year are diminishing. Instead, the Forest Zone should be imagined as the area with climatic and soil conditions which will support a particular range of crops and encourage particular farming systems. Similar provisos are made for the other zones or regions.

Like the climatic zones, which they obviously reflect, the principal vegetation zones are aligned east and west. They can be recognised as:

1. Forest
2. Guinea Savana Woodland
3. Sudan Savana
4. Sahel Savana

In addition we can recognise certain distinctive and important vegetation regions, which are either discontinuous or too limited to be described as zones.

a. Strand and lagoon margins
b. Coastal Savanas of the Accra-Dahomey dry belt
c. Montane Vegetation

These regions may not exactly coincide with those recognised on a phytogeographic basis, and may not reveal sufficient diversity for a biogeographical study, though they follow closely the work of at least one botanist, H. G. Baker.[17] Many botanists and biogeographers distinguish between Tropical Rain and Moist Semi-deciduous Forest, and between a Northern and a Southern Guinea Savana.[18] But these distinctions do not appear to have any reflection in crop distribution.

1. FOREST. In natural conditions the Forest has a storied structure. The larger trees form with their crowns a continuous canopy about 40 metres high, through which the crowns of

'emergents' occasionally project up to 60 metres above ground. Many writers recognise a lower canopy at about 18 metres, which is very dense and is responsible for casting the deep shade characteristic of the forest floor, though others consider there is no statistical evidence for this. Beneath the trees is a shrub layer, but insufficient light reaches the ground and the undergrowth is seldom thick enough to prevent easy movement.

Agricultural practice aims at clearing the lower layers and replacing them with cultivated plants. Useful natural plants, notably the oil palm (*Elaesis guineensis*), are preserved from felling and firing and so multiply at the expense of other species. Where tree crops have been planted, the ground is 'brushed' or cleared of woody weeds annually, permitting no natural growth. Eventually only residual upper canopy and emergent trees remain to shelter the cocoa, cola (*cola nitida*) or oil palms. Where food cropping is the rule, provided the land is allowed to revert to fallow for sufficient periods, regrowth is assured. But if the fallows are short and if the soils are degraded by over-cultivation, the regrowth will cease and the forest will give way to thicket or even grassland.

The Forest Zone coincides with a rainfall of over 125 cms. and, more important, with nine or more humid months. Its extent is somewhat limited, while areas of true forest are even more so. An extension of the main Equatorial Forest runs through southern Nigeria, narrowing westward until finally petering out in the region of Porto Novo in Dahomey. To the west is an isolated block in southern Ghana, Côte d'Ivoire and Liberia. In Côte d'Ivoire an embayment of the savana, the Baoulé Salient, almost divides this block into two. The only considerable areas of high forest remaining are:

1. The Eastern Cross River Basin in Eastern Nigeria
2. The Niger Delta
3. The Forest Reserves of Ondo Province in Western Nigeria
4. Southern Western Ghana
5. South Western Côte d'Ivoire and Liberia

Apart from timber supplies, these areas are important as the last supplies of virgin land for cultivation.

The extent to which both northern and southern boundaries

of the Forest Zone have retreated over the past century is a matter of speculation, as is the possibility for regeneration around the periphery. Keay[19] recognises a Derived Savana Zone on the northern edge up to fifty miles wide, though Morgan and Moss[20] argue for greater stability in the northern boundary. Either way, the transition is sharp, the boundary being crossed in a few miles, though beyond this galleries of forest extend along the water courses far out into the savana, while higher ground is crowned with isolated forest patches.

In the south the extensively cultivated *terre de barre*, with relict oil palms and fetish groves of forest species, is not really savana country, though shown as such on the small scale vegetational maps.[21] Along the northern boundaries of the Accra Plains there is evidence that the coastal savanas have replaced forest in the past fifty years and the same can be said for the coastal-thicket zone between Accra and Takoradi.

2. GUINEA SAVANA WOODLAND. In this context, in the absence of any marked socio-economic consequences, there is no need to distinguish a Derived Savana Zone.[19]

The Guinea Savana is a woodland, that is to say, the tree canopy is broken and there is a herb layer. The woodland is continuous over vast areas though tree densities vary widely. The natural appearance is hard to reconstruct, for there are few reserves and these are mostly planted with exotics. Everywhere drastic modification has resulted from the annual burning, which no government measures have succeeded in reducing. Burning is not only for cultivation, but is to stimulate grass growth for grazing. It is also carried out for hunting, the grass being fired to drive out game.

The tree species are naturally more limited than in the Forest, and the numbers are further reduced to the more fire-resistant ones. In addition, the trees tend to be stunted. Only a few species which augment the food supply, notably the shea (*Butyrospernum parkii*) and dawadawa (*Parkia spp.*) are preserved as far as possible. Under the trees the ground is normally covered with annual grasses, which grow tall during the rains, but which wither away during the dry season. The irregular fodder supply is one of the difficulties in keeping animals.

In Western Sierra Leone and the coastlands of Guinée and Portuguese Guinea oil palms are a feature of the thicket and savana lanscape, and it would seem meaningful to distinguish as some workers have, a Casamence Woodland. Here, too, the concept of Derived Savana would appear more meaningful. In Port Loko District of Sierra Leone vegetation catenas can be distinguished, consisting of barren interfluves with a thick lateritic crust supporting a thicket growth of useless *Lophira alata*, cultivated mid-slopes with oil palms and occasional forest trees, and broad, swampy bottoms with grass and raphia palms, used for rice cultivation.

3. SUDAN SAVANA. Again it is very difficult to reconstruct its natural appearance. In places it may have been a true savana, grasslands with tree-clumps. In others a woodland with a herb layer. The tree species would, however, have been thornier than those of the Guinea Savana. The influence of man is virtually universal, however, in particular in modification by fire. In addition, large areas of the Sudan in Northern Nigeria, Northern Dahomey, Haute Volta and Northern Côte d'Ivoire have been so extensively cultivated that only scattered trees still remain among vast stretches of crops and grass fallow.

4. SAHEL SAVANA. The low rainfall and length of the dry season prohibit cultivation, except in areas of natural flooding and of irrigation. The vegetation is mainly thorn scrub and annual grasses which grow in clumps. It shades out by slow degrees into the desert. For convenience the boundary is usually taken to be Lake Chad—the Niger Bend—the mouth of the Sénégal. But there is some nomadic cattle herding well to the north of this line, and the northern limit of this activity might be said to be the real limit of West Africa.

a. STRAND AND LAGOON MARGINS. There are three sub-divisions, the sand dunes, salt water swamps drying out seasonally, and permanent salt water swamps. The coconut palm is exotic to West Africa, but since it is the only large plant which will grow on the dunes and since the coconut crowned dunes have been the first sight of West Africa for so many travellers, it is fair to regard them as typical. The seasonal swamps have a vegetation of reeds and grasses, but the permanent swamps are characterised by mangroves (*Rizophera spp.*) The main areas of mangrove are the Rivières du Sud and the Niger-Cross Delta. Here the swamps are very extensive and form real barriers between land and sea.

b. COASTAL SAVANAS. These are the response to the Accra-Dahomey dry belt. They extend from Winneba, west of Accra to Lomé, for, as we shall see (p. 85), the *terre de barre* of Togo and Dahomey is not true savana from the economic viewpoint. Because the wet season is so long the short grass remains green for most of the year. Tree and bush species differ from those of the interior savanas.

c. MONTANE VEGETATION. Seldom in West Africa is the land sufficiently high to result in modification of the vegetation. The main areas of land over 900 metres are:

1. The Futa Djalon and Mount Nimba plateaux of middle Guinée and the Guinée-Sierra Leone-Liberia boundary.
2. The Jos Plateau of Northern Nigeria
3. The plateaux of the Nigeria-Cameroun border

Up to 900 metres there is scarcely any floristic modification as a result of climatic change. Above that level a thick tree cover is usually found, because of increased rainfall. Over about 1,500 metres trees are found only in gulleys. The plateau surfaces are normally under grass, though this has probably been created by Man. An important aspect of these tsetse-free highlands, scattered amongst tsetse-ridden areas, is their possibilities for stock rearing and for growing a different range of exotic crops, such as the Irish potatoes cultivated on the Jos plateau.

STRUCTURE & PHYSIOGRAPHY

The geological structure and physiography have been adequately described elsewhere[22]. There is no need to repeat the work here as their effects on differential economic development have been much less than in regions such as North West Europe. Thomas,[23] however, has evolved a useful working hypothesis which bases land classification surveys undertaken for development purposes on the geomorphology. The nature of the geology of course effects the distribution of economic minerals, but this aspect is dealt with in Chapter 6. The African surface evolved over a very long time and has developed almost irrespective of structure. It presents a monotonously rolling plateau of moderate height with wide shallow valleys and broad, flat interfluves, with an occasional inselberg or mesa rising above, or more rarely a scarp edge. Apart from the occasional river crossing this landscape presents few obstacles to communication.

The drainage pattern, however, has evolved in recent times and has resulted in the connection by trunk streams of inland drainage with the sea. Thus river profiles are interrupted by breaks of slope which provide barriers to navigation and possibilities for power generation.

The coast, which has important implications for port development, stretches for some 2,400 miles (3,860 kms.) from Cape Verde to Mount Cameroon and can be divided into three sectors:[24]

1. CAPE VERDE TO CAPE ST. ANNE (650 miles: 1,050 kms.). Here submergence has created a series of vast rias, the *Rivières du Sud*. Impressive as they may appear on the map, their utility is reduced by the formidable estuarine bars and fringe mangrove swamps. There are only two good natural harbours, the Rade de Dakar and the Sierra Leone River. The swell from the south west gives way to one from the north west, north of Freetown between October and May, but breaks with less violence than in the Gulf of Guinea. The tidal amplitude is high by West African standards, but does not exceed two metres.

2. CAPE ST. ANNE TO THE BENIN RIVER (1,350 miles: 2,170 km.). Throughout, the smooth, almost featureless coastline is continually beaten by the fierce south westerly surf, which has amplitudes of up to 250 cms. This prevents any but small, specially designed boats from being able to land. This stretch has two contrasting types of coast.

The first is the dune and lagoon coast, called the *Dahomey type*. The sea has piled up a continuous littoral dune complex backed by seasonal swamps or lagoons. The latter are both longitudinal and transverse, the estuaries and minor *rias* of the small rivers entering the longitudinal lagoons, which may be continuous over long distances. It is possible to travel by launch 275 miles (442 kms.) between Cotonou and the Niger along them. This coastal type extends from Cape St. Anne (Sierra Leone) to Southern Liberia, from Sassandra to Cape Three Points and from the Volta to the Benin River.

The second is called the *Elmina type*, and here variation is provided by the close approach of low plateaux to the coast. While dunes form across estuaries and valley mouths, usually backed by small lagoons, the dunes are interrupted by low bluffs. These protect beaches to the leeward from the full force of the surf. Along the Gold Coast between Cape Three Points and Ada these formed the sites of the early European castles, the first of which was Elmina, built in 1482. Along the other section of Elmina coast, between Cape Palmas and Sassandra, there are no such castles, as the hinterland was more inhospitable. This was the *Côte des Mals Gens*, whose inhabitants were suspected of cannibalistic tendencies.

3. THE BENIN RIVER TO MOUNT CAMEROON (400 miles: 640 kms). Here offshore depths increase more gently and the swell breaks with diminished violence. There are 18 entries to the Niger listed in the 'Africa Pilot'. Most are 'dead' but all these mouths are open to the sea. But the eastward coastal drift, estimated to move 1·0 to 1·5 million tons of sand a year past any given point along the Guinea Coast, forms wide, shallow and continual changing bars. The channels, too, are lined with continuous mangrove swamps. The estuaries of the Cross and Rio del Rey are of similar nature.

ENDEMIC DISEASE IN THE ENVIRONMENT[25]

Attention was drawn in the Introduction to the proliferation of pathogens and the vectors by which so many are transmitted. We can divide them into three groups, those affecting human beings, domestic animals and crops.

Of human diseases associated with a tropical environment, malaria is most widespread. The breeding activity of the anopheline mosquitoes closely follows the rainfall regime. Along the Guinea Coast activity is continuous, but inland it gradually declines to only five months of the year in the Sudan and Sahel, provided there is no standing water. In contrast with the Far East, malaria in West Africa is a killing disease of infants rather than a debilitating one of adults. Surviving infants build up a considerable immunity. In human beings, sleeping sickness (*trypanosomiasis*), spread by the tsetse fly, tends to be most common in the Guinea Savana and to be rare in the Forest. Most widespread of all are the debilitating filarial diseases. These include hookworm, guinea worm, bilharzia (with its water-snail vector), and *filariasis*, which in the form of *onchocerciasis* may cause widespread blindness (transmitted by the *simoleum* fly).

These diseases, together with those generally associated with low standards of living and hygiene, notably cerebro-spinal meningitis, of which there are annual epidemics in the Guinea Savana and Sudan, and smallpox, of which there are occasional outbreaks in the larger towns, are greatly reduced by rising living standards. Almost full protection is given by the taking of anti-malarial prophylactics, wearing of shoes as a protection against hookworm and guinea worm, and avoiding rivers. Unfortunately, much of the social life revolves round river and well, the principal sources of infection.

Malnutrition, both a cause and a consequence of other diseases, is widespread. Calorific intake is seldom deficient, but protein is notably so. A single example will suffice. Due to the prevalence of animal *trypanosomiasis*, milk is almost non-existent in the Forest and Guinea Savana. Infants are breast fed for three years, then forcibly weaned on a most unsuitable diet of starch and pepper, very deficient in protein. There is no doubt that over much of West Africa debilitating disease, malnutrition and agricultural practice have formed a vicious circle only slowly being broken. A complete remedy requires the environment as a whole to be improved, not just a particular factor within it.

The principal animal disease, *trypanosomiasis*, spread by the tsetse fly, is widespread everywhere except in the Sudan and Sahel. It affects chiefly cattle and horses. Rinderpest is endemic but can be more easily controlled by inoculation. International co-operation in disease control is vital. In the 1950s along the Ghana-Haute Volta frontier, the British authorities were attempting to control *trypanosomiasis* by eradicating the habitat of the tsetse, while the French were trying to do the same job a few miles away by inoculating the cattle! A happier example is the success of international locust control.

Plant disease may be even more troublesome. The threat of swollen shoot to Ghana's essential cocoa crop is sufficiently well known. In the early 1950s maize rust threatened to wipe out this staple food crop in the Accra-Dahomey dry belt. An unidentified virus destroyed the coconut groves in Ghana east of the Volta, and the *cigatoka* is a constant threat to the banana industry of West Cameroun.

CONCLUSION

The natural and the human ecology and their inter-relationship is a complex study. An outline of this relationship, which is vital to the understanding of the West African economy has been given on a scale broad to the point of superficiality. On a very broad scale, too, some indications have been given of this relationship as a factor in spatial variations in the economy. On a local scale areal differentiation is even more complex. An impression of monotony within the major regions can easily be given, but this is the result of constant repetition over wide areas of considerable minor variations. In south west Nigeria, Moss has related land use, soils and geomorphology and has mapped them in detail.[26] In an area of some 1,200 square miles (3,100 square kilometres) of the south western end of the Cocoa Crescent, he recognises 17 biogeographical regions of considerable contrast, and this excludes the coastal regions.

The ecological balance within the natural environment is essentially a fragile one. If the relationship between vegetation, soils and water balance is disturbed by clearance or over-cultivation, the whole complex can be destroyed and the area rendered infertile by soil degradation and erosion. Thus in the Densu valley near Accra high forest has been replaced by infertile *imperata* grass in less than fifty years. Over-simplification of the human-natural ecology has led to the failure of many land re-settlement schemes and better understanding to the success of at least one, the Anchau scheme of Northern Nigeria.[27]

In general, the Forest offers the greatest opportunities. Soils are more fertile and the rainfall regime allows the greatest range of crops, including the high-value tree crops. The likelihood of seasonal failure of the rains is minimal and the dry seasons short. Crops are therefore maturing and can be harvested over the whole year. The food supply is thus constant, plentiful and reliable. Apart from agriculture, the forests provide a source of timber. Finally, proximity to the coast reduces the cost of imports and exports.

The Guinea Savana has perhaps the most difficult environment of any zone. Savana soils are poorer and the dry season longer than in the Forest zone, which precludes the tree-crops of that zone, while the annual crops of the Sudan, notably ground-nuts, are not suited to the longer wet season of the Guinea Savana. Diseases are even more serious than in the neighbouring zone. The range of crops is even more limited than in the Sudan, few cash crops can be grown and virtually none is suitable for export. Animals are prohibited by tsetse and timber products are limited.

Possibilities in the Sudan are greater, though more limited than in the Forest. Tree crops are impossible and the annual plants suitable for cash crops are of lower value. There are additionally the heavier burdens of transport costs to and from the ports. Annual harvests also lead to seasonal food shortages.

The Sahel is an area of very restricted possibilities. Without irrigation cultivation is impossible, and stock rearing, because of limited water supply and seasonal fodder shortage, must be on a very extensive scale.

REFERENCES

1   Climatic statistics are published by the Meteorological Departments of most West African governments. *See* also: Meteorological Office, '*Tables of temperature, relative humidity and precipitation—Part 4. Africa, etc*'. London, H.M.S.O., 1958

2   Clackson, J. R., '*Seasonal movement of the boundary of northern air*', Accra, Met. Dept., Tech. Notes 5, 1957 (mimeo)

3   Fosber, F. R., Garnier, B. J. & Kuchler, A. W., '*Delimitation of the humid tropics*', Geog. Rev., *51*, 1961, pp. 333–347

4   Walker, H. O., '*The Monsoon in West Africa*', Accra, Met. Dept., Tech. Notes 9, 1958 (mimeo)

5   White, H. P. & Gleave, M. B., '*The West African Middle Belt—environmental fact or geographers' fiction?*' Geog. Rev., *59*, 1969, pp. 123–139

6   Mohr, E. C. J. & Buren, F. A. van, *Tropical Soils*, The Hague, 1954, (esp. Chap. 3)

7   White, H. P., '*Environment and Land Utilization in the Accra Plains*', W. African Sci. Assoc., *1*, 1954, pp. 47–62
———— '*Terre de Barre, the basis of a West African agricultural region*', Bull. d'IFAN, *27*, 1965, pp. 169–182

8   Brückner, W., '*The Mantle Rock ("laterite") of the Gold Coast and its origin*', Geologische Rundsch., *43*, 1955, pp. 307–327

9   *see* Brammer, H., '*Soils*'. Chap. 6 in *Agriculture and Land Use in Ghana*'
    Wills, J. B. (Edt.), London, 1962

10   Milne, G., '*Some suggested units of classification and mapping, particularly for
    E. African soils*', *Soil Res.*, *4*, 1935, pp. 183–198

11   Nye, P. & Greenland, D. J., '*The soil under shifting cultivation*'. Tech.
    Comm. Commonw. Bur. Soil. Sc., Farnham Royal, 1963

12   Grove, A. T., '*Soil Erosion in Nigeria*' in *Geographical essays on British
    tropical lands*, Steel, R. W. & Fisher, C. A. (Edts.) London, 1956

13   Hilton, T. E., '*Land Planning and resettlement in Northern Ghana*', *Geog.* *44*,
    1959, pp. 227–40
    Clancey, J. L. & Ramsey, J. M., '*Land use, soil and water conservation in the
    Northern Territories of the Gold Coast*', *African Soils*, *3*, 1954, pp. 338–353

14   Pullan, R. A., '*The soil resources of West Africa*'. Chap. 7 in *Environment
    and Land Use in Africa*, Thomas, M. F. & Whittington, G. W. (Edts.),
    London, 1969

15   Combeau, A., '*Contributions à l'étude de la fertilité des terres de barre*', *Agrm.
    Trop.*, Nogent, *11*, 1956, pp. 490–506

16   Moss, R. P., 'The ecological background to land use studies in tropical
    Africa, with special reference to the West'. Chap. 8 in Thomas &
    Whittington, *op cit.* (14)

17   Baker, H. G., 'The ecological study of vegetation in Ghana'. Chap. 7
    in Wills, *op cit.* (9)

18   Keay, R. W. J., *An outline of Nigerian vegetation*, Lagos, 1953
    —— *Explanatory notes on the Vegetation Map of Africa*, London, 1959
    Note. In his later work Keay makes no distinction between the Tropical
    Rain Forest and the Moist Semi-Deciduous Forest.

19   Keay, R. W. J., '*Derived Savanna—derived from what?*', *Bull. d'IFAN*, *21*,
    1959, pp. 427–438

20   Morgan, W. B. & Moss, R. P., '*Savanna and forest in Western Nigeria*',
    Africa, *35*, 1965, pp. 286–294

21   White, H. P., '*Terre de barre—the basis of a West African agricultural region*',
    Bull. d'IFAN, *27*, 1954, pp. 169–182

22   Richard-Molard, J., *Afrique occidentale française*, Paris, 1952. Harrison
    Church, R. J., *West Africa*, London, 1963

23   Thomas, M. F., 'Geomorphology and land classification in tropical
    Africa', Chap. 6 in Thomas & Whittington. *op cit.* (14)

24   White, H. P. '*The ports of West Africa, some geographical considerations*',
    Tijd v Econ En Soc Geog, *50*, 1959, pp. 1–9

25   Moss, R. P., *op cit.* (16)
    May, J. M. (Ed.), *Studies in disease ecology*, New York, 1961
    Davey, T. H. & Lightbody, W. P. H., *The control of disease in the tropics*,
    London, 1956

26   Moss, R. P., '*Soils, slopes and land use in a part of south-western Nigeria*',
    Trans. Inst. Brit. Geogr. *32*, 1963, pp. 143–168

27   Nash, T. A. M., *The Anchau rural development and resettlement scheme*,
    London, H.M.S.O., 1948

D

CHAPTER 3

Indigenous Society

In order to understand development of the West African economy, it is necessary to consider certain aspects of indigenous society. As Polanyi observed,[1] the primitive subsistence economy is embedded in the society and does not exist as a separate set of practices and relationships apart from the social organisation. Thus land is acquired through one set of social relationships (e.g. membership of the clan or other social group), while the labour to work it is obtained through another (e.g. the acquisition of wives from other social groups). Again, the employer-employee relationship is unknown. Men work together because they are related or have other social obligations to each other. An individual works to fulfil his social obligations, or to maintain his prestige and the status to which he is entitled and not for a monetary wage.

'Indigenous' presents problems of definition when applied to society or economy. 'It is common,' writes Southall[2] 'to regard tribal Africa as timeless and unchanging.' In fact, however, African societies and their economies have always been liable to change. Of the changes resulting from internal influences, the gradual evolution from hunting and gathering, through shifting agriculture to rotational bush fallowing even to permanent cultivation[3] is, perhaps, the most important. On the other hand new crops, tools and weapons have been introduced from outside West Africa and integrated into the traditional economy. Indeed, things introduced in one century have come to be considered as indigenous in a later one. But such changes have taken place within a system characterised by a kin-bound social structure and largely self-sufficient economy, and it is this system we describe as indigenous and traditional.

Since 1885, the pace of change has quickened. The traditional social system had been transformed and with it the character of the economy in large parts of West Africa. These changes have resulted in participation in exchange economy and in industrialisation. Thus towns have become more numerous and larger and therefore have become more important than formerly as agents of social and economic progress. New centres of employment have been created associated with plantations, mines and forests. Tribal systems, no longer politically autonomous, have changed under these external stimuli with which they have become interlocked. Finally new political and social systems have grown up to challenge the traditional ones.

THE DISTRIBUTION OF POPULATION [4]

West Africa has 31·7 per cent. of the total population of the continent living on 20·2 per cent. of the continental area, and overall population density is 16 per square kilometre compared with 10 for the whole continent. Within West Africa, however, population is unevenly distributed among nations and relative to area. National populations (1964 estimates) vary from 324,000 in Gambia to 56·4 millions for Nigeria, although most are small. Indeed only Ghana, with a population of 7·5 millions, and Nigeria have populations in excess of 5 millions (Table 3.1). In terms of the relationship between area and population there is a major contrast between anglophone West Africa which has 69·1 per cent. of the population on 17·4 per cent. of the area, and the remainder. Thus population densities range from 61 per square kilometre in Nigeria to less than 1 per square kilometre in Mauritanie, with the former British territories the most densely populated in the sub-continental area, if the Cape Verde Islands are excluded (Table 3.1).

We have seen in Chapter 1 that, viewed on a continental scale, the distribution of population in West Africa has a marked west to east alignment, with belts of relatively dense population, one in the Forest Zone and one in the Sudan separated by the more sparsely settled Guinea Savana Woodland. These population belts reflect the differing agricultural opportunities of the zones. The Forest has the greatest range in terms of choice of crops, especially those produced for export, while yields of food crops are greater and reliability of harvest is more assured than in the other zones. The Sudan Zone, whilst lacking this breadth of opportunities, enjoys advantages not found in the Guinea Savana Zone in the production of annual cash crops such as groundnuts and cotton. These population belts also reflect external trade relations. The traditional markets for exchange with North Africa lay in the Sahel and Sudan Zones. Whereas some have declined with the disappearance of trans-Sahara traffic others have flourished after road and rail connections were established with the coast. Modern markets lie overseas and demand is strong for the products of perennial plants grown in the Forest, while proximity to ports has led to early exploitation of its mineral resources.

But population distribution is not so clearly zoned as the factors of the physical environment may appear to be. Closer examination of distribution patterns reveal a tendency towards concentration into discontinuous 'islands',[5] separated by areas of much lower densities. The largest and most important islands, the cocoa belts of Ghana and Western Nigeria, Iboland in Eastern Nigeria, and the south-eastern parts of Côte d'Ivoire are to be found in the Forest. But here also are the sparsely populated areas of Southern Liberia and South Western Côte d'Ivoire, of South-Western Ghana and the Cross River Basin of Nigeria. There are also important 'islands' in the Sudan zone, notably the Mossi area of Haute Volta and the Sokoto and Kano regions of Northern Nigeria. In the Middle Belt, which Harrison Church equates with the Guinea Savana, such 'islands' are few, small and less important. They are confined to the agglomerations around Korhogo and Bouaké in the Côte d'Ivoire, to the Yoruba, Nupe and Tiv lands of Nigeria and to certain upland areas, such as the Jos Plateau and the central Atakora Mountains in Dahomey where physiography provided a refuge for small tribes.

A second major feature of the general distribution of population is the contrast between east and west. The area east of a line running north from Abidjan to the Niger Bend contains most of the large population 'islands' and supports approximately two-thirds of West Africa's population. Such a line also approximates to a cultural divide separating peoples of eastern and western origin. To the north-east the Hausa are culturally

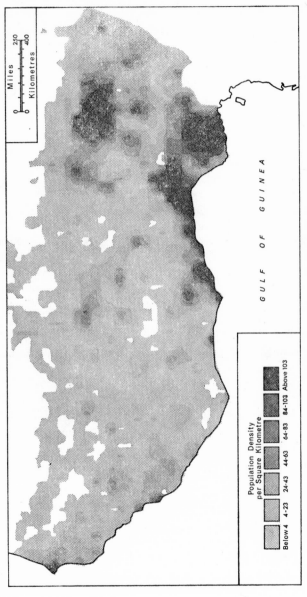

Figure 3.1. Population density

linked more with the peoples of Bornu and the Nile basin than with their western neighbours. Whereas to the north-west the Songhay and Malinké have developed their population 'islands' in the floodplains, the Hausa cultivated both the floodlands and the rainlands of the plateau east of the Niger and Sokoto valleys. In the south the line separates the rice cultivators of the western forests from the yam cultivators to the east.[6]

A third feature of population distribution is the marked density gradients from very high to very low densities associated with population 'islands' both large and small. Thus densely settled areas lie cheek by jowl with sparsely settled areas. The former occupy relatively small areas of West Africa, the latter are extensive even in countries such as Ghana with overall population densities which are high by West African standards.

Viewed on regional and local scales, population distribution is influenced by many factors both physical, social and economic. Fundamental is the collection of people into tribes, some of which form the basis of the large population 'islands' discussed above. Others form the basis of smaller nucleii which do not show up on maps in which administrative units form the statistical frame. Further, some of the large tribes are subdivided into smaller groups so that the structure of some of the larger 'islands' is multi-nuclear. Densities tend to be highest in the centre of these nucleii and diminish away from the centre. Until recently it has been common to leave a less densely occupied 'no-man's land' of forest or thick 'bush' between neighbouring tribes, such as that between the Yoruba and the Bini. Where tribes are small, on the Jos Plateau a single tribe may inhabit only a single village, this may be surrounded by such a no-man's land. A reserve of land is thus provided into which peoples have migrated after the establishment of peaceful conditions during the Colonial Period.[7]

Some tribes were able to support large population concentrations, either by enslaving their neighbours, thus depopulating the surrounding areas, or by relying upon their crops exacted as tribute. The Hausa city states had clearly defined roles, Zaria being one of the slavers. The low overall densities of much of the Guinea Savana Zone in Nigeria and the concentration of peoples upon defensive sites in upland areas is thus partly a consequence of Zaria's warrior activities. Peaceful conditions have resulted in movement from these nucleii into the sparsely settled plains. Simultaneously the population has spread more evenly over the tribal area.

Other factors influencing population distribution include the character of the soils, supply of drinking water and distribution of disease pathogens and their vectors. Light, easily worked soils are preferred, which are generally to be found on the erosion surfaces and their dissected remnants rather than in the river valleys. Consequently many of the concentrations of population occur on plateaux and hilltops, not, as in Western Europe, in the river valleys. These latter are generally narrow, except in their upper reaches in the north. Here the Manding and Songhay live in the only major riverain concentrations of population. Drinking water supplies are particularly critical during the dry season and, along with other factors notably slave raiding, account for the low densities in the 'Middle Belt'. The incidence of disease is more local in its effects. It has recently been shown, for example[8] how river blindness has resulted in a withdrawal of settlement in the Red Volta valley in Nangodi, Northern Ghana, leaving a totally depopulated area cheek by jowl with a densely settled one.

Several consequences follow from the pattern of population distribution and from the changes just indicated. The concept of overpopulation is a difficult one to define precisely but it seems clear that a few areas are overpopulated, notably the Ibo and Ibibio heartlands, where densities are locally over 360 per square kilometre. But areas of underpopulation are much more extensive. It is paradoxical, in view of the proximity of population concentrations, that agricultural development schemes in these underpopulated areas, the Niger Agricultural Project at Mokwa is an example, have failed partly because they were unable to attract labour. The more successful settlement schemes have been those set up across a path of spontaneous migration such as the Shendam scheme in Nigeria and those associated with the Cabrais movement in Togo. It is also paradoxical that the level of tsetse infestation remains high in much of the Guinea Savana Woodland Zone because the levels of population density are below those necessary to reduce the 'bush' sufficiently to restrict the fly's breeding grounds, when densely settled areas exist not far away.

Perhaps the most important feature of the distribution pattern is that it has always been liable to change. Certain recent changes have been indicated, but important changes also took place before the Colonial Era. Population distributions were constantly in flux, strong tribes extended their tribal area at the expense of weak. Migration in search of fresh farmland was common. The grasslands north of the forest margins were more attractive for settlement than the forest itself, which was difficult to clear.

This is illustrated in Nigeria, where the powerful Yoruba kingdom of Oyo was established in the grasslands. The Ibo are also a Savana people. But both are to be found at the present time mainly in the Forest. Before European influence was intensified, the Forest was only sparsely settled by peoples who were as much hunters and gatherers as cultivators. Exceptions were Ife and Ilesha, just within the Forest, and the Benin kingdom which grew up on light soils of the tertiary sandstones where the Forest was possibly less dense. In addition, Benin had ready access to trade routes and to the fish supplies of the Niger delta.

The Ibo appear to have invaded the Forest from the seventeenth century onwards. They cut down the forests, which were probably easy to clear as they were developed on soils consisting mainly of deep well-drained sands, and replaced them with villages, hamlets, oil palm groves, and farmlands. The southward migration of the Ibo took place at the expense of the Ibibio.

In the south-west of Nigeria large scale clearance of the Forest took place in the nineteenth century when the Fulani armies overthrew the Oyo kingdom, and was facilitated partly by the import of steel cutlasses. The Oyo Yoruba withdrew into the forest margins where they founded a new capital, the present Oyo, displacing the Egba southwards, where they founded Abeokuta.[9] Subsequent expansion of the Egba has resulted in the southward displacement of lesser peoples such as the Aworri. Thus the present location of the Ibo and Yoruba concentrations is of relatively recent origin although increasing density also reflects the development of cash cropping in the forest areas.

Numerous economic consequences stem from the distribution

of population. The separation of large population concentrations directly or indirectly influences the cost of providing power and of transport. It also affects the location of modern industry by fragmenting the bulk of the market. These aspects will be considered in greater detail in subsequent chapters.

While European intervention and later colonial administration has had marked influence on population distribution, it has also fundamentally affected the demographic situation in West Africa. The suppression of the slave trade, cessation of inter-tribal warfare and the increasing application of advanced death control techniques have undoubtedly reduced death rates considerably. But birth rates have not apparently begun to fall, so that rates of natural increase are high. There are numerous data problems associated with precise determination of death rates, birth rates, rate of natural increase and population growth which have been summarised recently by Caldwell.[10] The results of E.C.A. studies are presented in Table 3.2 although it should be noted that they differ in detail from those of the African Demography Project, Office of Population Research, Princeton University. The results given in the table are all based on sample survey data except for Nigeria, Gambia and Portuguese Guinea, for which other techniques of estimation were used. One consequence of rapid population growth having economic implications both at the present, in terms of provision of social facilities such as schools, and in the future, in terms of job provision, is the marked juvenility of the population (Table 3.3). Thus the dependency ratio, i.e. the population below the age of fifteen years added to that above age sixty years as a ratio of those between fifteen and sixty, is everywhere high. Consequently a relatively low proportion of the population is economically active in the accepted sense of the term.

SOCIAL STRUCTURE

The basic unit in West African social systems is the *extended family*, which includes people who in Western Europe would be considered only as distant cousins. The extended family has economic significance as it is the primary unit of production. It provides a labour force for food-crop farming and affords a

means of collecting enough cultivators for the heavier agricultural tasks such as fallow-clearing and weeding. In specialist
craft industries it provides both the organisational framework
and the units of production. In terms of consumption it is the
primary unit since production of foodstuffs is mainly for
subsistence. It also provides a system of social security, the fit
and the capable being obliged to care for the old, the crippled,
and the orphaned.

It is a matter of some controversy as to whether the extended
family system is breaking down or not. Its influence is still
powerful, more so in rural than in urban areas. Whilst its
egalitarianism is humane, it can become a hindrance to progress
in a developing economy. The wealthy—and the domestic
servant earning $35 a month is wealthy in the eyes of his
brethren in the rural areas—are called upon to contribute to
school fees for nephews or to the upkeep of the feckless. Those
in positions of influence are under pressure to appoint
relatives rather than the best qualified applicants, or to
divert profits from re-investment in business to undeserving
kinsmen. Similarly civil servants are made to feel that it is less
of a crime to embezzle public monies than to fail in supporting
less fortunate kinsfolk. Thus nepotism, bribery and corruption
are rife and, indeed, have contributed to the downfall of elected
governments in Ghana, Nigeria and Dahomey.

The extended family and others accepted into the family
group, such as servants or slaves, normally lived in a compound,
the basic unit of settlement. In rural areas the compound
performed the function fulfilled by the farmstead in more
advanced parts of the world. Within indigenous towns, where
these existed, it served as craft workshop or farmstead according
to the occupation of the inhabitants. There was, therefore,
great variety in the detailed form of compounds which still
persists. This variety reflected the nature of the rural economy,
the influence of social conventions and customs, and defensive
needs.

Extended families are grouped into *lineages* or *clans* that
claim a common ancestor in the recent past and form the local
community. These have economic significance because they
form the basis of the system of land-holding. The concept
of land ownership in the European sense is alien to West

Africans except in those restricted areas where economic and social change has proceeded farthest, notably in urban areas and the surrounding countryside and in the cocoa belts.

Tenurial practices vary in detail but have broad common principles. Traditionally land is owned by the community (normally the lineage or clan) made up, as a Nigerian chief told the West African Lands Committee in 1912,[11] 'of a vast family of which many are dead, few are living and countless members are unborn'. Rights in the use of land are granted to the living by the chief or village elders. Where population densities are very low and shifting agriculture is practised, rights are granted only for the period of cultivation. With increasing population density this practice gives way to one by which the cultivator maintains his rights in the land while it lies fallow. In such situations the land is still communally owned but the rights in it are vested in individuals or families. Thus improvements made in the course of cultivation can be passed on from one generation to the next whilst the interests of the community are safeguarded by the lapsing of such rights should the land be left fallow for too long.

Where population densities were high, indigenous tenurial systems evolved to embrace the gift, pledging and loan of land, so that an embryo land-market developed. This evolution was given added impetus in the Colonial Era by further pressure on land resources and by the introduction of cash crops, with the result that land came to be bought and sold in those areas where pressure is greatest. Amongst the Hausa, for instance, the customary tenurial system still operates in areas of moderate population density, as at Soba in Zaria Province, whereas outright sale was taking place in the 1920s in those parts of the Kano Close Settled Zone close to the city. Nadel[12] points to a similar contrast in Nupeland between 'trans-' and 'cis-' Kaduna, i.e. west and east of the Kaduna river respectively.

Rights in crops, trees and houses are separable from those in the soil upon which they stand. Thus tree crops may be individually owned although they stand on *usehold* land, that is land owned by the community in which cultivation rights have been granted. Similarly, the pledging or leasing of land does not necessarily give rights in the trees on it, which may be retained by the owner. On usehold land, harvesting rights of trees in cropland normally belong to the cultivator, in fallows they belong to the community. This concept has undoubtedly led to the expansion of individual land ownership.

The widely held view of communal land tenure has been challenged by Paul Bohannan[13] as a 'silly concept'. He argues that in a community based on kinship, the land is an aspect of the group but is not the basis of the grouping. Using the Tiv of Central Nigeria as an example, he argues that descent and genealogy provide the basis for both lineage and territorial grouping. A 'genealogical map' consisting of lineages juxtaposed in a fixed arrangement includes all the Tiv and moves about the surface of the earth in response to changing demands arising out of farming or migration. Its relation with specific pieces of ground is brief indeed but the position of a man's farm in relation to that of his agnatic[14] kinsmen and his rights do not change. The Tiv are said to have 'farm tenure' but not 'land tenure'. With the development of Western ideas of property, lineage groups such as the Yoruba *ebi* have become legal entities. The *ebi* is an agnatic descent group with rights in a more or less precisely determined area of land which they farmed. From being a social group that owned nothing it has become a corporate body before the law owning land, the transformations taking place under the Communal Land Rights (Vesting in Trustees) Law of 1958.

Sometimes, but by no means universally even among the people of one tribe, specialist craft industries may be the prerogative of certain lineages to the exclusion of others. In such cases, the lineage provides the organisation for the craft. Thus amongst the Oyo Yoruba large compounds of blacksmiths and male weavers are commonly confined to a few lineages and tend to be concentrated in certain quarters of the town. The craft skills are passed from one generation to the next within the kin group and boys begin to learn their craft at an early age. The *bale*, or lineage head, had considerable influence in settling disputes, in maintaining standards of workmanship and in regulating relations with other groups through the medium of the lineage meeting.

But among other Yoruba sub-groups such as the Ekiti, where cognatic[14] as opposed to agnatic descent groups were the rule, the lineage was less important in this respect. The traditional crafts, with notable exceptions such as weaving, are tending to decline but have been joined by a whole host of modern crafts. These are organised in guilds or associations which perform functions very similar to those of their medieval European counterparts.

Lineages and clans are grouped together to form *tribes*, politically or socially coherent and autonomous groups occupying or claiming territory. The tribal area need not be occupied solely by members of one tribe. The Fulani, for instance, graze their herds on pastureland of other tribes such as the Hausa and Gbari whilst Ewe and Ga fisher-communities are found along the length of the coast and of the Volta river on the lands of other peoples. Further, tribes are capable of absorbing strangers who settle within the tribal area, and who inter-marry into the tribe. Formerly they also assimilated groups that were conquered by the tribe. Thus tribal communities are fluid and dynamic. Some are small, and may be nothing more than collections of kinsfolk who may inhabit a single village. Others are very large, composed of peoples of various origins and have extensive tribal areas.

Anthropologists commonly distinguish between *acephalous* (without rulers) segmentary tribes and centralised tribes that recognise a traditional head. The former lack centralised authority, administrative machinery and constitutional judicial institutions, whereas the latter possess all these. Furthermore, within acephalous tribes there are not the sharp divisions of rank, status or wealth, found in centralised tribes.

In addition some of the larger centralised tribes evolved sophisticated political institutions leading to the development of traditional *states*. Contrary to the view of Meyer Fortes and Evans Pritchard,[15] the development of centralised states is associated with higher than normal population densities. The 'islands' of high population density in the Sudan Zone bear a close relationship to the former existence of states such as Old Ghana, Mali, Songhay, Mossi-Mamprusi-Dagomba, Hausa-Fulani and Bornu-Kanem. Those of the Forest and the coast are the result both of indigenous state formation and of commercial development in the Pre-Colonial and Colonial Eras. Along the Atlantic Coast, the Serer and Wolof of Sénégal and the Temne of Sierra Leone evolved indigenous states. Along the Guinea Coast and in the adjacent Forest Belt the Yoruba states are noteworthy. The states of Cotonou, Ouidah, Allada and Abomey were organised into the Dahomey kingdom, and in present-day Ghana the Akan, Fanti and Ashanti states evolved. Frequently, however, there is a very marked fall in population densities beyond the borders of large states of powerful tribal groups.

The expansion of the larger states sometimes stimulated pockets of higher densities immediately beyond their borders and in the area between them, either by the compression of smaller neighbouring tribes into a smaller tribal area, or by the grouping of those weaker neighbours for protection. Furthermore, and significant from our point of view, the evolution of states was not caused solely by population density but by a three-way interaction between this factor, evolving trade and trade routes, and developing political and economic organisation.

The Ibo and Ibibio concentrations are major population groups which do not appear to fit this notion. These have hitherto been reckoned to be acephalous and segmentary societies, but R. F. Stevenson[16] has shown how, during the slave trade, the main arteries of trade, major markets and main sources of slave supply were controlled by the Aro (an Ibo people), which, he suggests, in terms of their organisation and functions must be considered a state. It differed from other states, such as Dahomey, in that the Aro concentrated on 'crucial nerve centres, trade routes, and markets rather than on a circumscribed and bounded region as such'.

THE SOCIAL ORIGINS OF TRADE

The states engaged in long distance trade and within their bounds there evolved a network of local markets. As the result of the development of a market economy there was division of labour, with specialised craftsmen making goods and agriculturalists producing foodstuffs for sale on the market. The stateless societies engaged in trade only when they bordered states and were drawn into the economic system of their powerful neighbours. Many were outside the traditional market economy and it is unlikely that they developed market institutions. Skinner's claim,[17] therefore, that 'markets were ubiquitous in West Africa' appears to be somewhat exaggerated.

The power and influence of the states and empires fluctuated partly with the importance of the trade routes which they commanded. Three groups of routes developed between the Sudan and North Africa.[18] Initially the western group from Morocco to the country west of the Niger Bend was most important. But by the eleventh century, the central routes, from Tunisia to the country between the Niger Bend and Lake Chad, had become more important and Tombouctou had become one of the chief foci of caravan traffic. The third group consisted of routes from Tripoli and Egypt southwards to the areas around Lake Chad. It had become important by the seventeenth century when Bornu-Kanem was at its most powerful and it continued to be important in the following century when the Hausa states were in their prime. Gold, slaves, ivory, ostrich feathers, and hides moved northwards along these routes while salt from the mines at Taodenni and luxury goods, such as red cloth, looking glasses, cutlery, tobacco, calico, silk and precious stones came from the Mediterranean.

Trade between the states of the Sudan Zone and those of the Forest margins developed from the thirteenth century. Ivory, kola-nuts and gold moved northwards. In return the products of the savana and goods that had been traded across the Sahara moved southwards. Thus by the fifteenth century, when the Portuguese began trading on the coast, an indigenous trading structure had already evolved, long distance trade was well developed and currency of various kinds was in use, including cowries (shells), gold dust, manillas (bronze or brass bracelets), blocks of salt, *umumu* (arrow-shaped pieces of iron), copper and cloth.

In the Proto-Colonial Era from the fifteenth and nineteenth centuries, European trading activities were confined to the coast, where traders were supplied with slaves and other goods by African middlemen. This trade had three major effects. First, it strengthened existing trade routes by providing increased and regular demand for the products of the interior. Secondly, it provided the interior with luxuries, which gradually became common, such as hardware, firearms, spirits and Virginian tobacco. And thirdly, it led to a coastward shift of the emphasis in trade in West Africa as the trade of the immediate interior, if not of the Sudan, was being diverted increasingly to the European trader from the traditional Trans-Saharan routes.

The nineteenth century witnessed the gradual suppression of the slave trade and expansion of legitimate trade, the two existing side by side through the first half of the century. Legitimate trade was based particularly on palm oil. Whereas the slave trade had benefited only the wealthy and had been readily controlled by powerful groups of middlemen like the Aro in Iboland or the coastal peoples of Dahomey, the export trade in palm oil was of interest to the populace at large and could not be controlled so readily. Thus a much more fluid distributive system evolved and local trade was stimulated. But the grip of powerful middlemen on the import trade was maintained, to be broken only by the penetration of European traders into the interior immediately prior to and during the Colonial Era.

In association with long-distance trade a network of local markets developed. Hodder[19] concludes they originated only where certain conditions were fulfilled. These include a political organisation able to guarantee peaceful passage to and from the market, a sufficiently high density of population and location on or near trade routes. Markets, it is argued, can develop only where exchange external to the community occurs. The markets were of two types, daily and periodic. The former were normally held in towns, were large and provided the goods for long-distance trade. The most usual type were held throughout the day but others, of lesser importance were held in either the morning or evening only. Periodic markets were held on 3, 4, 5, 8 or even 16-day cycles, and were arranged in rings so that no place was far from a market for more than a day or so. In rural areas they often served as feeders to the larger urban daily markets. Periodic markets were also found in towns.

Thus by the sixteenth century the periodic rural markets of the Edo, organised on a four-day cycle, apparently acted as feeders to the two urban markets in Benin City. From there goods were traded to neighbouring areas, particularly Iboland and Yorubaland. Similarly, in the mid-nineteenth century the periodic markets of Hausaland, also organised on four-day cycles, acted as feeders to urban markets in Katsina, Kano and other centres. From there Hausa merchants traded the goods to other peoples in what is now Nigeria such as Tiv, Nupe, Ibo and probably to the Yoruba and Edo, as well as peoples closer at hand. In addition they traded the goods to Dendi in northern Dahomey, to Gao, Zinder and Dori in the Songhay lands, to Ouagadougou in Mossi country and to Salaga in present-day Ghana. In the latter's markets they entered the trading system that connected the western coastal and forest zones and the Sudanese states of the Niger valley.

But the importance of rural periodic markets was not confined to their role as feeders to urban markets. Long distance trade was carried on by caravans of as many as 600 people which were 'moving markets, buying and selling everywhere along the road'.[20] These halted in rural periodic markets as well as in urban markets.

THE ORIGIN OF TOWNS

High population density, centralised political organisation, stratification of society, and long-distance trade were found in association with indigenous urbanism. Towns developed at nodal points in the network of trade routes, themselves often the political centre of states. There was a line of towns extending from Tombouctou through Northern Nigeria to Khartoum, including such notable centres as Gao, Katsina, Kano and Maiduguri. These were the 'ports' along the southern border of the Sahara on the old trade routes across the desert. Their size and influence fluctuated with the importance of the route with which they were associated as well as with their political fortunes.

Thus, the Songhay capital of Gao, founded in the ninth or tenth century, was an important trade centre until overrun by

E

the Moors in 1591, from which it never recovered. Tombouctou, which long held a fascination for Europeans, was founded by the Tuareg in the twelfth century. It was an important centre of trade and scholarship with a population in the sixteenth century estimated by Leo Africanus at 45,000. Like Gao it suffered from Moorish and later Fulani conquest and the first European visitor to the city, René Caillié, was bitterly disappointed by the squalor and ugliness of the town.[21] As Tombouctou and Gao declined with the growing importance of eastern trade routes, so first Katsina and later Kano developed as the dominant centre of trans-Saharan traffic.

There were also towns associated with the Guinea states Kumasi, Abomey, Porto Novo, Benin and the city states of the Niger delta, for example. But the most notable are the Yoruba towns. Many of the latter are of some antiquity, others are of recent origin. Bascom[22] has suggested that the development of the Yoruba town took place in four stages. The initial settlement was often a hunters' camp to which newcomers were attracted by good farmland, population pressure in the parent town or a good trading position. The second stage was one of consolidation and growth in which some became metropolitan in that they served as centres for an entire kingdom. The third, a period of inter-tribal warfare, invasion and the collapse of central authority lasting for much of the nineteenth century, which placed a premium on adequate defence, size and political affiliations. New towns were formed from war camps and by the grouping of peoples for defence. The fourth stage began with British administration and continues in the Independence Era. Interposed between the towns of the Sudan and of Guinea were those of the interior such as Djenne, Bida and Salaga which acted as staging posts in the north-south trade. This last town has been described as having a unique role in the economy of West Africa.[23] Unlike the other centres it stood on a cross-roads on the north-south route, trading with both Kano and Tombouctou.

Trade and commerce were vital for indigenous urbanism but so also was the political and religious aristocracy who established a social hierarchy and the market-peace conducive to the development of trade. The importance of these two

aspects of the social system is reflected in the juxtaposition
of palace and market place, a characteristic feature of many
indigenous towns. The aristocracy also provided the market
for the luxury goods, which were traded over long distances.
In order to survive, the non-agricultural aristocracy exacted
tribute from surrounding rural peoples, a transfer of food
from rural to urban dweller which was but a short step from
local exchange. They also used serfs and slaves to grow
foodstuffs, some of which were sold locally or to passing
merchants or caravans.

Within such an exchange economy specialisation of labour
was possible. Specialist craftsmen were an important factor
in the emergence of urbanism in the larger states of the Guinea
Coast and Sudan. In many states, amongst them Nupe,
Benin, Dahomey and Hausa, particularly in Katsina and
Kano, the various crafts were grouped in individual quarters
or wards of the town often reflecting their organisation into
guilds. The importance of craftsmen in the urban economy
varied. The eastern states produced more manufactured
goods than did those in the west. Crafts were more numerous,
occupied more people and were better organized in Katsina,
Kano, Bida, Benin or Oyo than in Djenne, Tombouctou or
Kumasi.

In the smaller centralised tribes, such as the Ewe, Birom,
Ga or Tallensi, and in the acephelous segmentary societies
such as the Tiv, crafts tended to be secondary occupations
to agriculture or sometimes trading. Craft products were
produced by the individual or community largely for his
or its own use although some were marketed and often found
their way into long distance trade.

RURAL SETTLEMENT

It is tempting to account for rural settlement patterns by
suggesting a relationship on the one hand between nucleated
or village settlement and centralised systems and on the other
between dispersed or hamlet and isolated compound settlement
and segmentary acephalous systems. But this cannot be
sustained. The Serer, Ouolof and Mossi, all state societies,
have dispersed settlement patterns. The Mossi, for instance,

live in scattered compounds grouped socially, but not morphologically, into 'villages' and it is difficult to tell where one village
begins and another ends.

The Ibo, on the other hand, are traditionally described as a
segmentary and acephalous people. In the most densely
populated portions of their territory they live in compounds
closely scattered amongst the compound-land. Udo,[24] however, has recently shown this may be a modern settlement
pattern resulting from the disintegration of nucleated villages.
Outside the most densely settled portions of their territory,
they live in villages. The character of these villages differs
from place to place in both size and morphology. Close to
the most densely settled areas they consist of dispersed but
closely spaced hamlets and compounds grouped into amorphous
villages rather like those of the densely settled areas, but
separated from each other by the outer farmlands. These
villages contrast with both the 'grassland towns' of the north-
western savana plateau and the medium sized compact villages
of southern Owerri and Ahoada Divisions to the south.[25]

In the Sudan, dispersed settlement is traditionally a feature
in areas of high population density. The patterns characteristic
of the Serer, Ouolof and Mossi have already been mentioned,
but in Hausaland and along the margins of floodlands along the
Niger and in the Lake Chad Basin village settlement is common.

Among the communities of the Guinea Savana, dispersed
settlement is traditional in two situations, firstly where central
authority was weak and where the extended family, the unit
of labour for cultivation, was more or less independent of
external forces. It is characteristic among the Lobi and
Dogarti of northern Ghana. Here, too, population densities
are generally low and agriculture tends to be on a true shifting
basis. Secondly, it is found where there was a strong tradition
of occasional migration to new farmlands within the tribal
area, involving movement of compounds, as among the Tiv
of central Nigeria. Nucleated villages are characteristic of the
upland refuge areas of the Guinea Savana, such as the Atacora
of Togo, and wherever defence has been an important influence
on the settlement pattern.

In the forest, semi-dispersed settlement in small hamlets is
characteristic of areas with low population densities where

shifting agriculture still survives, as in south-west Côte d'Ivoire and the neighbouring parts of Liberia. Elsewhere villages occur in association with medium and high population densities as in south-east Côte d'Ivoire and Ghana, and where defence or trade have had an important influence. Villages are also characteristic of coastal fishing communities of strand and swamp.

Settlement patterns in West Africa, however, are very dynamic and traditional patterns, when inappropriate in modern conditions, have often been changed. The fixation of shifting cultivation has led to fixation of settlement and, in some cases, a tendency to greater nucleation. Peaceful conditions have permitted the movement of settlements from upland areas to surrounding plains, often accompanied by dispersal of many of the compounds over the farmlands.[26] The commercialisation of the economy has led to concentration of settlement around railway stations and road junctions. Villages have also been moved to roadside locations and the development of linear villages on main roads is now a wide-spread feature. The movement of settlements to more accessible sites has sometimes been forced upon unwilling people by Colonial Administrations, but more commonly it has been a spontaneous response to changing economic and social conditions.

The concentration of settlement has also been encouraged by colonial officers. It is sometimes argued, usually by African scholars, that the sole reason for this was ease of tax collection and administration.[27] There is some evidence to suggest, however, that it was to facilitate the provision of basic services such as water supply, schools and clinics and thereby reduce their cost.

The development of the economy thus cannot be understood without reference to the consequences of the social structure upon it. In addition some social customs have a clear economic significance.

SOCIAL CUSTOMS

These fall into one of two categories, those concerned with labour and those with exchange. The extended family is traditionally the basic unit in the labour force. It is not, however, the sole unit and the individual may draw upon other groups in the community for labour. Amongst the Yoruba the labour of extended families grouped into lineages is traditionally supplemented by two other kinds of group farming, *airo* and *ebese*. *Airo* is the occasional association of agnatic kins, farm-mates or members of an age-set who work on each other's farms on a reciprocal basis. It is usually a small group of younger men. In Ekiti, according to Ojo,[28] it varied from four to 30 members. *Ebese* on the other hand, may be large, from 20 to 100 or more, depending upon the popularity of the man raising the group. It consists of agnatic kins, affines, in-laws and other associates and was generally raised by elder men. Payment takes place at the end of the working day in the form of food, palm-wine and kolanuts. Other examples were the Dahomean *dopkwe*, the Nupe *egbe*, the Mossi *sosol*; in some cases these produced surpluses for sale in the markets.

But the foundation of such labour groups has been eroded by social and economic changes, particularly in areas where cash cropping is important. Families are tending to become nuclear rather than extended; primary education has reduced the number of young men remaining on the land; the introduction of the money economy has resulted in the growth of non-agricultural activities so that labour cannot be exchanged on a direct basis; and finally the introduction of cash cropping makes possible the discharge of obligations by cash payment and the hiring of workers to replace group labour. For these reasons the traditional groups are rapidly becoming a feature of the past.

Everywhere in West Africa a well-marked division of labour between the sexes was customary. The details of this division however, varied from people to people and in some cases has influenced the acceptance of cash cropping. Amongst the small tribes of the Bamenda Highlands, such as the Nsaw and Ngembe, most of the agricultural activities are traditionally the concern of the women, who are responsible for providing food for the menfolk. This left the men with a comparatively light work-load and, with the introduction of *arabica* coffee, this enabled them to take to cash cropping with alacrity.[29]

In southern Dahomey, on the other hand, the men are mainly responsible for agriculture. They provide their families with food surpluses and palm products, although the women may help in sowing and harvesting. In the forest areas of Ghana the men are responsible for the cocoa cultivation and for the clearing of the fallows for food crops. The women, however, cultivate the vegetable farms near the compounds. In the Kadjebi area of Trans-Volta, the men are responsible for bush clearing and yam mounding, but men, women and children alike engage in planting, weeding and harvesting.

Similar divisions of labour existed and continue to exist in other spheres of economic activity. In many societies trading is a woman's occupation, and women are overwhelmingly predominant in the Yoruba market. In southern Dahomey where trading is a woman's occupation, those embarking on their career and those who are old specialise on trading products gathered from the bush, whereas those specialising on the cooked food trade are younger. On the other hand trading is both a male and female occupation among the Ibo, but certain commodities are the preserve of each sex and others are reserved for young boys.

All tribes distinguish between men's and women's craft activities. For example, among the Limba of northern Sierra Leone[30] men are blacksmiths, do leatherwork, weave and sew native cloth, dye cloth (red), make large baskets, mortars, stools and musical instruments. Limba women, on the other hand, engage in dyeing (indigo), spinning and carding cotton, weaving, bead-work, making of mats and small baskets, soap making and palm-oil processing. Again the details differ from tribe to tribe, but cloth weaving is generally undertaken by women. Smithing, like hunting, is always a preserve of the men, and potting nearly always that of women. In fishing communities, the men are concerned with bringing in the catch and repairing boat and nets, the women with curing and marketing.

Polygamy is a social custom which has economic consequences[31]. In pre-colonial times wives and slaves were for the agriculturalist the only capital investment, for land was freely available to all members of the group. A man commonly had as many wives as his economic position would permit, for in taking several he increased his social standing amongst his fellows, and also increased the size of labour force available to him for cultivation of his farms, not simply by the addition of wives but subsequently by the contributions of children born by the wives. Polygamy was also advantageous for the preparation of the food given in payment for farm work: lavish entertainment on such occasions increased a man's social standing. Children traditionally entered the labour force at an early age as they learned the skills associated with the various forms of economic activity from their parents. Thus five and six-year-old boys often accompany their parents to the farms or assist in lighter aspects of craft industries. As they grow older and more skilled their responsibilities increase until marriage, when they begin to work on their own account. The training of girls similarly begins early in life when they begin to help around the compound.

The rights and duties of man and wives in marriage are generally clearly understood. Although the wife's first responsibility is to the husband in terms of domestic and farming duties, this does not preclude her from having her own farms or engaging in other activities, such as trading. This is so, for instance, among the Ewe of southern Togo and south-east Ghana and the Limba. The proceeds of these activities remain her sole property to be disposed of as she wishes. This is particularly the case in societies such as the Fanti and Ga, where a wife is responsible for feeding herself and her own children.

There is a host of minor social customs and taboos related to labour and agricultural practices and involving distribution of produce. These vary from tribe to tribe. Some affect the role of women in the labour force during pregnancy and following childbirth. In some cases the woman withdraws for periods which may be as long as six months when she returns to her mother's compound prior to the birth. A wife too, on moving to live with her husband, does not shed her responsibilities to her own lineage, clan or family. Mother-daughter links are commonly strong and result in extended visits by the daughter to her mother which again may result in temporary withdrawal from the husband's labour force. This is an added incentive to take more than one wife.

Social customs give rise to non-economic exchange of goods and services, by reciprocity and redistribution. Reciprocity is obligatory, mutual giving of goods or services between persons who have some socially defined relationship to each other. Such gift-giving was much more important in many West African communities than market exchange. Mechanisms for redistribution involve the chieftainship, 'secret societies' and 'bride-price'. Where there were powerful chiefs, tribute was commonly exacted and in addition the chief was often entitled to labour service on his farms. But, conversely, the contents of the chief's granaries and stores were distributed as rewards and gifts with the result that local inequalities of production were evened out.

In addition those in hardship could expect assistance from the chief who was also able to call on his more prosperous subjects for supplies. 'Secret societies', associations of leading men, were found in many West African communities and afforded an element of redistribution because entrance to them was gained by payment of fees. These fees were shared equally by all members so that the accumulated wealth transferred in fees was widely redistributed. Finally, to win a wife a man had to present gifts to his betrothed's parents or engage in a long period of labour service on their farms. In some communities both gift and service were required. The precise nature of the bride-price and the levels charged for a wife vary from people to people and with time. But the institution of bride-price, linked to polygamy, leads to considerable redistribution of wealth within a given society. Recently both payments in kind and labour service have tended to be replaced by money payments. With the introduction of the money economy, there has been marked inflation in bride-prices particularly in the more wealthy parts of West Africa.

The distribution of people and of communities together with the nature of social institutions and customs are as vital to an understanding of the economy as are the conditions of the physical environment. In the space of one chapter it has not been possible to present a comprehensive picture of the social factors influencing indigenous economies.[32] We have merely attempted to indicate the kind of social influences operating.

Furthermore the close relationships between society and economy make it difficult when considering economic and social change to determine whether economic influences have caused social change or *vice-versa*, although we suspect the greater influence of the former. Some of these changes have been indicated, others form the subject matter of subsequent chapters. Before considering the economic and geographical character of these changes we need to consider the variations in the nature of indigenous economies in West Africa and this is our task in the next chapter.

TABLE 3.1

AREA, POPULATION DENSITY & DISTRIBUTION, 1964

Country	Area		Estimated Population		Density of Population persons/ sq. km.
	Thousand sq. km.	Per cent. Distribution	Number in thousands	Per cent. Distribution	
Nigeria	924	15·1	56,400	58·7	61
Ghana	239	3·9	7,537	7·8	32
Gambia	10	0·2	324	0·3	32
Sierra Leone	72	1·2	2,200	2·3	31
Togo	57	0·9	1,603	1·7	28
Dahomey	113	1·9	2,300	2·4	20
Sénégal	196	3·2	3,400	3·5	17
Haute Volta	274	4·5	4,757	4·9	17
Port. Guinea	36	0·6	525	0·5	15
Guinea	246	4·0	3,420	3·6	14
Côte d'Ivoire	322	5·3	3,750	3·9	12
Liberia	111	1·8	1,041	1·1	9
Mali	1,202	19·7	4,485	4·7	4
Niger	1,267	20·8	3,250	3·4	3
Mauretanie	1,030	16·9	900	0·9	1
TOTAL WEST AFRICA	6,099		95,892		16

Source: Economic Bulletin for Africa, Vol VL, July 1966.

TABLE 3.2

FERTILITY, MORTALITY AND NATURAL INCREASE & GROWTH RATES

Country	Year	Fertility Measures			Mortality Measures			Rate of Growth	
		Crude Birth Rate %	General Fertility Rate %	Gross Reproduction Rate	Crude Death Rate	Infant Mortality Rate	Rate of Natural Increase	Period	Per cent. per Year
Nigeria	1952–53	53–57	—	3.6–3.8	—	—	—	1953–63	5.8
Ghana	1960	47–52	203–224	3.0	24	156	2.3–2.8	1948–60	3.2
Haute Volta	1960–61	53	212	2.9	35	182	1.8	1955–60	4.7
Mali	1960	61	240	3.8	30	123	3.1	1955–60	2.4
Côte d'Ivoire	1957–58	55	220	3.2	35	138	2.0	1955–61	2.3
Guinea	1954–55	62	223	3.5	40	216	2.2	1958–60	0.5
Sénégal	1960–61	43	174	2.6	17	93	2.66	1955–60	6.0
Niger	1959–60	52	232	3.5	27	200	2.5	1955–62	3.6
Dahomey	1961	54	227	3.3	26	111	2.8	1956–61	4.2
Togo	1961	55	228	3.5	29	127	2.6	1955–62	5.0
Mauritanie	1961–62	47	—	—	25	—	—	1958–64	2.2
Portuguese Guinea	1940–45	47	—	2.4	—	—	—	1950–60	0.4
Gambia	1962–63	39	—	2.5	21	—	1.77	1951–64	1.1
Sierra Leone	—	—	—	—	—	—	—	1956–63	0.5

Source: R. K. Som 'Some Demographic Indicators for Africa', in Caldwell, op cit., Economic Bulletin for Africa, Vol 6, 1966.

TABLE 3.3

PERCENTAGE OF POPULATION IN AGE GROUPS

Country	Year	Under 15 years	15–59 years	Over 60 years	Dependency Ratio
Togo	1961	47·9	46·8	5·3	113·7
Dahomey[1]	1961	46·0	48·4	5·6	—
Ghana	1960	44·5	50·6	4·9	97·6
Nigeria	1952–53	44·3	47·7	8·0	—
Mali	1960–61	43·8	51·2	5·0	95·3
Côte d'Ivoire	1957–58	43·6	52·9	3·5	89·0
Mauritanie	1960–61	43·0	52·3	4·7	91·2
Sénégal	1960–61	42·4	52·1	5·6	92·1
Guinea	1954–55	42·0	53·0	4·9	88·5
Haute Volta	1960–61	41·6	53·1	5·3	88·3
Gambia[2]	1963	37·6	49·4	13·0	—

Notes:
1. Age groups for Dahomey are under 34 years, 35 to 74 years and over 75 years.
2. Age groups for Gambia are under 15 years, 15 to 44 years and over 45 years.
Source: Economic Bulletin for Africa, 6 (2) July 1966.

REFERENCES

1   Polanyi, K, The Great Transformation, New York, 1944

2   Southall, A. W. (Ed.), Social Change in Modern Africa, London, 1961

3   This step by step evolution is not generally accepted by anthrop-
    ologists, who are concerned with people see Forde, C. D. and Douglas
    M. Primitive Economics, in Dalton, G. (Ed.), Tribal and Peasant Economics,
    New York, 1967. It is however accepted at least by some geographers,
    concerned with places, see Gleave, M. B. and White, H. P. Population
    Density and Agricultural Systems in West Africa in Thomas, M. F. and
    Whittington, G. W. (Eds.), Environment and Land Use in Africa, London,
    1969

4   Adams, J., A population map of West Africa. L.S.E. Graduate
    School of Geog. Discussion paper 26, published in Nigerian Geog.
    Journal, 12, pp. 87–97. We are grateful to Mr. Adams for permission
    to use his map

5   Hance, W. A., op cit. Chap 1

6   Miége, J., 'Les cultures vivrières en Afrique occidentale: essai de leur ré-
    partition géographique, particulièrement en Côte d'Ivoire', Cahiers d'Outre Mer,
    7, 1954, pp. 25–50

7   Grove, A. T., 'Land Use and Soil Conservation on the Jos Plateau', Bull.
    Geol. Survey of Nigeria, 22, 1952

8   Hunter, J. M., 'River blindness in Nangodi, Northern Ghana: A Hypothesis
    of Cyclical Advance and Retreat', Geog. Rev., 56, 1966, pp. 398–416

9 Morgan, W. B., 'The Influence of European contacts on the landscape of Southern Nigeria', Geog. Jour., 125, 1959. pp. 48–64

10 Caldwell, J. C., Introduction, the Demographic Situation, in Caldwell, J. C. and Okongo, C., The Population of Tropical Africa, London, 1968

11 Quoted in Davidson, B., Which Way Africa? Harmondsworth, 1964, p. 31

12 Nadel, S. F., A Black Byzantium: the kingdom of Nupe in Nigeria, London, 1942

13 Bohannan, P., Africa's Land. in Dalton, G. (Ed.) op cit. See also Bohannan, P., Land Use, Land Tenure and Land Reform, and Biebuyck, D., Land Holding and Social Organization in Herskovits, H. J. and Harwitz, M. (Eds.), Economic Transition in Africa, Evanston, 1964

14 Agnatic. Kinship traced through the male line, sometimes called patrilineal. Cognatic. Kinship traced through both the male and female line

15 Foster, M. and Evans Pritchard, E. E. (Eds.), African Political Systems, London, 1946, pp. 7–8

16 Stevenson, R. F., Population and Political Systems in Tropical Africa, New York, 1968

17 Skinner, E. P., West African Economic Systems in Herskovits and Harwitz, (Eds.) op cit.

18 op cit. See also Hodder, B. W., West Africa: Growth and Change in Trade, in Prothero, R. M. (Ed.), A Geography of Africa, London, 1969

19 Hodder, B. W., 'Some comments on the Origin of Traditional Markets in Africa South of the Sahara', Trans. Inst. Br. Geogr., 36, 1965, pp. 97–105

20 Monteil, P. L., De Saint Louis à Tripoli par le Tchad, Paris, 1894, quoted in Skinner, op cit., p. 94

21 Gardner, B., The Quest for Timbuctoo, London, 1968, Readers Union edition 1969, Chapter 5 particularly pp. 120 et seq.

22 Bascom, W. R., 'Urbanism as a traditional African Pattern', Soc. Rev. n. s. 7, 1959, pp. 29–43

23 Skinner, E. P., op cit. p. 93. See also Dickson, K. B., A Historical Geography of Ghana, London, 1969, pp. 110–113

24 Udo, R. K., 'Disintegration of Nucleated Settlement in Eastern Nigeria', Geog. Rev., 55, 1965, pp. 53–67

25 A review of the literature on settlement patterns of the former Eastern Region of Nigeria forms Chapter 3 of Floyd, B,. Eastern Nigeria: A Geographical Review, London, 1969. See also, Karmon, Y., A Geography of Settlement in Eastern Nigeria, Jerusalem. 1966

26 Gleave, M. B., 'Hill Settlements and their Abandonment in Tropical Africa'. Trans. Inst. Bri. Geogr., 40, 1966, pp. 39–49

27 Udo, R. K., 'Transformation of Rural Settlement in British Tropical Africa', Nig. Geog. Jour., 9, 1969, pp. 129–144, reference at p. 138

28 Ojo, G. J. A., 'The Changing Patterns of Traditional Group Farming in Ekiti, North-eastern Yoruba Country', Nig. Geog. Jour., 6, 1963, pp. 31–38

29 Gleave, M. B. and Thomas, M. F. ,'*The Bagango Valley: an example of land utilisation and agricultural practice in the Bamenda Highlands*', *Bull. Inst. Fond. Af. Noire*, Sér B, *30*, 1968, pp. 655–81

30 Finnegan, R., *Survey of the Limba people of Northern Sierra Leone, Overseas Research Publication*, 8, H.M.S.O., London, 1965

31 Crook, J. H., '*Monogomy, Polygamy and food supply*', *Discovery* 24, 1963, pp. 35–41

32 For further details *see* Labouret, H., *Paysans d'Afrique Occidentale*, Paris, 1940.   This still remains the best general account.

CHAPTER 4

The Indigenous Economy

The commercialisation of the West African economy that has been going on at an ever increasing rate over the last half century has in some respects, such as increased urbanisation, been imposed from without. In other respects it has been grafted on to the pre-existing indigenous economy with a degree of intensity that varies regionally. This indigenous economy, though subsistence based, was rarely completely self-contained. There has always been some measure of exchange, long distance as well as local, and some specialisation. Of all the sectors, however, agriculture is universally the most important.

AGRICULTURE

Agriculture is the foundation of the economy of all West African countries. These countries produce all but a small part of their own food, while agricultural commodities are always significant and often dominant in the export economy. Whereas in Britain only 6·5 per cent. and in the United States only 16 per cent. of the active male population is engaged in agriculture, in all West African countries farmers comprise more than 70 per cent. of the working male population. But the greater part of the labour expended goes into obtaining food that is consumed by the families who actually grow it. Even in areas where most progress has been made in introducing cash crops, the farmers still produce much of their own food. Thus subsistence agriculture, by which we mean food production for consumption by the producer and his family, makes a contribution which, whilst extremely difficult to quantify, is vital to the gross national product.[1]

West African agriculture is characterised by low technological levels, low yields measured against either acreage or labour input, and low cash returns to the cultivator. The main implements are the hoe, the digging stick, the cutlass and the sickle. There are numerous varieties of each of these implements, designed to suit local methods of tillage, soils and crops. Indeed, some nine types of hoe have recently been noted in a list that is almost certainly not exhaustive.[2] Manure is scarce and artificial fertilisers impossible in a largely subsistence economy. Outside the principal areas of export or food cropping for cash, only the marginal surplus is available for sale and this will vary greatly from year to year.

Data on the size and structure of agricultural holdings are widely scattered in the geographical, anthropological and agricultural literature, where the results of innumerable case studies have been reported.[3] At the national scale, data on size of holding are usually based on sample surveys[4] and are subject to large sampling errors. Holdings are, however, small, varying in size from less than half an acre to over 20 acres, although the evidence suggests that the majority are between one and five acres in extent. Variation in size of holding is as much a feature of densely as of sparsely settled areas. Factors affecting these variations include the availability of land, the area that can be satisfactorily cultivated given the technical limitations and, in densely settled areas where land can be purchased, the wealth of the cultivators.

A subsistence area of half an acre per head of population is usual in the Forest regions. This is probably increased to three-quarters of an acre or more in the Savana regions for the root crops typical of the Forest yield more heavily than cereals, the task of clearance in the Forest is more burdensome, and fallow periods are shorter there. Holdings consist of small plots ('farms') widely scattered through the village lands. Fragmentation results from the process of allocation of lands to the cultivator. It is least where land is abundant and fallows are long, particularly where settlements are dispersed in small compound units. It is most marked where settlements are large and where there is pressure on land resources. Within this broad framework there is considerable variation within individual communities. In Kimbaw, a village in the Bamenda Highlands of West Cameroun, the

average acreage cultivated by each woman is 1·34 acres in
an average of eight farms. At one extreme is a woman with a
holding of four farms totalling 1·04 acres, all within ten minutes
walk of her hut. At the other, is a woman cultivating 1·8
acres in fourteen plots, the largest of which is some ninety
minutes' walk from the hut over two steep hills.[5] Amongst
the Lobi Birifor of Western Gonja in central Ghana, most
of the holding is made up of the family farm cultivated by
the farming group to supply foodstuffs. More scattered bush
farms are used to provide cash crops.[6] Similarly, at Wum
in the Bamenda Highlands one large block of land is cultivated
by the women, who grow the foodstuffs, and the cultivated
portion is rotated around the village area, as fallow follows
cropping in the cultivation cycle.

AGRICULTURAL PRACTICES & SYSTEMS

There are three main categories of cultivation practice in
West Africa, *shifting cultivation, rotational bush fallowing,* and
permanent cultivation. There is considerable confusion in the
literature surrounding the first two, since many authors
fail to distinguish between them. While the principles of
husbandry are similar, they are in fact two quite different
methods of land use and management, which present differing
economic opportunities.

SHIFTING CULTIVATION

Shifting cultivation has been described as the rotation of
fields in contrast to the rotation of crops.[7] But the use of the
word 'field' is misleading since it normally means a permanently
utilized, enclosed area. Better terms are clearing or garden-
area, but in West Africa the word 'farm' is invariably used.
The system depends upon the use of virgin or well-developed
secondary vegetation, and since it also depends upon burning
it is best suited to areas with a well marked dry season and
sparse population. It is, therefore, found mainly in the
Guinea Savana Woodland, particularly around the hill
masses that formerly served as refuge areas. It is also found
in the less densely peopled and less well developed areas of

F

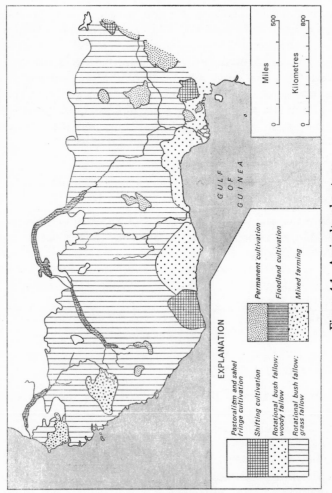

Figure 4.1. Agricultural systems

the Forest Zone, notably in the Cross River Basin of south-eastern Nigeria, in the south-west Côte d'Ivoire and in Liberia.

In the Forest, sites for new farms are selected at the end of the rainy season, according to the type, height, and density of their vegetation. Large trees are left but the smaller trees and the shrubs are felled and left to dry, the debris being burnt towards the end of the dry season. This destroys most of the available plant nutrients, but enough remain in the ash to afford modest prospects for the crops. As soon as the rains start, the first crops are planted in the rich layer of friable, humic, porous topsoil that has developed under the forest fallow. In the woodland areas cultivation sites are selected at the end of the rainy season, when yam mounds are scraped up while the soil is still moist. Trees are felled and the debris, together with the grasses, are burned at the end of the following dry season. The planting of yams and the cultivation of other crops is undertaken with the onset of the rains.

While traditional areas of shifting cultivation survive in the Guinea Savana Woodland, it has also developed during the past 60 years or so on the areas surrounding the hill masses. These latter were formerly inhabited by peoples seeking refuge from slave raiders. With the onset of settled conditions following the imposition of colonial rule, they have been abandoned in favour of the adjacent, unsettled plains. Shifting cultivation on the plains has replaced intensive agricultural techniques in the hill masses because labour inputs in the former are less and are more discontinuous.

Crop variety is everywhere limited, so that rotations are either not practised or are extremely rudimentary. The farm is usually cropped for two or three seasons, after which soil fertility declines because no manure, natural or artificial, is used, and it also becomes progressively more difficult to prevent the spread of weeds. The labour of cultivation is no longer justified by the return and the farm is abandoned, although in the forest areas the farmer may return to harvest the remaining root crops. The fallow period is always long, periods of 20 or 30 years being common, although this is usually related to lack of pressure on land resources rather than to the needs of the soil since periods of this order are needed to restore fertility only on the poorer soils. Soil

fertility is restored during the fallow period by the re-establishment of the natural growth cycle and the restoration of the
ecological balance between vegetation and soil. Deep-rooted
plants develop and reach nutrients leached down to lower
levels.

As we have seen in the previous chapter, tribes, clans and
lineages occupy apparently ill-defined areas of territory;
there is no concept of land ownership in the western sense.
The land is allocated by the chief of the group among its
members, all of whom have the right to clear land for their
own use. When the period of cultivation ends, their rights
over the now fallow land revert to the group. At the end
of the fallow cycle the land is re-allocated and not necessarily
to the previous cultivator. The farms, whether in forest or
in savana, are rarely more than an acre (·4 hectares). They are
scattered around the group area in a confused mixture along
with fallow patches in various stages of regeneration and with
uncleared forest or grassland. This both assists the rapid
regeneration of bush and secondary forest and helps to reduce
erosion hazards. New farms rarely maintain the same boundaries or have the same dimensions as earlier clearings. The
clearings thus rotate around the territory of the group, although
land nearest the settlement is most intensively used. When
this land is nearing exhaustion, or when the houses need
renewing, it may be decided to move the village to a part of the
group territory that has been little used and where soils are,
therefore, more fertile.[8]

In areas where the method is still practised, only a small
proportion of the land is under cultivation at any one time.
In an area of some 5000 square miles (12,950 square kilometres)
in East Dagomba District in Ghana, for instance, it was found
that only one per cent. of the land was under cultivation
in any one year.[9] This is less than the proportion, about
4 per cent. of the total, taken up by non-agricultural uses.
A very high proportion of the land was in grass, but although
most farmers kept cattle about 85 per cent. of the grassland
was not being used in any one year. Because so little land is
actually being used, the land use pattern is best described as a
mosaic of cultivated patches interspersed with fallows of
varying age and with uncultivated land.

THE FIXATION OF SHIFTING CULTIVATION

We have argued elsewhere[10] that increasing pressure on land resources results in a process of change from shifting agriculture through rotational bush fallowing to permanent cultivation. This pressure stems chiefly from population growth and from the introduction and expansion of cash cropping. Shifting agriculture is virtually unknown where population densities exceed 25 persons per square mile (10 per square kilometre) or in major areas of commercial agriculture.

Fixation comes in two ways; as population increases a greater proportion of the land must be cultivated and eventually fallow periods are reduced. Land develops a scarcity value which is reflected in rights over the fallow now being maintained by the original cultivator and his descendents. Agriculture is now fixed. But in addition a number of factors combine to fix the settlements themselves and with them their cultivated lands.

In the pre-colonial era the need for protection frequently led to population gathering in large groups, locally increasing densities while villages and towns were permanently located on defensible sites. In the colonial era the need to establish an administrative system, achieved by strengthening the powers of traditional chiefs and creating warrant chiefs where the former did not exist, reinforced by the need for social provisions, roads, schools, dispensaries and wells, all played a part in settlement fixation.

Commercialisation of agriculture (Chapter 5) has also been a fundamental factor. The introduction of cash crops operates in the same way as population increase, by intensifying land requirements. Where, as is often the case, cash crops are perennials, their influence in fixation is even greater. There is also increased need to locate the cropping areas near evacuation routes, markets and official buying-stations.

The greater the investment in a settlement, the less the tendency to shift. The greater permanency of buildings, the erection of trade stores, shops and market buildings all reflect this increased investment. The creation of large forest reserves in which cultivation is prohibited, the loss of land to public institutions, and the widespread use of the bicycle, which increases the area of land that can be cultivated from a settlement, have all played a part.

ROTATIONAL BUSH FALLOWING

Rotational bush fallowing is the most widespread cultivation system in West Africa although it is usually used in conjunction with permanent cultivation, in proportions which vary not only between communities but also from place to place within communities. The aim of the cultivators is to create a regular system of fallows. Usually the fallow periods are too short to permit a return to woodland or forest, thus differing from the fully developed secondary woodland and forest remaining in forest reserves, in the no-man's land between communities, and on slopes too steep or soils too poor for cultivation. In clearing, various useful trees are preserved and these are subsequently maintained in the fallows. Indeed, such trees are often deliberately planted in the fallows, as in those parts of Yorubaland within the Forest. Farms are more regular in shape and may have semi-permanent boundaries, although it is not usual for them to be hedged or fenced. The 'field' pattern, however, is not static, as changing demands for land are accommodated by adding new farms.

Bush fallowing is more intensive than shifting agriculture, so the problem of maintaining soil fertility is greater. Because of trypanosome infestation in the Forest and Guinea Savana and because of the split between crop and animal husbandry in the Sudan, the use of animal manure is not widespread, nor as yet are farmers inclined to spend money on artificial fertiliser. Renewal of fertility, therefore, depends upon the fallow period, as in shifting agriculture, but in addition crop mixtures and rotations are practised. Generally speaking the more demanding crops occupy the early years and are followed by less demanding ones. There is also evidence that rotations are longer in areas with a longer dry season, for this rest period acts as a short fallow which adds some nutrients to the soil. Since these areas are tsetse free, nomadic pastoralists are encouraged to graze their herds on the stubbles. Where the dry season is short, there is no rest period, the staple root crops take longer to mature, and tsetse infestation increases the difficulty of obtaining organic manure.

Fallow then still occupies the greater part of the available land. Given sufficiently long periods, woody regrowth in the Forest quickly re-establishes the nutrient and water cycles, while the floristic composition and the density and height of the plants change in a well-documented succession. Certain plants serve as indicators of restored fertility and in choosing areas for new farms the cultivator is guided by their presence. A period of between five and ten years is usually long enough to restore fertility. In the savana areas woody re-growth is much slower, or even absent, and restoration of fertility is correspondingly longer.[11]

Length of fallow periods is not controlled only by the need to restore fertility. Other factors are pressure upon land resources and accessibility. Where population densities are high, fallows are reduced, especially where cash crops occupy a significant proportion of the cultivable land. Thus W. B. Morgan[12] has examined the relationship between length of fallow period and population density in Aba Division of Eastern Nigeria and found a three-year fallow period where population density was 793 per square mile, (306 per square kilometre) five years where densities were 263 and 490 per square mile (102 to 189 per square kilometre), seven years where densities were 138 and 306 (57 and 118) and between nine and 15 years where density was 187 (72 per square kilometre) per square mile. In the *terre de barre* of Lower Dahomey and Togo, where population densities reach 130–260 per square mile (50–100 per square kilometre), fallow periods rarely exceeded three years after two years of cropping. Similarly fallow periods tend to be shorter on land close to settlements and to lengthen with increasing distance from them. In south-western Ghana it has been shown how cultivation takes place within easy access of roads so that fallow periods shorten close to the roads and lengthen away from them.[13]

Whether fallows are woody or grassy has significant implications. Woody fallows are normally restricted to humid areas, but over-cultivation may reduce them to grassy fallows however humid the climate. Clearance of grassy fallows obviously requires fewer labour inputs, but conversely they require more labour in cultivation to remove grass roots, and weeding is more arduous, especially if such grasses as *Imperata cylindrica* are present.

Planting, which follows the first rain, is usually in mixed stands. Whilst this reduces the yields of individual plants, it greatly increases the total yields of the individual farm. This in turn reduces demands for cultivation on the fallow areas. Labour requirements for clearing are also reduced, and, since the crops in the mixture are planted and harvested in succession, work is spread more evenly. The dense crop cover reduces competition for nutrients from weeds and the labour of weeding. This cover also reduces the rate of leaching and risk of erosion by reducing the impact of the heavy tropical rain and lessens the possibility of a lateritic crust forming. The mixed stands also reduce the possibility of total crop failure through weather conditions, disease, and pests, while individual crops are planted so that their varying demands upon soil nutrients are catered for, advantage being taken of different soil depths and drainage conditions on the mounds and ridges characteristic of cultivated plots.

More of the land is in cultivation in the rotational bush fallowing system than under shifting cultivation, the proportion of fallow is lower and patterns of land-use become discernible. At Soba in Zaria Province,[14] Northern Nigeria, where population density in 1952 was 103 per square mile (40 per square kilometre) about 6 per cent. of the village land was under cultivation. The land-use pattern of Soba is characteristic of large parts of the savana land of West Africa. Its dominant feature is the arrangement of uses in a number of concentric rings centred on the village. In central Ghana[15] the rings take the form of a permanently cropped garden area, a grazed grassland area formerly cultivated but now exhausted, and a ring containing the cultivated land interspersed with fallow; and the outer ring is unfarmed bush. Similar patterns have been identified elsewhere in West Africa and the literature has recently been reviewed by W. B. Morgan.[16]

PERMANENT & SEMI-PERMANENT CULTIVATION

Where these practices are carried on, fallows are either non-existent or occur at long irregular intervals. Only rarely can certain favoured soils, such as those weathered from basic volcanic rocks, sustain long periods of cultivation without resource to other methods of maintaining fertility. These include the application of organic manure, the collection and composting of night soil and household waste, the use of crop residues, crop rotation, and tree cultivation. Five forms of these practices can be identified.

The first and most common is *compound and kitchen-garden land*. Located close to the settlement, it is used to provide foodstuffs frequently used in small quantities for relishes and sauces, and for crops that require guarding, more fertile soils, or individual attention. In addition, tree crops are either preserved or planted on compound land, where they can receive individual attention and protection from the 'bush fires' of the cropland. Soil fertility is maintained or improved by the application of household refuse, ashes, crop residues and animal manure. Compound land generally occupies only a small proportion of a village's land and is almost invariably supplementary to crop production by shifting cultivation or bush fallowing.

The second form is found on confined sites in *defensible uplands* where small or weak tribes sought shelter from attack by more powerful neighbours. It is thus a feature of the Sub-Sudanic zone and is best developed in the Guinea massif, the Atacora range of Togo, the Jos Plateau and the Adamawa plateaux. It is also found in the smaller hill masses of the zone, such as the Birrimian inselbergs of northern Ghana. The most advanced agricultural system is perhaps found among the Dikwa of the Mandara mountains.[17] Stanhope White estimated that there are 20,000 miles (32,200 kms.) of dry-walled terraces in the area. Crops are grown in a three-year rotation, beans with some millet, followed by millet with some beans and, in the third year, guinea corn. Cattle are confined at night during the growing season and their manure carefully collected, and used together with night soil and household waste. Useful trees are planted, some of which provide fodder. These techniques allow the terraced fields to yield for ten years, after which they are left for a short period of fallow.

But such sophisticated systems are rare. Much more common are systems evolved in a peripheral manner by the clearing of stones from the area to be cultivated, laying them around the slope and allowing soil creep to bank the earth up behind them. It is thought that the systems in the Lere Hills of the Jos Plateau, of the Cabrais Massif of Togo and the Maku areas of Eastern Nigeria developed in this way. On these rudimentary terrace systems, however, advanced agricultural practices were common. The Cabrais[18] maintain the fertility of their soil by the use of leguminous crops in the rotation and by assiduous collection of manure and household waste. The Maku[19] peoples rely on crop rotation and composting, supplemented by the burning of weeds and trash to provide ash scattered on the fields and by the digging in of grass and leaves taken from the forest to maintain soil fertility. In other upland areas similar practices are employed but without terracing.

Thirdly there are *lowland areas of dense population*. These include the Kano Close-Settled Zone of Northern Nigeria,[20] the Mossi area of Haute Volta,[21] both in the Sudan, and the Ibo and Ibibio lands of the Eastern Nigerian Forest.[22] In these areas fertility depends upon the collection and application of all kinds of organic matter and in the Sudanic areas upon seasonal deposition of harmattan dust. Those parts of the Kano Close-Settled Zone near the city benefit from night soil brought out by the donkey-load. Crop rotations are also a feature of this form, while permanent cultivation in the Ibo and Ibibio lands is distinctive, as it relies on oil-palms in addition to field crops.

Finally, there are two special forms, *tree cultivation* and *floodland cultivation*. Tree cultivation is more a feature of commercial than of indigenous agriculture, but nevertheless the development of oil-palm bush, particularly in Lower Dahomey and Eastern Nigeria and of kola plantations in areas occupied or controlled by the Akan-speaking peoples should be noted at this juncture.

Floodland cultivation is widespread but is usually practised in association with other systems of cultivation. The use of annually flooded alluvium to produce supplementary foodcrops extends both the season of agricultural labour and the period when fresh food is available into the long dry season of the Sudan zone. But in three areas floodland cultivation is more important than the cultivation of adjacent rainlands. The first area is the Sahelian floodplains of the Sénégal, Niger and Chad Basins. In the valley of the Sénégal between Dagana and Bakel crops of guinea corn, cowpeas and maize are planted on the floodplain from October onwards and the cultivation season lasts until the final harvest in June. The rainland crops, chiefly bulrush millet, are planted in June and harvested in November. Fallows are long in spite of the application of manure and ashes on the cropland. In the middle Niger valley and in the inland Niger Delta rice is the chief crop in the floodlands.[23]

The second area is the smaller floodplains of the Sahel and Sudan, where lands under permanent cultivation are small in area and irregular in distribution. Practices and crops vary from place to place but cereals are dominant and wheat is sometimes important. Irrigation is also practised on these *fadama* lands, using well water and shadufs to produce vegetables, date palms and tobacco.

The third area is the estuarine floodlands, particularly the Rivières du Sud, where swamp rice cultivation pre-dates European influence. Methods of cultivation are thorough, occupy all the cultivators' time and impose their rhythm on the cultivators' life. There are no rotations and no fallow, the problem rather being to keep salinity within acceptable levels than to maintain soil fertility. The embanked polder lands on which the rice is grown are divided into small parcels which can be bought and sold whilst there are complicated rules governing their exploitation.[24]

SUBSISTENCE ECONOMIES

The farming practices outlined and the range of crops available[25] impose a common basic diet. This consists of a starchy base, composed of one or more of the range of staples locally available. In the Forest these are either plantains (*Musa paradisiaca*), roots, such as cassava (*Menihot utilissima*), cocoyam (*Xanthosoma sagittifolia, Colocasia esculenta*) and in Nigeria yams (*Dioscorea spp.*) or grains, chiefly maize (*Zea mays*) and rice (*Oriza spp.*). In the Guinea Savana Woodland the staples are yam, guinea corn (*Sorghum guineense*) and bulrush millet

(*Pennisetum cinerum*). In the Sudan these grains are supplemented by finger millet (*Eleusine coracona*).

These are usually eaten in the form of a paste or porridge flavoured by 'soups' made from pulses such as cowpeas (*Gigna unguiculata*), winged bean (*Psophocarpus tetragonolobus*) and groundnuts (*Arachis hypogaea*), vegetables such as onions and okra (*Hibiscus esculens*), pot herbs and vegetable oils. The soups are highly seasoned with peppers (normally *Capsicum spp.*; the indigenous *Piper guineense* and *Aframomum melegueta* are less common) and sometimes include small amounts of protein, fish or meat, in the diet. In addition a wide variety of fruits, bananas, citrus, mangoes and so on, is eaten.

Palm wine, the fermented liquor tapped from oil palms, is drunk in the forest areas, and millet beer in the Savanas.

Four major subsistence economies can be identified, using the staple starch crops as the key criterion and considering the other crops grown in association.

1. THE NORTHERN GRAIN-PULSE ECONOMY can be broadly equated with the Sahel and the Sudan. This economy is divisible into two categories, the first with bulrush millet, the second with guinea corn, as the dominant staple. The former is found north of 7° N., where the rainy season is less than five months in length and where the annual total is less than 750 mms of rainfall. Bulrush millet requires little moisture in the soil for germination, and while some varieties take up to 130 days to mature, others only take 60. It is thus a most suitable crop for the drier northern parts of West Africa. A wide variety of subsidiary crops is grown in association, including guinea corn, grown not only for food but also for beer making, *acha* (hungry rice) (*Digitaria exilis*) or *fonio* (finger millet), groundnuts, dry rice, cotton, maize, various legumes and cassava. The varieties and the rotations vary from area to area. Thus the Ouolof grow a quick growing and low yielding millet (*souna*) and high yielding millet (*sanio*), groundnuts and some guinea corn. The millets follow groundnuts in rotation and are grown in combination with cow peas or other pulses. There is little compound land and the cropland is usually cultivated for up to eight years before being fallowed for four years or less.[26]

To the south, with increasing resources of soil moisture, guinea corn increases in importance until it replaces millet as

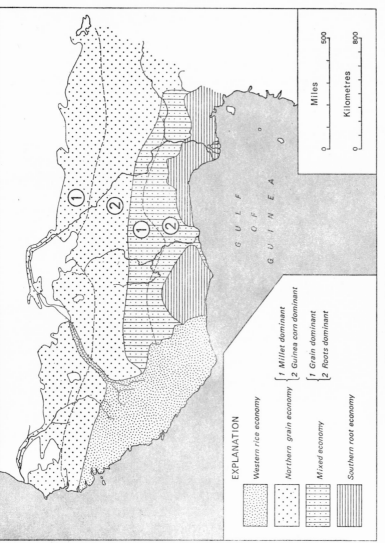

Figure 4.2. Subsistence economies

the dominant crop. The Mossi lands of Haute Volta straddle the transition zone and here both are staples while maize, beans, cotton, groundnuts, sesame (benniseed) (*Sesamum indicum*) and rice are included amongst the important secondaries. Maize, tobacco, vegetables and slower-growing varieties of guinea corn are grown on the compound land. The main cropland is cultivated by the bush fallowing system, although in some areas a semi-permanent system has evolved. In order to achieve more balanced use of plant food resources subsidiary crops are interplanted with staples, beans and sesame, for instance, with guinea corn. In the village of Taghalla (Haute Volta), maize and tobacco are grown by the women on compound-land whilst the surrounding large permanently cultivated fields are worked by family groups. On these a primitive rotation of millet, groundnuts and cotton is practised or alternatively millet and cotton alternate. On the main cropland, which provides the bulk of the food supply, millet is grown for up to four years and the land is then fallowed. On the low lying lands true rotation with fallow is practised. Millet alternates with beans and sesame for four years followed by two years of cotton and one of *tamba* (finger millet). The land is then fallowed for three years. Duhart[27] gives examples of pseudo-rotations practised in Mossi-land:

(i)   1. Bulrush millet   2. Bulrush millet or guinea corn
      3. Bulrush millet   4. Groundnuts   5. Fallow, 4–10
                                                years.

(ii) 1. Guinea corn   2. Guinea corn   3. Guinea corn
      4. Bulrush millet   5. Groundnuts   6. Fallow, 4–10
                                                years.

(iii) 1. Guinea corn   2. Guinea corn   3. Guinea corn
      4. Guinea corn   5. Cotton   6. Cotton
      7. Guinea corn   8. Guinea corn   9. Guinea corn
      10. Bulrush millet   11. Fallow, 3 years or more.

The Manding of the Casamance Basin[28] divide their main cropland into near and distant portions. On the former they cultivate groundnuts mixed with guinea corn until the soils are almost exhausted, when bulrush millet and *acha* are planted in successive years. On the latter millet, groundnuts, guinea corn and acha frequently rotate. They also cultivate compound land

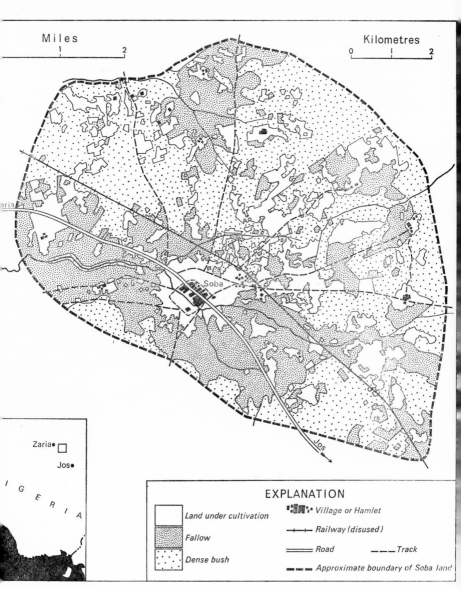

Figure 4.3. Land use in the Soba area, northern Nigeria (after Prothero)

and floodland. Where the latter is abundant rice replaces guinea corn as the staple food.

Prothero's study of Soba in Zaria Province[29] illustrates the form this economy takes in the moderately populated portions of Hausaland. There are four classes of land arranged in roughly concentric zones. The first is compound land within the village walls which is manured and permanently cultivated to produce tomatoes, calabashes (gourds) and tobacco; the second, immediately outside the village, is also manured and permanently cultivated and extends in a belt between half and three quarters of a mile in width and planted chiefly with guinea corn and cotton; the third is a ring, between half and one and a quarter miles wide, cultivated by rotational bush fallow methods and consisting of intermixed plots of land and fallow in various stages of regrowth; finally thick bush, extending in a ring one and a half miles wide, except in the south, where it is half a mile wide, intermittently cultivated by shifting cultivation methods. In these last two, guinea corn and groundnuts are dominant.

In certain areas, notably those of high population density, where pressure on land resources is acute, both bulrush millet and guinea corn have been replaced as the dominant crop by more poverty tolerant cereals, particularly hungry rice but also finger millet. The economy of these areas is illustrated by conditions in the closely settled areas of the Jos Plateau.[30] Amongst the Birom a distinction is made between the household farmland of about 2·5 acres (one hectare) and the bush farm, which may be as large as eight acres (3 hectares). The home farmland is often protected by euphorbia hedges and cultivated by intensive techniques. Amongst the eastern Birom a rudimentary rotation is practised in the bush farmland which involves fallow periods of three or four years. Hungry rice, the main crop, is sown broadcast. In addition, yams, cocoyams, bulrush and finger millet, beans and vegetables are grown in mixed stands. Manure is used only on the household farms. Cultivatable land in the Gyel District represents 60 per cent. of the total area. Of this, fallow occupies 28 per cent., hungry rice 40 per cent., millet 16 per cent., and other crops 16 per cent. Farms are cropped for 10 to 15 years and fallow periods are too short, so fertility is being depleted. The fallows are also over-grazed by Fulani cattle. Only on the household farmlands (10 per cent. of the cultivated area) is productivity being maintained.

2. THE SOUTHERN ROOT ECONOMY is found in an area extending eastward from the Bandama River in the Côte d'Ivoire. It occupies the two main areas of woody fallow separated by the coastal savana of southern Ghana and Togo. Plantains and cocoyams, and in Nigeria yams, are the traditional staples, but cassava has become increasingly dominant in the last 50 years and is now one of the chief food crops of West Africa.[31] Maize is the only staple cereal and is grown where the forest canopy is well broken. Two crops a year can be taken in this area of double rainy season. Both upland and swamp rice are locally important. Many vegetables are grown whilst fruits vary in importance from place to place. The oil palm is universally important.

There are several variants within the large area in which the economy is found. One such is practised along the fringes of the woody fallow in southern Ghana, in the *terre de barre* (Figure 4.5) and in south-western Yorubaland. Cassava and maize form the basis of the economy, and are cultivated under oil palms of greater or less density. In Egba Division of south-western Yorubaland yam as a dominant crop is now confined to the grassy fallow area, having been ousted by cassava from the woody fallow area. This has been a gradual process due to progressive decline in soil fertility, to the greater labour demands that yam makes and to the pattern of this labour demand, which clashes with that of the export tree crops, now dominant in the woody fallow areas. In addition both yam and cavassa have been partially displaced by hill rice. Yam is displaced because like rice it yields best on newly cleared land but has higher labour inputs. Cassava is replaced because of the greater ease of processing rice. Fresh cassava contains prussic acid and requires drying to get rid of the volatile but potent poison.

A second variant is found in eastern Yorubaland and Benin and is based upon yams, maize, cocoyam and cassava. Allison[32] has described this system as practised in Ondo Province: 'The area is cleared in February and the slash is burned soon after. The main crops of yams and corn are planted with the first rains

G

together with pumpkins, melons and calabashes. When the first corn is harvested about June, beans, cassava, okra and cocoyams may be planted. A second crop of corn is planted in August and harvested in October or November; yams are

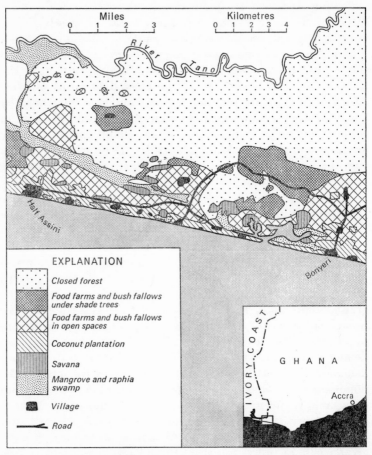

Figure 4.4. Land use in Western Nzima, Ghana, (after Varley & White)

harvested in September or October.' Similar systems are to be found in Southern Ghana. (Figure 4.4).

A third variant, based on yam and cassava, is found in Iboland, east of the Niger. There are two types of land, compound land, on which fertility is maintained by the use of

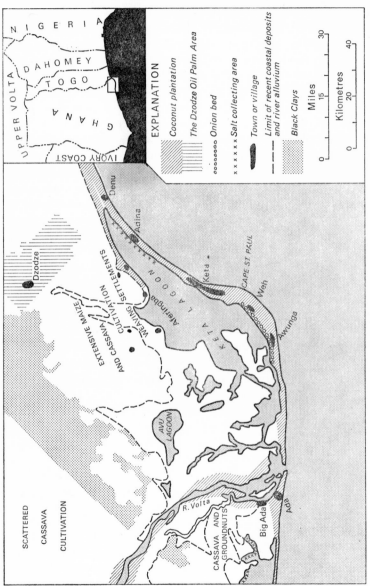

Figure 4.5. Land use in the Keta area of Ghana, (after Varley & White)

manure, household waste and vegetable waste, and the outer farmlands, which receive no manure but are planted with leguminous shrubs during the fallow periods. Compound land is permanently cropped with mixtures composed of yams, cocoyams, maize and vegetables grown in the shade of oil-palms and other trees. The outer farmlands are cropped once in four to six years with intercropped yams and cassava and some maize or beans. The farms then become fallow, with cassava in the second year before reverting to full fallow. Where population density exceeds 1,000 habitants per square mile (386 per square kilometre), as in parts of Orlu, Okigwi and Awka Divisions, compound land occupies almost the whole of the village area. Oil palms are planted in the open fields after manuring of the ground, and new compounds built when the palms are established. This process has recently been described for the Ozubulu village group, south west of Awka.[33]

3. THE WESTERN RICE ECONOMY occupies the coastlands west-ward of the Bàndama, a major cultural divide according to Miège.[34] It also extends, finger-like, along the Niger Valley to the Sahel fringe. Outside this large area rice is also important in the river valleys of the Sudan zone, and its cultivation is spreading in parts of the yam producing area beyond the Bandama River. Agricultural techniques and crops of this economy are similar to those of neighbouring economies. But it differs in the dominance of rice, the chief staple. There are two methods of cultivation.

Upland, hill or dry rice cultivation requires a minimum of 750 mms. of rainfall over at least five months. R. Portères[35] counted 37 varieties of rice in the north-west forest of Côte d'Ivoire and more in the Guinée forests, maturing in 90 to 170 days. Like any other grain, the rice is a part of the bush fallowing system.

In the forest portion of their territory the Gouro of the Bouaké Cercle in Côte d'Ivoire[36] grow rice with cocoyam, maize, plantains, legumes and vegetables. Land is abundant, permitting shifting cultivation of land newly cleared from high forest each year. After cropping for one year the land reverts to secondary forest. In addition to the main croplands the Gouro also use bush-fallowing techniques on land close to the village which they call *frita*. Here rice or maize is grown in association with plantain for one year, after which the land is fallowed for two to five years.

Wet rice cultivation takes place in coastal swamps, inland swamps and on riverain floodplains. It is a form of permanent cultivation in which rice is the sole crop. Swamp rice grown in coastal floodlands forms the basis of the economy in the Rivières du Sud (page 32). Here the silt laden rivers discharge into the rias through deltas. Mangrove swamps occupy the mud-flats of the coast, the *poto-poto*, washed by high tides but uncovered at low water and threaded with creeks and rivers, the *bolongs*. The influence of tidal range is twofold and a spring-tide range of 10 feet (3 metres) appears to be critical. A sufficiently great tidal range reduces to an acceptable level the free sulphuric acid in the mangrove swamp soils, whilst the flooding of the fields by salt water in the rest period reduces weed growth.

Polders are created from mangrove swamps, the banks equipped with sluice gates made of palm trunks and old canoes sealed with grass and mud. These are closed as the tides rise and opened as they fall. Canals are cut behind the dikes to effect drainage and irrigation. Desalination of the soil takes two or three years. Most of the ricelands occupy the low lands along secondary arms where the tide does not penetrate much and their utilisation is easy. In polders where the soil is salty rice is grown on ridges thrown up by a spade-like implement which needs two men to use it. The crop is transplanted onto the ridges from carefully tended, fertilized, nursery beds close to the villages. Yields average 900–1,700 lb per acre (1,000–1,900 kilos per hectare). After harvest the stubble is grazed by cattle and the land is further fertilised by the addition of manure, household waste, ashes, shells to provide lime, and by hoeing in of the trash from the previous crop.

The Baga of Guinée illustrate this general picture. They live in linear villages along the sand bars and ridges, planted with oil palms and running between the rice-lands which extend into the swamp at right angles to the village. Thus each compound has individual access to its fields. The land is held on a family basis, each cultivating 5 to 8 acres (2·0 to 3·25 hectares). The cultivation cycle begins in March and April, when the polders are ridged to take the first crop. Because water levels are lowest, dikes can be repaired and new polders cleared. Transplanting begins with the onset of the rains in May. Quick growing varieties are planted first for harvest in October but planting continues into June. Land from which a crop has been harvested in October is prepared and planted with a second crop for harvesting in January and February whilst harvesting of slower growing varieties proceeds through November. Between January and May cattle are pastured on the dried out rice-lands. Secondary crops, onions, fruits, maize, cassava, sweet potatoes (*Ipomaea batatas*), yams, cocoyams and groundnuts, have recently been introduced. They are grown on the higher floodlands and are planted as the water recedes in December and January and harvested from April to September. Their labour demands are thus complementary to those of the traditional crop.

The cultivation of swamp rice sometimes forms a mixed agricultural system with upland rice. Thus the Diolas of Casamance[37] practise swamp cultivation similar to that described above and upland cultivation of rice in association with maize, millet or hungry rice and groundnuts on farmlands beneath oil-palms. The location of their villages and the pattern of land use around them, reflect this mixed agricultural system. Amongst the Kissi of Upper Guinée a more complex system has evolved. Land is used in four ways. First, kitchen garden land, small and close to the village, is cultivated permanently, using animal manure. Secondly, the valley bottoms are devoted to swamp rice and are also permanently cultivated. Thirdly, on the plateau, in the forest and bush a five-year rotation of rice, groundnut, cotton, sweet potatoes and cassava is followed by a five-year fallow period. Finally, on the slopes patches are cleared by burning and cropped for a year.

4. THE YAM-GRAIN ECONOMY occupies a belt of West Africa between the northern grain-pulse and southern root economies. It has features of both its neighbours, and indeed it results from their overlapping. But it can readily be distinguished from them. There are two forms. In the southern part yams dominate. It differs from its southern neighbour by the absence of tree crops, except in narrow gallery forests along water courses, in the importance of guinea corn, and in the grassy as opposed to woody nature of its fallows. This economy has

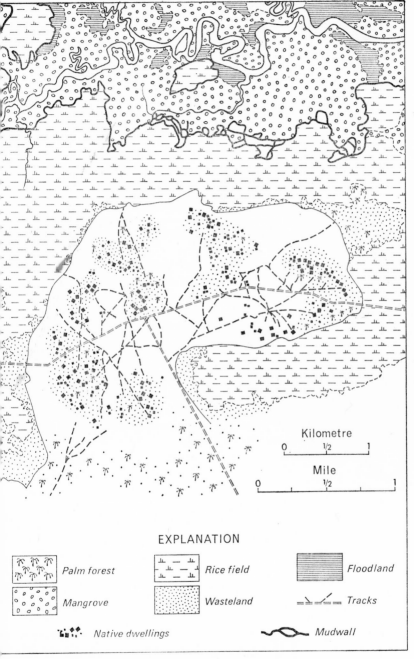

EXPLANATION

Palm forest		Rice field		Floodland	
Mangrove		Wasteland		Tracks	
Native dwellings				Mudwall	

Kilometre

0   1/2   1

Mile

0   1/2   1

Figure 4.6. Diola land use, Casamence (after Pélissier)

several variants. In Ghana, in a broad belt of northern Ashanti adjacent to the Forest edge, yams form the basis of the economy. They are grown under shifting cultivation and are followed by maize in the southern portion and guinea corn in the northern and in the third year by upland rice and cassava before the land returns to fallow. A second variant is found in the grassland portions of Yorubaland where the first crop is yams whenever sufficient tree stumps to serve as supports for the vines are available. Where supports are not available, maize is planted during the first rainy season followed by maize or guinea corn during the second. The stalks of the grain crops are carefully interwoven to provide yam supports for the following season. At the close of the cultivation cycle cassava is planted and remains in the fallows until needed. Many minor crops—cotton, groundnuts, melons, spring onions, various leaf vegetables, okra, peppers—are interplanted with the main crops. Grain and legumes such as cowpeas, interplanted or in pure stands, follow in the second season. Tobacco as a cash crop has supplanted yam as the first crop in the rotation wherever it is grown. A third variant is found on the Accra plains where the economy is based on cassava. It is grown wherever soil texture is suitable, friable sandy loams being preferred and damp avoided. In the western part of the plains it is virtually the sole crop, in the eastern part groundnut is also important. Other variations are found in Tivland, where sesame (benniseed), a cash crop, follows yams and the cereals in a three course rotation, and in northern Iboland, where the yam-cassava economy extends beyond the woody into the grassy fallow areas.

In the second type of yam-grain economy cereals are dominant. It differs from its neighbour to the north, the grain-pulse economy, chiefly in the importance of root crops. It is found in a belt narrowing eastwards and extending from northern Côte d'Ivoire, through northern Ghana, Togo and Dahomey into Nigeria. Yam is the main root crop and it usually occupies the first year of the rotation. Thus in eastern Dagomba yams are planted on mounds on newly cleared fallow in late December and intercropped with acha and millet, sown in June and July, and with Bambara groundnuts (*Voandzeia subterranea*) and with okra. Cassava is planted as a farm boundary. Early yams are harvested in August and September, whilst harvest of later yams continues into the dry season. That of cassava begins in December and lasts until the rainy season. The yam mounds are reduced through intercropping and by rainfall during the first year. Prior to cropping in the second year these are broken down and made into ridges on which maize is interplanted with guinea corn, groundnuts, and other legumes. For the third year little seed bed preparation is undertaken and the second year's crops are repeated. The land reverts to fallow in the fourth year.

The economy of the Nupe of central Nigeria illustrates a variation of this sub-type and also the mixed nature of agricultural systems. The staple crops are millet, guinea corn, yam and to a lesser extent rice, some of which are sold, though groundnuts and cotton are the main providers of cash income. The Nupe cultivate three types of land, namely compound and village land, *fadama* or marshy valley bottom land, and main cropland. The compound and village land is fertilised with household waste and is permanently cropped with vegetables, peppers, cassava and maize. Normally the compounds are in scattered villages and the compound crops are grown round them. Where compounds are closer and in Bida town the compound land is in small plots. The *fadama* occupies 10 per cent. or less of the cultivated area. But its importance is far greater. It is cropped with a mixture of cassava and sweet potatoes, followed by rice for 10 years or longer. The main cropland is cultivated for between four and seven years and is fallowed for a period varying from four to 15 years. Cultivation techniques are similar to those described above for Dagomba and a strict rotation of crops, with intercropping and succession planting, is used during the cultivation cycle. Nadel[38] lists four main rotations in which yam, cotton, and groundnuts are always grown in the first year and only once in each cropping cycle. These are:

(i) 1. yam, 2. maize and guinea corn or bulrush millet, late millet and guinea corn, 3 and 4. bulrush millet, late millet and guinea corn.

(ii) 1 to 3. bulrush millet, late millet and guinea corn, 4. as in 3, or cassava, sweet potatoes or beans.

   (iii) 1. groundnuts and cassava, 2 and 3. bulrush millet and maize, late millet and guinea corn, 4. cassava, sweet potatoes and beans.

   (iv) 1. cotton, 2 and 3. bulrush millet, late millet and guinea corn, 4. cassava, sweet potatoes and beans.

STOCK REARING[39]

The keeping of animals is widespread, but only in the Sudan and the Sahel is it an important sector of the economy. Small stock, sheep (estimated at 14 million), goats (26 million) and, in non-Moslem areas, pigs (1 million) together with chickens are kept everywhere, but are not integrated into the agricultural economies. They are left to scavenge for food around the compounds, on the stubble after harvest and on the fallows. They are killed and eaten on ceremonial occasions and provide the main source of meat. There is a contrast between the larger breeds of goat in the Sudan and the smaller animals of the south. Sheep are more numerous in the Sudan zone, where they are kept by nomadic pastoralists, particularly the Fulani. Again there is a contrast in size between the larger northern and the smaller southern animals. Productivity of all small stock is low. Of the larger stock, donkeys of which there are about 2 million, and camels, numbering about 200,000, are the beasts of burden of the Sudan and Sahel zones respectively, the half-million or so horses being kept for ceremonial purposes and for riding by the nobility, while oxen are still used for riding and as pack animals on the fringes of the Sahel particularly by the Moors and by the Shuwa.

There are about 21 million cattle belonging to four major types. The most important is the humped or zebu. The southern limit of its distribution coincides with the northern limit of the tsetse fly. Like the much less numerous *kuri* type, found only in the marshes and islands of Lake Chad, these are large. They form the basis of Fulani herds, and are found particularly north of latitude 12°–14° N. The other two types are humpless, one the *ndama*, a native of the Guinée highlands, the other the widespread West African Short-Horn, are small and are tolerant of trypanosomiasis. Cross types between humpless and zebu, having incomplete resistance to fly are

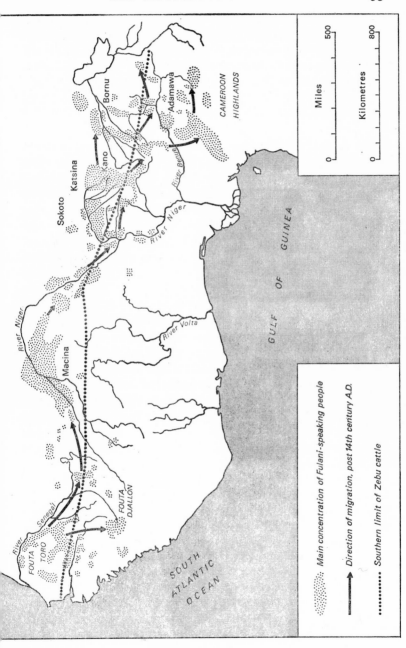

Figure 4.7. Fulani migrations (after Prothero)

found between latitudes 10° N. and 12°–14° N. Yields of both meat and milk are low and the animals are slow to mature. Even the superior northern stock yields only one-third as much beef and only one-quarter as much milk as its European counterpart whilst yields from humpless cattle are even lower.

Generally there is a clear division between livestock and crop husbandry. Usually, but not invariably, stock rearing is carried on by nomadic pastoralists, notably the Fulani. The Fulani are found throughout West Africa and were originally all nomadic cattle-herders, racially and culturally distinct from the cultivators. They spread outwards from a nucleus in the Sénégal River basin after the fourteenth century A.D., gradually dispersing across the Sudan plains as far as Cameroun. During this process many settled in the sub-Saharan towns and some lost their herds and integrated with the cultivators. These are referred to as the 'town Fulani'. Only a minority, in Northern Nigeria some 8 per cent., now remain as 'cattle Fulani' or *Bororo*.

The cattle Fulani live off the milk of their cattle. They also exchange milk and butter for grain and other foodstuffs, selling only enough cattle to pay their taxes. They are restricted, therefore, to areas free of the tsetse fly and live mainly in the Sahelian zone. Here are the wet-season pastures where they have a semi-permanent home. They move in bands of between 10 and 20 households over an area of several hundred square miles, seeking water and dry-season pasture on the former cropland and fallows in the Sudan zone. In northern Nigeria some groups of pastoral Fulani have their wet season pastures in the Sudan zone and move southwards within the zone or into the Guinea Savana zone where dry season pasture is found in the valleys of the Niger and Benue rivers and of their main tributaries. This is tsetse country in the wet season but during the dry season the distribution of fly is more concentrated. Nevertheless contact between the fly and both stock and men occurs as the fly breeds in the areas where water is available.

Small groups of cattle Fulani have also penetrated the upland areas of West Africa. Some of these, such as the Jos and Bamenda Plateaux, are fly-free, others, such as the Fouta Djallon, are not. In the latter case they adapted, exchanging their zebu cattle for ndama. In these upland environments,

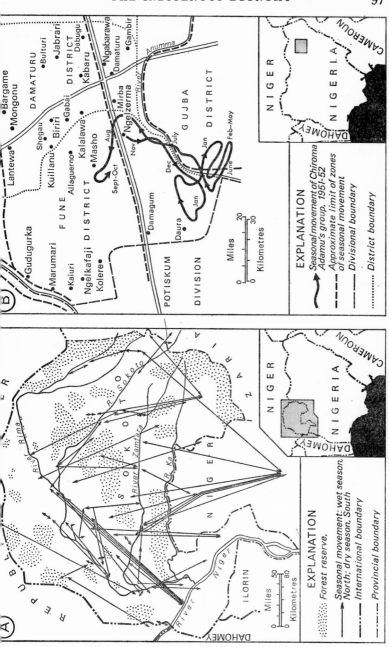

Figure 4.8. Patterns of pastoral nomadism. (A) Sokoto Province, Nigeria (after Prothero). (B) Bornu Province (after Stenning)

transhumance takes the form of movement downwards to dry season pastures. In the Fouta Djallon it is from the treeless high plateau to the valley bottoms, on the Jos Plateau it is on a smaller scale but again from upland to valley bottom, and in the Bamenda Highlands from the high Lava Plateau to the granite plateau of the Gondwana surface.

In addition to the Fulani, the Moors of the west and Tuareg and Toubou of Mali and Niger are nomadic pastoralists. The Moors may be divided into a Saharan group who are camel herders and wander over thousands of square miles and a southern group who like the Fulani, herd cattle and sheep and wander over small areas. The Tuareg and Toubou either wander over vast areas of the border zone between desert and Sahel herding cattle, camels and sheep or are sedentary and occupy oases in the Saharan massifs.

MIXED FARMING

Mixed farming in the usual sense of the term, the integration of crop and animal husbandry whereby the animals are used to fertilise the crops and some of the crops are used to feed the animals, does not exist in the indigenous economy. There are, however, a few instances of partial integration.

We have pointed to numerous examples of permanent cultivation with the aid of animal manure, but in no cases are fodder crops grown. Livestock are allowed to graze the stubbles and fallows, that is all. In addition most of the cattle are not owned by the cultivators, and if they are integration is not practised.

Perhaps the Serer of Sénégal approach closest to true mixed farming. For them crop production and stock rearing are of equal importance. Cattle graze throughout the year on the fallows and on cultivated land in the dry season, but fodder crops are not grown, though leaves are gathered. Settled Fulani in the Futa Djallon and Shuwa Arabs south of Lake Chad combine but do not integrate the cultivation and livestock sectors. Other cattle owners have them tended by Fulani.

OTHER ECONOMIC PURSUITS

GATHERING[40] is widespread as a supplement to agricultural produce. It is of greatest importance in the grassy savanas of the

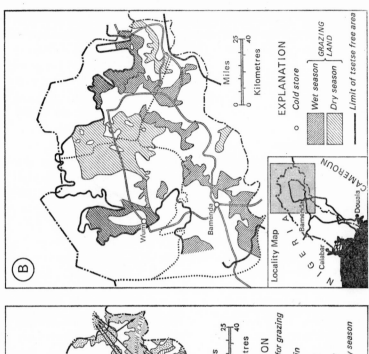

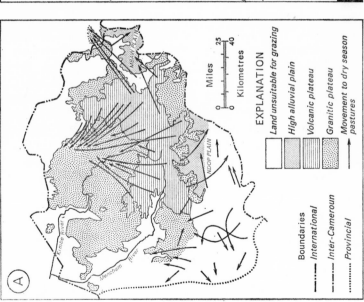

Figure 4.9. Patterns of pastoral nomadism in the Bamenda area of West Cameroun

Sudan and in the Sahel, where agriculture is interrupted by the very long dry season, but is also carried on in the woody savanas and even in the Forest. The Songhay of Mali gather roots, seeds and leaves of a great variety of plants between February and August. Useful plants include grains such as *Digitaria spp.* and *Brachiaria deflexa* in the grassy savanas. Wild yams and pot herbs are everywhere important. In the woody savanas there is a wide variety of useful trees which yield oil seeds, fruit, edible leaves, drink, fodder, fibre, medicines, gums, building timber and firewood. The most widely used include the shea (*Butyrospernum parkii*)—oil seeds, baobab (*Andansonia digitate*)—fruit, leaves, fibre and cloth, fan palm (*Borassus aethiopum*)—palm wine, bombax (*Bombax buonopozense*)—leaves and kapok, and tamarind (*Tamarindus indica*) oil, leaves, tannin. In the Forest the *Ceibe petandra* is valued for kapok, but the main trees are oil-palm and kola, which are also important in agricultural systems. Honey and snails are also gathered.

HUNTING, like gathering, is a dry season occupation carried on after harvest and when drinking points are reduced. In the savanas it is normally a group activity. The bush is fired to flush the game which are shot with muzzle-loading guns, or with bows and arrows. Spears, often tipped with vegetable poisons, clubs and traps are also used. In the Forest, where the dry season is short, it is often a specialist activity. Groups or guilds, possessing monopoly rights in certain methods or over certain animals, are formed of hunters who practise little or no cultivation. Almost anything that moves is considered edible, monkeys, deer, 'cutting-grass' (*Thyronomys swinderianus*), rats and snakes. Professional hunting is declining because of expansion of cultivated areas and increasing population density.

FISHING[41] may be a part-time activity of agriculturalists, but it is normally engaged in by communities of specialists. It is of great importance since fish provide some of the chief sources of animal protein and in many communities it plays a more important part in the diet than meat. Sea and lagoon fishing is mainly a wet season occupation engaged in by specialists. There are about 200 edible species of fish found in West African coastal waters. Greatest landings are made in Sénégal, where the waters abound in species such as sea bream, mackerel and sardines. Both lines and nets are used. The drift net, used mainly from large canoes, originally powered by sail but nowadays by outboard motors, and the seine net, used mainly from the beaches, were introduced in the late nineteenth century. In lagoons and estuaries lines, nets, traps of various kinds and sizes, together with poison, spears and harpoons are used. The smoking and salting of fish is an important activity in the fishing villages along the coast, whilst associated activities include canoe building, the preparation of tannin for net treatment and the production of salt. The fish is traded throughout West Africa.

Fresh-water fishing is mainly a dry season activity carried on in conjunction with cultivation during the wet season. Only in the larger river valleys such as the Niger and on Lake Chad is it a specialist occupation. Methods of catching fish are similar to those used in the lagoons. As it is a seasonal occupation strongly influenced by river regimes, it frequently involves extensive migration and the construction of temporary camps on levees and sandbanks. Thus the Sorkawa have their base along the Niger between Ayuna and Bagarua and along the Gulbi-n-Kebbi, but their migration in search of fish extends over 1,500 miles from Tomboctou to the coastal delta.

With the exception of fishing, these activities are often neglected in the literature, but their contemporary importance should not be under-rated. Gautier has shown they provide about 20 per cent. of the Mossi food supply. They are particularly important in reducing the shortages of the 'hungry season' of the savanas, when, between sowing and first harvest, food from the previous harvest is short at a time when labour demands are at their maximum.

MINERAL WORKING [42] was formerly of local importance. Gold mined in Ashanti, at Bambouk in the Sénégal basin, and at Bouré on the Bakhay headstreams reached North Africa and Europe. Gold from the Akan states of present day Ghana, produced from alluvial or pit and shaft workings, reached Hausaland and Mali, while Yoruba goldsmiths, using alluvial gold won from small valleys near Ilesha, have a high reputation throughout Nigeria.

Working of concretionary iron ores was widespread, but ceased at an early date when imported bar-iron or local scrap-iron became available. Copper, tin, lead, silver, zinc and

H

antimony ores have all been worked at a few locations during the pre-colonial era and galena is sold in most markets as an eye cosmetic. Finally, salt is an item of trade with a history about as long and important as gold. The Sudan is notably deficient and imports salt from oases in the Sahara and the coastal salt pans, such as the ones in the Keta area of Ghana. It is also worked at inland locations such as the 'salt lakes' of Ogoja Province in southern Nigeria.

MANUFACTURING is dealt with later, but its early importance in the indigenous economy must be mentioned. Craft industries of all kinds were widespread and many survive. The most important were the production of iron goods and textiles. The former used charcoal to smelt local ores, but nowadays scrap is the normal raw material. Smithing is the monopoly of specialised clans and some achieved a wide reputation for their products. The Banjeti in northern Togo supplied the whole of northern Togo and Dahomey, Ashanti and Mossi. The usual products were the simple agricultural tools. Spinning and weaving of locally grown cotton is long established and some peoples notably the Ashanti, Yoruba, Edo, Akiete Ibo and Hausa developed long distance trade. Other widespread crafts included building, carving, pottery and canoe building. Some, such as smithing, were the preserve of men, others such as pottery that of women, some were the prerogative of specialists, others were carried on as a part-time occupation, but most were confined to certain areas and villages.

A few of the more skilled crafts were even more highly localised. These included the making of brass-ware by the Edo and Nupe, the latter also being famous for their glass beads, the casting of bronze at Ife and Benin, the production of gold jewellery by the Ashanti and Yoruba and leatherwork by the Hausa. All these formed, and still form, important items of long distance trading.

The indigenous economy, which varies greatly from area to area, is the basis of the present-day economy of all West African countries. But it is evolving rapidly. Agriculture has been widely transformed by the introduction of cash cropping. Other sectors capable of development, certain craft industries and fishing, are being modernised and expanded. Those not capable of development, gathering, hunting, other craft industries which are in direct competition with factory production, and mineral working, are in decline. But the availability of external capital, of skills and enterprise harnessing modern technology, and the increasing place of the profit motive, together with the desire of all governments to increase local wealth, has resulted in the emergence of modernised sectors of the traditional economy. West African economies are consequently of a transitional nature, embodying in close juxtaposition the indigenous and the exotic, the subsistence and the commercial, the traditional and the modern. The relative importance of the old and the new varies both from sector to sector and from place to place both within West Africa and within the individual countries.

REFERENCES

1 *See inter al:* Clark, C. and Haswell, M., *The Economics of subsistence agriculture*, London, 1964

2 Morgan, W. B. and Pugh, J. C., *West Africa*, London, 1969, p. 67

3 *Agricultural sample surveys* of Western and Northern Regions of Nigeria, 1955 onwards (mimeo)

4 *See* for example, *Report of the sample census of agriculture*, Nigeria 1950–51: *Agricultural sample surveys. op cit.* No. 3

5 Gleave, M. B. and Thomas, M. F., '*The Bagango Valley: an example of land utilisation and agricultural practice in the Bamenda Highlands*'. *Bull. Inst. Fond. Afr. Noire*, Sér. B. *30*, 1968, pp. 655–81

6 Manshard, W., '*Land Use Patterns and Agricultural Migration in Central Ghana (Western Gonja)*', *Tijdschrift voor Economische en Sociale Geografie*, 52, 1961, pp. 225–230

7 Schlippe, P. de., *Shifting Agriculture in Africa: The Zande system of Agriculture*, London, 1956

8 Froelich, J. C., '*La Tribue Konkomba du Nord-Togo*', Mém, Inst. Française d'Afrique Noire, 37, 1954
Tait, D., *The Konkomba of Northern Ghana*, London, 1961

9 *East Dagomba agricultural and livestock survey, Northern Ghana*, Min. of Food and Agriculture, Kumasi, 1959 (mimeo)

10 Gleave, M. B. and White, H. P., '*Population density and agricultural systems in West Africa*', Chap. 10 in Thomas, M. F. and Whittington, G. W. (Eds.), *Environment and Land Use in Africa*, London, 1969

11 Nye, P. H. and Greenland, D. J., '*The soil under shifting agriculture*', Commonwealth Bureau of Soils, Technical Communication 51, Farnham Royal, 1960

12 Morgan, W. B., '*Farming practice, settlement patterns and population density in S. E. Nigeria*', *Geog. Journal*, 121, 1955, pp. 320–333

13 Ahn, P., *Soil Vegetation relationships in the Western Forest Areas of Ghana*, Kumasi, Division of Agriculture, Soil and Land Use Branch. (Mimeo), 1959

14 Prothero, R. M., *'Land Use at Soba, Zaria Province, Northern Nigeria'*, *Econ. Geog.*, 33, 1957, pp. 72–86

15 Wills, J. B., *'The general pattern of land use'* in Wills, J. B. (Ed.), *Agriculture and Land Use in Ghana*, London, 1962

16 Morgan, W. B., *'The zoning of land use around rural settlements in Tropical Africa'*, Chap. 11 in Thomas and Whittington *op cit.* 10

17 White, Stanhope, *'The agricultural economy of the hill pagans of Dikwa Emirate, Cameroons'*, *Empire Journal of Experimental Agriculture*, 9, 1941, pp. 65–72

18 Enjelbert, H., *'Paysans Noirs: Les Kabré du Nord-Togo'*, *Cahiers d'Outre-Mer*, 34, 1956, pp. 137–180: Froelich, J. C., *'Généralités sur les Kabré du Nord-Togo'*. *Bull. IFAN*, 11, 1949, pp. 77–105. *Idem. 'Densité de la population et methodes du culture chez les Kabré du Nord-Togo'*, *Compte Rend. Cong. Int. de Géog*, Lisbonne, 1949, 4, (Section 5), pp. 168–80

19 Floyd, B., *'Terrace agriculture in Eastern Nigeria: the case of Maku'*, *Nig. Geog. Jour.*, 7, 1964, pp. 91–108

20 Mortimore, M. J. and Wilson, J., *'Land and people in the Kano Close-Settled Zone'*, Ahmadu Bello University, Dept. of Geog., occ paper 1, 1965

21 Dubourg, J., *'La Vie des Paysans Mossi: Le Village de Taghalla'*, *Cahiers d'Outre-Mer*, 10, 1957 pp. 285–324: Gautier, E. F., *'Les Mossi'*, Chap. 5 in *Afrique Noire Occidentale*, Paris, 1943

22 Forde, C. D. and Jones, G. I., *'The Ibo and Ibibio-Speaking Peoples of South Eastern Nigeria'*, London, 1950

23 Gandet, C., *'Les sédentaires du Cercle de Tombouctou'*, *Cahiers d'Outre Mer*, 10, 1957, pp. 234–256: Dresch, J., *'Le Riziculture en Afrique Occidentale'*, *Annales de Géographie*, 58, 1949, pp. 295–312

24 Paulme, D, *'Des Riziculture Africains Les Baga'*, *Cahiers d'Outre Mer*, 10, 1957, pp. 257–278

25 see Johnson, B. F., *'The staple food economies of Western Tropical Africa'*, Stanford, 1958: Schnell, R., *'Plantes alimentaires et vie agricole del 'Afrique Noire'*, Paris, 1957: Morgan, W. B. and Pugh, J. C., *op cit.*

26 Dumont, R., *'Etude de Quelques Économies Agraires au Sénégal et en Casamence'*, *Agronomie Tropicale*, 6, 1951, pp. 229–238

27 Duhart, A. J., *'Rapport sur l'État Actuel de la Conservation des Sols en Territoire de la Haute Volta'*, *Proc. 2nd Inter-African Soils Conference*, Leopoldville (Kinshasa), 1954, Vol. II, pp. 1291–1300

28 Dresch, J., *'La riziculture en Afrique Occidale'*, *Annales de Géographie*, 58, 1949, pp. 295–312

29 Prothero, *op cit.*

30 Suffill, T. L., *'The Biroms—a pagan tribe on the Jos Plateau, Nigeria'*, *Farm & Forest*, 4, 1943, pp. 179–182: Davies, J. G. *'The Gyel Farm Survey in Jos Division'*, *Farm & Forest*, 7, 1946, pp. 110–113: Grove, A. T., *'Land Use and soil conservation on the Jos Plateau'*. *Bull. Geo. Survey*. Nigeria, 22, 1952

31 Jones, W. O., '*Manioc in Africa*', Stanford, 1959

32 Allison, P. A., '*From Farm to Forest*', *Farm & Forest*, 2, 1941, pp. 95–6

33 Udo, R. K., '*Disintegration of nucleated settlement in Eastern Nigeria*', *Geog. Rev.*, 55, 1965, pp. 53–67. *See* also, Grove, A. T., '*Soil Erosion and population problems in South East Nigeria*', *Geog. Jour.*, 117, 1951, pp. 291–306

34 Miège, J., '*Les Cultures Vivrières en Afrique Occidentale*', *Cahiers d'Outre-Mer*, I., 1951, pp. 25–50

35 quoted in Dresch, J., *op cit.* p. 304

36 Meillassoux, C., *Anthropologie économique des Gouro*, Paris, 1964

37 Pélissier, P.,'*Les Diola: étude sur l'habitat des riziculteurs de Basse-Casamance*', *Cahiers, D'outre Mer*, 11, 1958, pp. 334–388

38 Nadel, S. F., '*A Black Byzantium*', London, 1942

39 The best work is Doutressoule, G., '*l'Élévage en Afrique Occidentale*' Paris, 1947. *See* also Mason, I. L., '*The Classification of West African Livestock*', Commonwealth Bureau of Animal Breeding, 7, 1951: Stewart, J. L. & Jeffreys, M. D. W., '*The Cattle of the Gold Coast*', Accra, 1956

40 There is very little on gathering in the economy. Lists of plants are contained in Dalziel, J. M., '*The Useful Plants of West Tropical Africa*', London 1937: Schnell, R., '*Plantes Alimentaires et Vie Agricole de l'Afrique Noire*', Paris, 1957: For a detailed study *see* Ryssen, B., '*Le Karité (Shea) au Soudan, Agronomie Tropicale*', 12, 1957, pp. 143–172 and 279–306. *See* also Morgan and Pugh, *op cit.* pp. 153–155

41 For a more detailed general account *see* Morgan, and Pugh, *op cit.* pp. 157–162. For regional accounts *see* Manshard, W., '*Die Küsten und Flüss Fischerei Ghanas*', *Die Erde*, 89, 1958, pp. 21–33, Guilcher, A., '*La Région Côtière du Bas Dahomey Occidental, Bull. Institute Française d'Afrique Noire*', Sér B, 21, 1959, pp. 357–424: Ruch, J., '*Les Sorkawa, Pêcheurs Itinérants du Moyen Niger*', Africa, 20, 1950, pp. 5–25

42 There has not been much written on mineral workings as part of the indigenous economy other than gold. The best account is in Junner, N. R., '*Gold in the Gold Coast*', Mem. Geol. Survey, Accra, 4, 1935

CHAPTER 5

Cropping & the Commercialisation
of Agriculture

By its very nature subsistence agriculture must remain nearly static, any evolution taking place only over very long periods. It is impossible to improve productivity of either land or labour inputs by means such as mechanisation, artificial fertilisers or scientific husbandry. For, by definition, there can be neither capital investment nor recurrent expenditure. But, even with the introduction of cash cropping and with it the possibility of capital investment, the physical and the socio-economic environment of West Africa raises problems. In common with most countries concerned with a rapid development of their economy, USSR and China among them, the West African countries have found their agricultural sector the most intractible.

The possibility of effecting spectacular and lasting improvements to agriculture, one of the great achievements of the Netherlands and of Great Britain, over the last two centuries, is in West Africa a challenge to cultivator, scientist and administrator alike. It must be admitted that so far response has been patchy. There have been outstanding successes such as cocoa cultivation in Ghana and Western Nigeria and coffee growing in Côte d'Ivoire. But these have been balanced by more numerous failures.

The introduction of cash cropping into a subsistence economy is an essential preliminary to any economic development. Trade then becomes possible as farmers sell crops and buy food, clothing and consumer goods, though it is true to say that it is the simultaneous appearance of consumer goods in the local markets that stimulates the farmers to sell. Trade can grow only as farmers accumulate a greater cash surplus. Taxation also becomes possible to raise the funds necessary for social services and infrastructure.

The appearance of a specialist, non-farming work-force, another essential to economic and social development is not possible without a surplus of food that can be sold. As the economy becomes more sophisticated, the import of capital goods, upon which modernisation depends, becomes possible. But this is possible only to the extent to which a country's products can be exported. Again, the circulation of consumer goods, both imported and home produced, is possible only to the extent of the local cash surplus.

In West Africa commercialisation of agriculture takes two principal forms. The first and by far the most common is the introduction of cash cropping into the subsistence systems examined in Chapter 4. The second is the establishment of commercial agriculture as a complete break from previous systems.

Obviously, the introduction of cash crops into a subsistence economy involves at least some modifications, which are increased as the proportion of the production disposed of for cash increases. Peasant farmers thus raise crops for sale as part of a cash-subsistence economy of infinitely variable proportions from the disposal of the small surplus their families cannot consume to concentration on export crops to the exclusion of subsistence production. We can distinguish four ways in which this process occurs.

First, a surplus of staple crops is produced from a largely unmodified system. In most cases this is marginal and liable to seasonal fluctuations. In good years it may be considerable, but may disappear when harvests are bad. Since, however, large numbers of cultivators are involved, the total tonnage entering the market can be very heavy. It is in this way that much of the food supply for urban areas is produced. In the Middle Belt[1] yams are produced for sale from areas not only of bush-fallowing, but in Ghana even from surviving areas of shifting agriculture. Traditionally it is the marginal surplus of subsistence palm-oil production that is sold. Even the million tons of groundnuts entering the Nigeria exchange economy in 1967–68 came from largely unmodified indigenous systems.

The trend, however, must be to a greater modification of the system. Cash cropping was a major force in the fixation of shifting agriculture. Oil-palms from selected seeds replace the semi-wild groves. The migrant *navétanes* of Senegambia[2] cultivate specialised groundnut farms. In general, an increasing proportion of the total output is sold.

Secondly, exotic crops have been introduced into existing systems. Success has varied greatly and is by no means automatic. As far as annuals are concerned, they may be an entirely new crop or improved strains to replace indigenous species. They may come from overseas or from other parts of West Africa. They include American varieties of cotton, Virginian tobacco, Sierra Leone rice, and numerous species of oilseeds.

The introduction of tree crops usually results in the considerable modification of an existing system rather than the emergence of a new system, even in the case of cocoa and coffee. Trees are planted in pure stands on farms separate from those used for food crops. They have inevitably led to the fixation of shifting agriculture, to the emergence of permanent cultivation and to freehold land-ownership.

But tree-crops have also led to the third type of change, the development of new systems. The plantation, using the term in a broad sense, has been introduced into all countries concerned with tree cropping. But completely specialised peasant holdings of cocoa and coconuts, in fact small scale plantations, have also emerged.

Fourthly, we must mention changes which come about in already established commercialised systems. The devastation caused by swollen shoot disease in the older cocoa areas of Ghana and Nigeria led to the substitution of kola for cocoa and, in parts of Ghana, of staple food crops.

As the exchange economy replaces the subsistence one, a system of trade has grown up which has been represented in Figure 8.1. Within this system inter-continental trade has been most widely studied as statistics are the most plentiful and reliable. Intra-continental movement is smaller and figures are less reliable. Detailed studies of local exchange have been made in the field by geographers and social-anthropologists. But until recently the internal exchange economy has not received much attention.

A particular crop may enter only one sector. Cocoa, for instance, is grown only for inter-continental trade. But others may enter two or more sectors. Yams are produced for both local and internal exchange and may even figure in intra-continental exchange. Palm-oil enters all sectors.

The distribution and the level of production of a cash-crop may be physical, a matter of soil, periodic fluctuations in rainfall, and the activity of plant pathogens. These factors, however, offer only a partial explanation. Other limiting factors are access to markets, price levels, opportunities for spending income derived from cash sales, willingness and ability on the part of the peasants to accept the results of scientific research, and the policies of governments.

Access to market implies transport that is adequate in capacity and low in cost. Thus distance from ports and from the larger urban markets, themselves mainly coastal, places an automatic handicap on produce from the Sudan. Furthermore, crops from that zone tend to be of lower value per unit weight than the tree-crops of the Forest. In 1966 groundnuts grown in the Kano area were fetching about N£65 ($182) per ton on the world market, as opposed to an average of about N£200 ($560) for cocoa. The rail rate for groundnuts Kano-Apapa was N£7 12s. ($21·28) per ton and to this was added the cost of lorry transport to railhead. For this the official rate was 7d. (8·16 cents) per ton mile on tarred roads and 1s. (14 cents) on dirt ones. Assuming 30 miles on the latter and 20 on the former, usual figures, the total transport cost from buying station to port would have been N£9 13s. 8d. ($27·07) or 14·9 per cent. of the selling price.

Again, primary agricultural produce is subject to greater price fluctuations on world markets than are manufactured goods. While, in this inflationary period, the prices of the latter show a steady upward trend, produce prices in 1965 were often lower in real terms than in 1955, representing a heavy fall at constant prices. A typical example is that of cocoa, for which the price fluctuations are shown in Figure 8.2. For a country dependent on the export of agricultural produce to obtain the capital and consumer goods necessary for economic development this is serious. For the peasant producer these fluctuations have been damped down by the Produce Marketing Boards of the anglophone countries and by guaranteed prices on the Metropolitan markets for the francophone (pages 205–207). They have not been eliminated, however, and the response of the producer is not always that of the model Economic Man of the textbooks. Because the wants he can satisfy by money are simple and limited, in times of high prices he may prefer to produce less, and when prices fall he can and does expand output to maintain income. Thus during the 1960s the tonnage of cocoa harvested rose as prices fell.

Cocoa growing has spread rapidly from Ghana into Côte d'Ivoire, which enjoys a preferential market in France for both cocoa and coffee. The anglophone countries, while enjoying some degree of Commonwealth preference, have lower margins of preference and are in competition with a wider range of countries, some of which may have natural conditions more suited to a particular crop. Thus Ghana has never developed coffee on anything like the scale of Côte d'Ivoire. Again, the climate of the Dahomey-Nigeria border is marginal for oil-palm products. On the Dahomey side are extensive palm groves, but on the Nigerian side these are replaced by kola and cocoa. It is useless to seek an explanation in differences of physical environment, but rather in differences of policy by the respective governments.

With these generalisations in mind, we will review the distribution and production methods of the principal cash crops.

COCOA[3]

Theobroma cacao is a native of tropical Africa. An evergreen tree, averaging 6·0–7·5 metres high, it flowers twice a year on the trunk. The pods, red, yellow and purple in colour, weigh two or three pounds. Cocoa requires very warm, shady conditions with almost constant dampness. Temperatures must not vary greatly from a mean of 27° C. and there should be between 100 and 160 cms. of well distributed rainfall. Exposure to wind, strong sunlight and low humidities will lower yields and may prove fatal. But conversely excessive rainfall encourages fungoid disease. Thus exposure to harmattan provides one climatic limit and an appreciable rainfall in January the other.

Cocoa is a tree of the lower layers of the forest, and agricultural systems mainly aim at replacing those layers with cocoa, leaving the upper and the ground layers in a semi-natural condition. Mature cocoa will survive without shade, but yields are badly affected. It is essential that for the first two or three

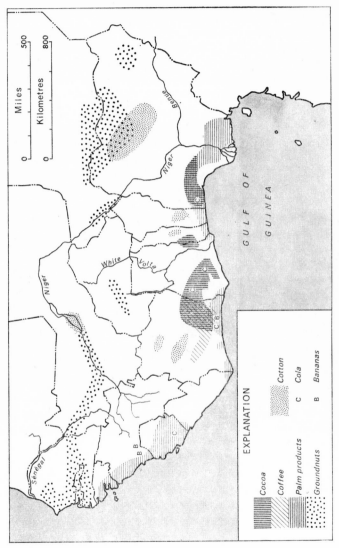

Figure 5.1. The principal areas of cash cropping

years seedlings are protected by cocoyams and bananas. This also means that the farmer's food supply is assured, and even some cash income may be got from the nurse crops until the new trees come into bearing.

Distribution of cocoa is further controlled by soil conditions. It requires a moderately deep soil overlying friable rock rich in nutrients and with plenty of freedom for root development. Stiff clays, free draining sands and waterlogged alluvia are all unsuitable. Even in the areas of greatest concentration of cocoa, therefore, the crop seldom covers extensive areas continuously. Between the plantations food crops are raised by the normal bush fallowing system.

The chief producers are Ghana, Nigeria and Côte d'Ivoire, which together accounted for 65·6 per cent. of world exports in 1966. Production trends have been upward over the period 1945–66 and this will probably continue (Figure 5.2)

In Ghana, the *Main Cocoa Belt* is the dryer part of the Forest Zone. To the south-east it coincides with the edge of the closed forest, which from Accra to the Volta tops the Akwapim Ridge. North-westward to Mampong-Ashanti the northern boundary is the foot of the Kwahu scarp, not the forest edge, for the Voltaian sandstone plateau is too exposed to harmattan and the soils unsuited. From Mampong to the frontier the boundary again coincides with that of the forest. The south-western limits are much less well defined, but the belt can be said to peter out along the southern boundary of Brong-Ahafo and Ashanti and along the Pra River. Beyond, the dry season is too humid. The outlying *Volta Region Cocoa Belt* extends northward from the Volta through Ho and Hohoe as far as Poasi.

On the average there are some 0·4 hectares of cocoa on each holding. It may be in one block, but is more likely to be in several. Some holdings may exceed 20 hectares and are in fact small plantations. At the other end of the scale, a farmer may have only a few trees. At Suhum a cadastral survey found 5,605 holdings covering 6,593·77 hectares, an average of 1·17 hectares, not all under cocoa.[4] For though cocoa dominates the economy and the farming system, it is never planted to the exclusion of other crops. Charter[5] estimated that of 80,290 square kilometres of the Forest Zone only some

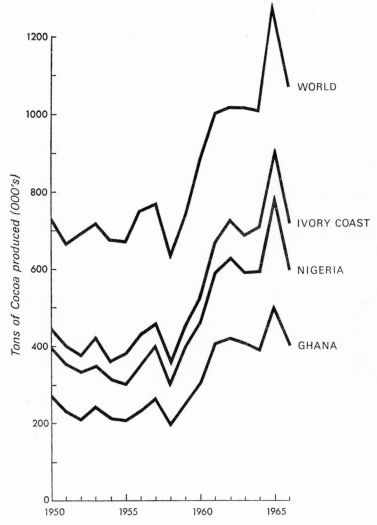

Figure 5.2. Cocoa production, 1950–66. *Source: Cocoa Statistics*

7,770 were under cocoa, and individual studies have shown the extent to which each village is self supporting in food.[6] Probably 80 per cent. of the staple foods are produced locally, at least for villages and small towns. Work on cocoa farms is complementary to other activities on peasant holdings, as is shown in Figure 5·3.

Cocoa was first cultivated along the Akwapim Ridge and from there spread to New Juaben and Akim Abuakwa. In Ashanti cultivation, centred on Kumasi, developed simultaneously. Polly Hill[7] has shown how the inhabitants of Akwapim and Krobo, driven to emigrate by pressure on land, gradually extended the cocoa area north-westward, buying land and planting cocoa. Hunter found in 1960 that migrant farmers cultivate 98·6 per cent of the land in Suhum. Migrants from Krobo and Shai formed 'companies' to buy large blocks of land from the Akan owners. The land was divided in proportion to the money each member contributed. The frontage along a stream was measured in 'ropes' and the members then cleared strips back to the watershed or some other landmark. Thus the *huza* system produced a characteristic landscape of strip holdings, each with a compound, aligned along the stream or a road[8]. Cultivation also spread outward from Kumasi, the Ashanti also being vigorous pioneers. Migrant farmers reached the Côte d'Ivoire frontier in the middle 1950s and it can be said that there are no new cocoa lands left in Ghana.

When migrants made enough money, they retired to their home villages. The visible signs are the large houses, many unfinished. But large sums of money flowed back into the original cocoa areas of the south-east, particularly important as these areas were worst affected by swollen shoot. The disease was first officially recognised in 1936, but not until 1940 was it proved to be a virus transmitted by the mealy bug. Unfortunately trees could be fatally infected before they showed any symptoms, and 'cutting-out' of all trees around a diseased one was resorted to.

This policy was bitterly unpopular and seemingly unsuccessful. Cocoa was apparently doomed to die out in the 'Special Area' of the south-east, and during the 1950s the whole industry was threatened, and with it the whole Ghana

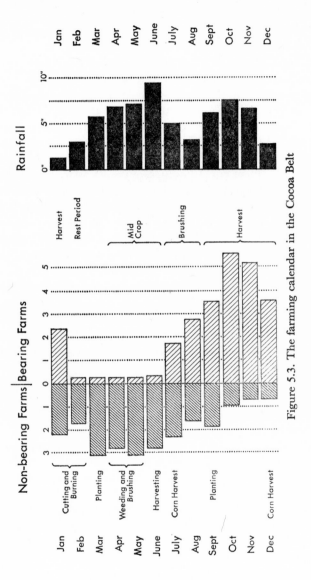

Figure 5.3. The farming calendar in the Cocoa Belt

economy. By the early 1960s, however, control had been achieved and replanting was proceeding apace, except in the 'Abandoned Area' of the extreme south-east, where control measures had to be abandoned.[9]

In Nigeria, cocoa cultivation is with few exceptions confined to the *Cocoa Crescent* of the Western Provinces. This extends along the axis of the Lagos-Abeokuta-Ibadan-Ife-Owo road. The northern limit of cultivation is that of closed forest, closely following the 115 cm. isohyet. To the south, especially in Ondo Province, the limit is set by increasing rainfall with greater liability to fungoid and capsid diseases. Little cocoa is grown south of the 175 cm. isohyet. Eastward the crescent peters out between Owo and Benin, less because of increased rainfall than because of the infertile soils of the Benin Sands. Similarly, south of Abeokuta high rainfall and unsuitable soils have led to replacement of much of the cocoa by kola.

Cultivation methods are similar to those of Ghana, though holdings would appear to be generally smaller. About 1,000 square miles (2,590 kilometres) are under the crop and the average size of holdings is just under two acres (0·8 hectares). Cocoa never occupies all the land of a village, and, except for the larger Yoruba towns, the communities are largely self-supporting in staple foods. By 1950 swollen shoot had reached very serious proportions, there being two main centres of infection, north-east and south-east of Ibadan. Control proved difficult in the face of opposition from farmers, but has broadly been achieved.[10]

Cocoa in Côte d'Ivoire was introduced from Ghana, but its spread was encouraged by preferential treatment on the French market. Cultivation spread across from Sunyani District in Ghana to the axis of the Bondoukou-Abengourou road, *'la route de cacao'*, and thence westward to Bongouanou and Ouellé. Subsequently cultivation spread southward, but not westward beyond the railway. To some extent the crop is in competition with coffee, but the heavier *assié-blé* soils are preferred.

The stock of many millions of trees represents a vital capital asset. Hitherto profits have been employed either to invest in new land, a source rapidly drying up, or in the replanting of devastated areas with second generation cocoa. Otherwise they have not been returned to the land. Increased production has come mainly from new and second generation planting. There is thus scope for increasing productivity by using fertilisers and a more scientific husbandry.

As we have seen, cocoa cultivation led to the breakdown of traditional land ownership and the emergence of individual freeholds. It has also modified the system of labour. Increased demands have led to the use of non-family labour, mainly of migrants, not only from other parts of the Forest but also from the Sudan and Middle Belt. In Ghana there are four classes of paid labour. *Abusa* is a share-cropping system. The farms of absentee owners are cultivated by 'caretakers' for one-third of the crop. *Ale* labourers are hired for an annual sum, mainly to clear land. *Afe* labourers are daily rated and hired for short periods. The *nkotokuala* labourer is paid on piece work for preparing the cocoa.[11]

PALM PRODUCTS[12]

The oil palm (*Elaesis guineensis*) is indigenous throughout the Forest and much of the bordering Derived Savana. Providing one of the earliest exports to replace the slave trade, palm products remain important in the export economy of a number of countries. As a rule the palms are not cultivated, but rather allowed to survive when the fallows are cleared. They tend to be low yielding and their height precludes easy harvesting of fruit. Much of the produce is consumed locally and in many areas does not enter the export market at all. Efforts at rehabilitation of the natural groves by encouraging the planting of high-yielding strains and by the use of fertiliser have been constantly pursued by all governments concerned, but have been only sporadically successful.

The palm requires a minimum of 100 cms. of well distributed rainfall, but yields increase rapidly as rainfall increases. Bunch yields on agricultural stations average 34·1 kgs. at Ibadan with 107 cms., but 68·2 kgs. at Benin with 177·8 cms., and are even higher in Cameroun with over 250 cms. Rainfall is more important than soil, for in spite of its demands on potash, the palm will flourish on very poor soils, including

I

the Benin Sands of Eastern Nigeria. Densities vary greatly from dense and continuous groves to a scattering of a few palms per acre. The former, however, are restricted and normally palms grow on crop and fallow land, while food crops are raised under them.

Wherever the palm grows, pericarp oil is extracted, but most is consumed within the country in which it is produced and exports are the marginal surplus. The kernels have less place in the local and internal exchange economy and production for export is more widely distributed. Unless output is increased, population growth, rising living standards and tapping for palm-wine tend to reduce the available surplus of pericarp oil, which becomes all the more susceptible to seasonal variations in yields.

The most notable concentration of production is in the Eastern Provinces of Nigeria. The palm belt is associated with the densely peopled Iboland, with high rainfall and poor soils. The main area is bounded by the towns of Port Harcourt, Oron and Onitsha. This produces virtually all the exports of pericarp oil and most of the kernels, but the latter are also produced from a much wider area north of the Delta and west of the Cross River. Within the palm belt the groves cover most of the cultivable land and the area is one of considerable deficit of staple food. Elsewhere food crops are grown under the more widely separated palms.

Until the exploitation of petroleum began in the 1960s, the crop formed the basis of the economy of the then Eastern Region. But the exports of pericarp oil, 165,438 tons in 1964–65, had a falling trend through increased local consumption. Exports of kernels remained more steady at just under 200,000 tons a year. The Regional Government had a programme of palm grove rehabilitation, with subsidies for replanting and for fertilisers, which was beginning to have results. Of necessity all this applies to conditions before the outbreak of the Civil War in 1967.[13]

In both Mid-West and Western Nigeria only kernels enter the export exchange, local consumption accounting for all pericarp oil produced. Exports of kernels even have been declining and in 1966 fell below 100,000 tons for the first time since the Second World War. With the completion of the present programme of crusher construction (page 177), virtually all Nigerian kernels will be processed before export.

Palm products form the basis of the economy of Dahomey. In 1966 they accounted for 53 per cent. by value of the exports, and the processing plants produced 8,890 tons of pericarp oil, 18,846 tons of kernel oil and 19,212 tons of kernels. Production is confined to the *terre de barre* soils of the south and is under rather marginal conditions, 90 to 115 cms, though well distributed over two wet seasons a year. For the most part the palms are under-cropped, but there are extensive areas

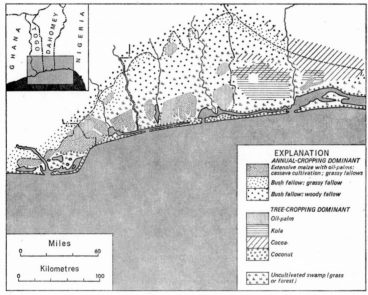

EXPLANATION

ANNUAL-CROPPING DOMINANT
Extensive maize with oil-palms: cassava cultivation; grassy fallows

Bush fallow: grassy fallow

Bush fallow: woody fallow

TREE-CROPPING DOMINANT
Oil-palm

Kola

Cocoa

Coconut

Uncultivated swamp (grass or forest)

Miles
0 — 60

Kilometres
0 — 100

Figure 5.4. Agricultural systems in the 'Terre de Barre'

of dense groves around Porto Novo and Abomey.[14] Encouragement for the use of high yielding strains is given from the I.R.H.O. research station at Pobé. In addition there were plans for the establishment by 1970 of 13,000 hectares of plantations, including 7,000 hectares at Agonvy. In Togo also, production is confined to the *terre de barre*, but rainfall is even less and palm densities and yields are both lower than in Dahomey. Exports are virtually confined to kernels.

In Ghana only a few thousand tons of kernels are exported,

and exports from Côte d'Ivoire do not exceed 20,000 tons. In both countries production of pericarp oil has hitherto been only for local and internal exchange, efforts having been concentrated on tree crops of higher value. But in recent years Côte d'Ivoire has aimed at even further agricultural diversification by increasing output of palm products. The plan is to produce 135,000 tons of oil by 1975, 90,000 being for export. By 1967 40,000 hectares had been planted. about one-third by peasants and two-thirds on state plantations, while the European Development Fund (page 166) had provided $29·5 million.

Peasant exports of all kinds from Liberia are small. But kernels for long formed the staple export of Sierra Leone. Since the War, however, they have tended to form a declining proportion, relatively and absolutely, of the exports and in 1967 accounted for only 2·2 per cent. by value. In 1966 55,198 tons of kernels, kernel oil and cake were exported, but there are considerable fluctuations from year to year, and in the succeeding year only 11,588 tons were exported. There are also some exports from Guinée and Portuguese Guinea. The area of production may be equated with the Casamance Woodland, an area of Derived Savana and degraded forest associated with the coastal lands of the two latter countries and of Sierra Leone. Throughout the area the palms are scattered, normally thinly, through the farmlands cultivated on the bush fallow system. Sierra Leone, however, aims to double production by encouraging plantations.

COFFEE

There is only one major exporter of coffee, Côte d'Ivoire, which shipped 181,460 tons in 1966. Both *robusta* and *liberica* varieties are grown, mainly on small peasant holdings. In contrast to cocoa, much coffee is also produced from the dryer parts of the Forest west of the railway within a triangle Dimbroko-Gagnoa-Man. Eastward of the railway the lighter *assié-kokoré* soils are preferred. The crop has always received preference on the large French market and now can enter the whole of that of the E.E.C. Guaranteed prices have been paid to producers since 1955. Arabica coffee is grown in southern Guinée, chiefly on fallows which follow rice growing. There is a small production in Togo and Dahomey, but the climate is on the whole too dry for successful cultivation.

Attempts have been made to introduce coffee in order to diversify the export economy of the anglophone countries, but without the success enjoyed by Côte d'Ivoire. The main market is the U.K. which, though expanding, is still limited, and the quality is inferior to coffee from Kenya, India and Jamaica. Exports have therefore remained small and subject to fluctuation. The 1966 exports from Sierra Leone and Ghana were 9,511 and 5,779 tons respectively. The figures for the previous year were 4,956 and 2,040 tons.

When they were under British administration, coffee was successfully introduced into the small area of the Bamenda Highlands of West Cameroun. High quality *arabica* is grown on the small peasant holdings and forms a valuable cash resource which requires lower labour inputs than do the staple food crops of the steeply sloping farms.[15]

KOLA[16]

The nuts of the *Cola nitida* tree, a native of the Forest, are mildly stimulating when chewed. Its importance as a cash crop is twofold. In the first place it is one of the few which enter long distance internal and intra-continental exchange (page 195), for kola nuts are in demand in the Sudan and Sahel, where they are used to relieve thirst and hunger during the long dry season. The kola trade has always been wholly in African hands, the merchants normally coming from the consuming areas of the Sudan. In the second, kola is a possible crop where cocoa has been introduced, but where it failed later. There are four main centres of production.

The first is along the southern edge of the Forest in Western Nigeria from Shagamu, on the Ibadan-Lagos road, westward to the frontier. Expansion took place mainly during the inter-war years encouraged by government policy concerned with reducing imports from Ghana. Planting spread particularly on soils unsuited to cocoa, and has taken the latter's place in the farming system. The trade is described on page 209.

The second is in the Forest of Ghana, where there are two areas of cultivation. In the south-eastern part of the Forest kola has replaced cocoa in some of the area devastated by swollen shoot around Kibi. The other area is centred on Sunyani and Mampong-Ashanti. The trade is with northern Ghana, Haute Volta and Mali, though it is not so extensive as that of south-western Nigeria.

The third area is in Côte d'Ivoire where the main centres are again in the southern part of the Forest, Agboville and Gagnoa. The trade is mainly with Haute Volta and Mali. The final area is the southern part of Sierra Leone and the adjoining parts of Liberia, but the trade from here has declined with the rise of the Côte d'Ivoire and Nigerian areas. Production figures for kola are scarce and unreliable, obscuring its importance in the economy.

GROUNDNUTS[17]

Groundnuts are in fact underground fruits of a leguminous annual (*Arachis hypogaea*), which is a native of the New World and was introduced by the Portuguese. It is widely grown among other pulses throughout the Sudan as a subsistence crop and mainly as a garden crop elsewhere. The surplus over subsistence requirements enters local exchange almost everywhere. But in parts of northern Nigeria and in Senegambia the peasant-grown crop enters the inter-continental exchange to such an extent that it dominates the economy. In 1966–67 some 2·25 million tons were marketed. Development became possible after the early 1900s as a result of the introduction of the hydrogenation process for oil extraction and of rail connections from producing areas to the ports. Expansion was steady during the inter-war years and after 1945 West Africa replaced India as the main world supplier.

In northern Nigeria production is centred on the Kano Close-Settled Zone and extends north-westward to Katsina and to Kaura Namoda and also north-eastward along the railway to Nguru. Bornu is of lesser importance, though production is now rapidly expanding, especially around Potiskum and Maiduguri. The use of lorry transport to railhead or even all the way to the port has extended the opportunities for raising groundnuts as an export crop. The limiting factor is the cost of concentrating the crop on the railway stations or main roads, for local transport charges per ton-mile are three to four times those for the trunk haul.

The main feature has been the spectacular growth in production over the last thirty years. Purchases for export averaged 213,100 tons over the period 1935–39, but by the 1952–53 season had risen to 435,300 tons. Growth continued steadily, the figures for 1960–61 being 625,200 tons, while those for 1966–67 reached 969,600 tons in spite of the political difficulties of the time.

The trend in production has been calculated at an annual compound growth rate of 5·1 per cent.[18] While there are no accurate figures, it is possible to make some deductions as to how this growth has been achieved. There are large annual fluctuations, for in addition to variations in yields due to climatic factors, when harvests are bad groundnuts grown for sale are used for food. The effects are carried over, for consumption of seed may affect the next harvest. The fixed prices at reasonable levels paid by the Marketing Board, however, have attracted land from alternative crops, especially guinea corn. Increasing population has also meant more land brought into cultivation. It is only to a much lesser extent that increased yields have been achieved. While consumption of fertilisers had been only a few tons in 1960, in 1966 it was estimated that 35,000 tons were used, 75 per cent of Nigerian consumption, but even this amount is insignificant compared with the acreage under the crop.

Groundnuts for export are invariably produced from a multiplicity of small peasant holdings, never more than a few acres in extent. Their cultivation is integrated into the traditional systems already described (pages 74–8). They are inter-cropped with grain on bush fallowed land and also as one of the main crops of permanently cultivated compound land. Mortimore and Wilson found at Dame Fulani, on the northern outskirts of Kano, that there were 203·26 hectares held in 183 *gonaki* (plural), or unitary parcels of land, by 103 farmers. Cultivation was permanent, with the aid of manure from Kano City applied at about 4·1 tons per hectare.

The average production of groundnuts per *gona* (sing.) in 1962–63 was 2·5 sacks sold at $7·3 per sack.

The Nigerian production area can be said to extend across the border into Niger. Groundnuts are the mainstay of the economy of that country, accounting for 58·4 per cent. by value of total exports in 1965. Here, too, production has risen, exports of groundnut products increasing from 79,000 tons in 1956–57 to 192,000 tons in 1966–67. The crop is grown in a narrow zone immediately north of the Nigerian border, the main centres being Magaria and Maradi. The main problem is the high cost of transport (page 253).

Production in Sénégal has a much longer history, exports dating back to 1840. But the initial impetus to growth was given by the opening in 1885 of the Dakar-St. Louis railway, though consequential overproduction led to a decline in the importance of this area. The present industry stems from the opening of the railway from Thiès to Tambacounda by 1914 and from subsequent road building. This extended the producing area south-westward from Thiès and this is still the main axis of production (Figure 5.1). In 1966–67 46·1 per cent. of the sown area and 57·0 per cent. of the production was accounted for in Siné Saloum Cercle, centred on the railhead at Tambacounda. A further 23·2 per cent. of the crop was harvested in Thiès and Diourbel Cercles, also along the axis of the railway. 14·8 per cent. came from Casamance in the far south.

The soils of Senegambia are mainly sandy and therefore well suited to the crop, but they are impoverished, being particularly deficient in phosphates. Fertilisers are necessary for good yields and it is fortunate that there are extensive local deposits, though as yet insufficient quantities are used. Much of the crop is produced by the indigenous farming system. But there is a large seasonal demand for labour in cultivation and harvest. This is satisfied by annual migrants, originally from Mali, but now mainly from the Guinea Savana zone of the Guinée Republic and from Cayor north of Dakar. Known as *navètanes*, they work either for wages or for an allocation of land for groundnut cultivation.

As in Nigeria, production has shown a great increase in recent years. The average for the period 1949–50 to 1953–54 was 565,000 tons. A decade later, 1959–60 to 1963–64 this had risen to 912,000. In 1965–66 over a million tons was harvested for the first time. The increase has been achieved partly by increased yields, from 836 kg. per hectare over the first period to 910 over the second. It has, however, been mainly the result of an increase in the sown area, from an average of 676,000 hectares to one of 1·0 million.

The Serer of Siné Saloum employ a rotation of grain, groundnuts and pasture on a 'three field' system on the main croplands, with food crops and cotton on the compound lands.[19] In Casamance Mouride Brotherhood colonisers have been persuaded to adopt co-operative methods using mechanisation.

Gambia is almost completely dependent on the export of groundnuts, which account for over 95 per cent. by value of total exports. Cultivation developed early along the axis of the navigable river, which provided a convenient evacuation route. Groundnuts occupy two-thirds of the planted area on the 'uplands away from the flood plain', used for rice growing. As in Sénégal, the industry largely depends on migrant labour, called here 'strange farmers'.[20] Exports rose from 90,000 tons in 1964 to 130,000 tons in 1967.

Groundnuts also form an important resource of Mali. The long and costly haul to the ports, however, places the country at a disadvantage compared with Sénégal and has put a brake on development. Mali's choice not to be associated with the EEC and its preferential market has also contributed. The crop is grown on light soils in the western part where rainfall is higher.

COTTON[21]

Cotton (*Gossypium spp.*) is well suited as a cash crop to the Sudan, not only from the viewpoint of climate and soil, but also because its high value-weight ratio enables it to bear the heavy transport costs from interior to port. Increasingly, too, it provides locally available raw material for import-substitution industry. (pages, 175, 183).

Native varieties have long been grown within the subsistence farming systems and are woven on the narrow African looms into coarse cloth (page 195) for local exchange. Traditional centres of such cotton growing are to be found in northern Nigeria, northern Togo and in Haute Volta. For commercial manufacture or for export, however, these varieties are of too short staple. Production for these purposes depends on the successful introduction of longer staple American varieties.

Nigeria has always been the principal producer, a tribute to the early and sustained work of the British Cotton Growers' Association, founded in 1903, which established ginneries and distributed selected seed. This work was first based on the Forest border and Guinea Savanas of Western Nigeria and of Ilorin and Kabba Provinces, but the attractions of cocoa and the prevalence of diseases led to the decline of the crop and the transfer of the work to the North. Here the main producing area is along an axis from Kaura Namoda south eastward through Zaria towards the Jos Plateau. More recently the sown area has increased in Bornu, centred on the ginneries at Gombe, Misau and Kumo. Further extensions, especially in southern Bornu and in the far north-west are inhibited by transport costs.

There are wide variations in the annual yields, but there is a steady upward trend. The average production of 'seed' cotton (before ginning) in the period between 1951 and 1956 was 71,100 tons a year, while that of the period between 1961 and 1966 was 123,900 tons.

The only other major producer is Mali (4,500 tons exported in 1964). Production is either from the irrigated lands of the *Office du Niger* (page 130) or from normal dry farming methods along an axis from San through Koutiala to Sikasso. Cotton has also been widely tried in the Guinea Savana, but with much less success than in the Sudan. In Côte d'Ivoire it is chiefly grown in the Bouaké salient and in Korhogo Cercle. There have been attempts to establish the industry in Dahomey, Togo and in northern Ghana. Like most attempts to provide a cash crop for the Guinea Savana Zone all these have largely failed. The physical environment is unsuited, due to infertile soils and a climate that is sufficiently humid to encourage disease, but insufficient to allow tree cropping, yet is on the whole too wet for groundnuts and cotton. There is also an absence of a cotton growing tradition.

STAPLE FOOD CROPS

It will be seen that crops entering the inter-continental exchange are either exotics grafted onto the indigenous peasant economy with greater or lesser consequential modification, or are themselves the surplus of crops from the indigenous system. In the same way there is a surplus of staple food crops available for internal exchange and even for export to other parts of West Africa, though unknown in inter-continental exchange, either because there is no overseas demand (e.g. yams) or because comparative production costs are too high (e.g. rice).

With a few exceptions, it is only the surplus that is available. White has shown that for Ghana this is always marginal,[22] estimating in 1956 that staple food requirements for all towns over 5,000 and for the mining compounds would be 380,750 tons against an estimated total food production of 3·2 million tons. Thus seasonal variations in the harvest have a very marked effect on the amount of foodstuffs sold and therefore on prices, which fluctuate widely and rapidly. The amount of foodstuffs sold is also the result of competition between food and other annual cash crops. Thus high prices for groundnuts may result in land being used the following season for that crop in preference to guinea corn; the available surplus of the latter is then reduced and prices rocket.

The increasing quantities of food crops entering internal exchange are a comparatively new phenomenon and are due mainly to the growth of towns, chiefly the ports and those of the Forest (Chapter 10). For example, Accra Municipality grew from a population of 133,000 in 1948 to 388,000 in 1961. The *per capita* consumption of Forest people in Ghana has been estimated at 794 kgs. a year. Thus the demand for food would have expanded from 104,000 tons to over 303,000 tons in the 13 years, assuming static living standards and purchasing power.

Since the surplus available from each holding is very small, the area from which food moves to a large urban area is a very wide one. In 1956 White[23] traced the relative importance of the areas concerned in the supply of Accra, which extended far into the Forest and across the border into Togo (Figure 5.5). Later Gould adopted similar methods to show how staples reached the whole of southern Ghana.[24] Abidjan[25] is supplied not only from the Forest, with yam and plaintain from east of the Bandama River and rice from the west, but with yam and rice from the Bouaké salient of the Derived Savana and with grain from Korhogo in the north of the country. Similarly towns in Iboland were largely supplied from the Mid-West,

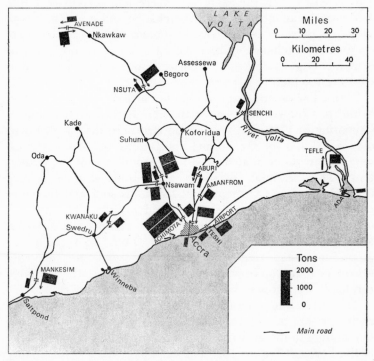

Figure 5.5. Movement of staple foods in the Accra area, July 1–14, 1953

while Ibadan and even Lagos received yams from the area north of Kaduna. All this has been made possible by the development of road transport, which ensures speedy and regular transits of the numerous and small consignments. In addition, the creation of a network of feeder roads in the producing areas is as necessary as the provision of trunk highways.

The possibility of selling a surplus of normal food production creates an economic resource of increasing importance, but of particular value to those areas unsuited to the production of export crops. Three instances may be cited. The Guinea Savana Zone has, so far, proved most intractable for those seeking to establish export cropping. Its chief subsistence crop is yam, and today yam sales to the towns and the tree-cropping areas of the Forest form a major source of cash income to the more accessible parts of the whole Middle Belt. Secondly, in the devastated cocoa area of south-eastern Ghana food cropping for cash sale has provided a substitute basis for the economy. In southern Akim Abuakwa some 45 per cent. of the production enters internal exchange, mainly for the feeding of Accra. This is an unusually high figure and is obviously more than the marginal surplus of production. In the village of Akotuakrom Hunter[26] found in 1960 a sample of 20 farmers holding 142·7 hectares in amounts varying from 38·4 hectares to 0·8 hectares. 88·1 hectares were under fallow, 28·2 hectares under cocoa and 47·3 under food crops. The farmer's income from the principal crop, cassava, averaged $2·8 to $4·2 a week from the sale of 4 to 6 baskets at 70 cents each. Finally, sales of food from the nurse crops over young cocoa is a valued source of income pending the maturing of the cocoa,

Food crops for sale may also occupy land hitherto unused, and thus become an additional resource. Rice can be grown in the swampy bottom lands of the savana areas suffering from population pressure. These lands would otherwise be useless, while the high value-weight ratio of the rice enables it to be transported long distances.

In the Forest Zone the chief staples entering the internal exchange are cassava and plantains, both of which are universally grown. Yams are the main produce sold from the Guinea Savana, and to a lesser extent grain, the latter being the main cash product of the Sudan. Rice is of growing importance in the coastlands, especially west of the Bandama River, where the *padis* of the Rivières du Sud are extensive. Maize is an important cash crop around large towns. Around Lagos, Accra and Abidjan it is grown in pure stands and the forest canopy has been almost completely destroyed. The *terre de barre* of Dahomey and Togo is another centre, where the crop is grown in conjunction with cassava and oil-palms.

The most important high value foodstuffs entering internal and intra-continental exchange are fish and meat. The former moves over great distances, northward from the coast and southward from the Niger. The trade is dealt with in greater detail on page 100. Since animals cannot be kept in the Forest, the growing demand for meat is met, apart from imports from overseas, by the movement of live cattle on the hoof southward from the Sudan and Sahel. The main currents are from the north to the south of Nigeria and from Haute Volta to southern Ghana and southern Côte d'Ivoire, forming the largest item of intra-continental exchange in West Africa (page 209). There are also some high value market garden crops, notably onions, produced on the *fadamas* of Northern Nigeria and of the Niamey area in Niger, which are distributed throughout West Africa.

Because of the farming methods and the marketing system, locally produced food is on the whole high priced, and seasonal fluctuations, in response to variations in supply, considerable. Home production, therefore cannot always compete with imports. While the estuaries of Sierra Leone are an important rice growing area, in the late 1950s the company working the Marampa iron mine found it less costly to import Italian rice in bulk to feed its work-force. More rice is imported from overseas into Sénégal than is provided from Casamance Province or from other West African countries.

Morgan[27] has shown that the import of food staples as well as of luxuries has grown fast in recent years, and this has had an adverse effect on the balance of trade. In 1967 rice imports into Gambia reached $840,000. Yet the Gambia farmer got $78·4 a ton for his groundnuts while he paid $172 a ton for his staple food, rice. In 1966 34,894 tons of rice were imported into Sierra Leone, 5 per cent. by value of total imports. In the same year food accounted for 13·4 per cent. of the total imports into Dahomey, yet these latter were three and a half times as great as exports.

In 1961 food accounted for 30 per cent. of Sénégal's imports and 19 per cent. of Ghana's.

OTHER PEASANT CASH CROPS

It has only been possible to outline peasant cash-cropping activities. Other crops enter the exchange system, but none is of more than local importance. *Tobacco* has long been grown in the subsistence economy of large areas of the Sudan and Guinea savanas. In recent years Virginian strains have been introduced as a cash crop into Northern Ghana, Côte d'Ivoire and Oyo, Zaria and Kano Provinces of Nigeria. The tobacco is sold for home manufacture. *Rubber* and *bananas* are mainly plantation crops, but rubber is produced on small holdings in the Mid-West and Delta areas of Nigeria and bananas are grown by peasants in Côte d'Ivoire and West Cameroun. *Coconuts* are the only possible crops all along the coastal dunes and oil is produced for the local exchange. There is also a small export of copra from Ghana and Togo. A good example of very localised crop production for export, is benniseed (sesamum) from Tiv-land in Nigeria. In 1962 exports reached 24,240 tons, but have since declined.

Altogether, there have been numerous attempts at the introduction of new crops and the development of indigenous ones to provide a cash income or to reduce dependence on a single crop. Few of these have succeeded, not only on the spectacular scale of cocoa and groundnuts, but even on the restricted scale of tobacco and benniseed. The promotion of ginger as a cash crop in Sierra Leone and the Jos Plateau has met with very limited success, while Sea Island and Egyptian cotton failed in Togo and Southern Nigeria and sisal in many parts of francophone West Africa.

COMMERCIAL FARMING

So far we have concentrated on the introduction of cash cropping into the traditional farming systems and on the consequent modifications. There have been notable developments achieved by the investment of human effort which have resulted in the accumulation of economic resources in the form of land cleared for annual crops or planted with tree crops. Output has constantly expanded, but more from new land brought into cultivation by an increased work force than by any intensification of production.

In contrast, capital investment has been much more limited. More of its profits have been diverted away from agriculture than have been ploughed back and it is not easy to attract outside capital. Tools and farming methods remain very simple and the pace of agricultural development tends to be slower than in other sectors of the economy. In 1953 Arthur Lewis[28] spoke of stagnating agriculture in Ghana at a time when economic expansion was otherwise gathering momentum in the early 1950s.

In all countries returns on capital are lower in agriculture than in other sectors of the economy, especially in the short run. In Great Britain massive investment has been made possible only by a favourable tax structure and a system of guaranteed prices for staple products. Even so, apart from wealthy 'hobby farmers', most investment is accounted for by ploughed-back profits. In West Africa the owner of tree crops may use his profits to buy more land, but otherwise tends to seek investment in road transport or urban housing, where returns are higher. Elsewhere peasants are either unable or unwilling to spend much money on tools, fertiliser and seed. Attempts at government investment have been made, but this has done little more than subsidise peasants in their economically inefficient ways. In the same way, overseas aid, with some exceptions, tends to be channelled into the provision of infrastructure, rather than in direct agricultural investment. When the latter has been made, it has sometimes taken the form of the provision of unwanted tractors and other equipment.

Attempts at introducing mechanised cultivation to peasant holdings typify some of the difficulties.[29] Most of these ultimately founder at the point of transferring the full costs to the farmers from the government agency initiating the scheme. The only possible way is through co-operatives, but even this presents problems resulting from small and fragmented holdings, the lack of capital and the shortage of expertise on the part of the co-operative. But in addition are the difficulties facing any mechanised system, liability to soil degradation by ploughing, high costs of clearing and stumping the woody vegetation, and the cost of maintaining the machinery. By no means least is the search for annual crops yielding a cash income sufficient to cover these outgoings.

Until recently the only alternative to peasant systems has been the commercial plantation. The British colonial governments consistently opposed their establishment, few concessions were granted and non-Africans were not allowed to own land. In Ghana during the 1930s there were some half-dozen rubber plantations, one of palm oil and one of limes. In Nigeria there were two large oil-palm and four medium sized rubber plantations and that was all.

Other administrations were more free with concessions and allowed land sales to non-Africans. In Côte d'Ivoire there were some 220 European holdings by 1955, totalling 30,000 hectares. Most of these produced bananas and were small, averaging 25 hectares. The coffee and cocoa holdings averaged 100 hectares. They accounted for about 50 per cent. of the banana exports, 7 per cent. of the coffee and 5 per cent of the cocoa.[30] Until Independence, there was a number of European banana holdings on the coastal plains of Guinée, averaging 12 hectares. In 1938 they exported 52,000 tons and in 1957 60,000, in addition to 15,000 tons from African small-holdings. In Liberia the two vast Firestone rubber plantations cover 43,000 hectares, produce over 40,000 tons of rubber a year and employ some 21,000 Liberians and 200 Europeans. The Liberian Government has, in recent years, granted other large concessions for rubber plantations. The island of Fernando Po, which forms part of Equatorial Guinea (granted independence by Spain in 1968), and the Portuguese island of Saô Thomé also have concentrations of plantations growing cocoa, coffee and bananas.

After 1945, however, there was a trend towards the investment of public funds in new plantations. On the volcanic soils at the foot of Mount Cameroon, German companies had established large plantations. Twice sequestered in the world wars, they were not again returned in 1945, but passed to the Cameroun Development Corporation, having been temporarily managed by the United Africa Company. The Corporation was financed by the British Government through the Colonial Development Corporation and this served as a model for investment in agricultural development by various West African governments.

After the creation of the Nigerian Federation in 1954, Agricultural Development Corporations were set up by each Region to direct and operate this investment. That of the Eastern Region was the most active in establishing what must

K

now be called 'estates'. By 1966 22 ventures had been launched, most of them in the sparsely peopled and economically under-developed East Cross River Basin. In the Western Region the Corporation established the extensive Ijebu Farm Project for palm oil and cocoa together with 15 other estates. In the North a 6,000 hectare sugar plantation was established at Bacita. In addition a few concessions were given to foreign firms, including that to Dunlop at Oban near Calabar (disposed of during the Civil War). The Mid-West has established a rubber estate in partnership with a foreign firm.[31]

Similar plantations were established in Ghana for the pro-duction of rubber and fruit. In addition, during the Nkrumah regime, large mechanised State Farms were set up, often with financial and technical aid from U.S.S.R. and Eastern Europe. By 1964 there were 290,300 hectares of plantations and state farms. Côte d'Ivoire has also been concerned with expanding palm-oil production by establishing estates.

As yet, however, estates are not making a large contribution to agricultural production, nor are they always a successful investment. It can be assumed that any surviving commercial holding is at least covering costs, but, as published figures are usually inadequate, it is difficult to assess the financial return from government estates. In addition, many commercial ventures have been abandoned and much government capital written off. The State Farms of Ghana have been ruinously costly and 60 of the 103 were abandoned in 1967, the year the Sierra Leone Marketing Board shut down its estates.

Attempts at the large scale production of annual crops in the savanas have been even less successful.[32] These attempts have taken two forms, either full scale mechanised agriculture or 'partnership' schemes, in which government agencies provide land, capital, overall management and, sometimes, mechanised clearing and ploughing. Some of these schemes employed irrigation, but in an area where water is a limiting factor in agriculture, these have been somewhat restricted.

The oldest scheme has been concerned with the utilisation of the interior delta of the Niger in Mali.[33] The *Office du Niger* was created in 1932 to carry out irrigation of a million hectares, half to be under cotton. By 1948 there were 6,600 hectares under cultivation, a small result for the vast expenditure. Even after the completion of the Sansanding Barrage in 1947, progress was slow. By 1962 $840 per acre had been invested, but cotton covered only 15 per cent. of the area, rice accounting for 60 per cent. Sugar is now being tried with aid from Communist China. The cotton failed partly because of low world prices and the excessive costs of transport to Dakar, partly because of soil conditions and weed infestation. Lack of success has overshadowed progress on the smaller, cheaper and more productive schemes for peasant cultivators in Guinée and Mali, amounting to 150,000 hectares.

The valley of the Sénégal has been the scene of the schemes operated by the *Mission d'Aménagement du Sénégal*, created in 1938. These included the large scale mechanised project at Richard Toll for rice production. Costs have been inflated by the need to pump the water and imported rice is cheaper. Experiments are being made in the cultivation of cotton, sugar and tomatoes. One again it is the smaller, peasant operated projects that have been more successful.[34]

The mechanised production of groundnuts was a goal that eluded governments in the years of vegetable oil shortage after 1945. The *Compagnie Général des Oléageneux Tropicaux* was formed to cultivate 200,000 hectares in Casamance. The Gonja project in Ghana and that at Mokwa in Nigeria were partnership schemes. All these projects were eventually much reduced in scope and survive only as high-cost operations.

More recently, in the 1960s, irrigated sugar plantations have been established at Bacita in northern Nigeria and at Komenda and Akuse in Ghana. The latter is on the Accra Plains, where there is a great potential for irrigation using water from the Volta River Project (page 154).

Farm settlement schemes have also been launched to provide rural employment in an effort to reduce the drift of young men to the towns (page 289). Drawing on Israeli experience, they hope to prove that peasant agriculture, using modern methods by co-operation, can provide higher living standards. Many schemes have been established in both western and eastern Nigeria[35] and in Ghana and Togo. Ghana is planning to establish 'agricultural communities', each with a nucleus plantation of 20,230 hectares with satellite farm settlements. With all these developments, we must not overlook the possibilities of peasant co-operatives as a means of administering investment. Progress, however, has been slow and a greater measure of success has been achieved by co-operatives in the marketing sphere (page 202).

Commercialisation of agriculture has proceeded apace in West Africa since 1920 and especially since 1945. The rate has, however, shown considerable regional variations. Because agriculture is the basic economic activity, commercialisation is the essential bridge between the indigenous economies and developed commercial economies. The problems of matching agricultural development with that of the other sectors of the economy and with social development are serious and require much more attention than they have so far received.

REFERENCES

1 White, H. P. and Gleave, M. B., 'The West African Middle Belt Environmental Fact or Geographers' Fiction?' Geog. Rev., 59, 1969, pp, 123–139

2 Jarrett, H. R., 'The Strange Farmers of the Gambia', Geog. Rev., 39, 1949, pp. 649–57: Péhaut, Y., 'L'arachide au Sénégal', Cahiers d'Outre-Mer, 14, 1961, pp. 5–25

3 For a general account of cocoa cultivation see Urquhart, D. H., Cocoa, London, 1955

4 Hunter, J. M., 'Cocoa migrations and patterns of land ownership in the Densu Valley near Suhum, Ghana', Trans. Inst. Brit. Geogs., 33, 1963, pp. 61–87

5 Charter, C. F., The nutrient status of Gold Coast forest soils, Report of Cocoa Conference, London 1955, pp. 40–48

6 Beckett, W. H., Akokoaso, London School of Economics and Political Science, Monographs on Social Anthropology, 10, 1944. Hunter, op cit.

7 Hill, P., Migrant Cocoa Farmers of Southern Ghana, Cambridge, 1963

8 Field, J. M., 'The Agricultural System of the Manya-Krobo of the Gold Coast', Africa, 14, 1943, pp. 54–65: Hunter, op cit. Hill, op cit.

9 Hunter, J. M., 'Akotuakrom: a devastated cocoa village in Ghana', Trans. Inst. Brit. Geogs, 29, 1961, pp. 161–186

10 Galletti, R., Baldwin, K. D. S. and Dina, I. O., Nigerian cocoa farmers, London, 1956

11 Hill, P., op cit.

12 Aubréville, A., 'Le climat écologique du palmier à huile dans l'ouest africain', Bull. d'Inst. Coloniale, Marseille, 1944: Broekmans, A. F., 'Growth flowering and yield of the oil palm in Nigeria', Journal W. African Institute of Oil Palm Research, 2, 1957, pp. 187–220

13   The best source for a general description is Morgan, W. B., 'The *Nigerian Oil Palm Industry*', *Scot. Geog. Mag.*, 71, 1955, pp. 174–7

14   Brasseur-Marion, P. and Brasseur, G., '*Porto Novo et sa Palmerie*', *Mem d'IFAN*, 32, Dakar, 1953. Other regional accounts include: Roy, J., '*Situation de palmier à huile en Guinée*', *Bull. agronome française d'outre-mer*, 14, 1957. pp. 120–5: Jarrett, H. R., '*The oil palm and its changing place in the economy of Sierra Leone*', *Geography*, 42, 1957, pp. 50–59

15   Gleave, M. B. and Thomas, M. F., '*The Bagango Valley, an example of land utilisation and agricultural practice in the Bamenda Highlands*', *Bull. Inst. Fond. Afr. Noire*, Sér B., 30, 1968, pp. 655–81

16   Russell, T. A. '*The kola nut in West Africa*', *World Crops*, 7, 1955: '*The kola of Nigeria and the Camerouns*', *Tropical Agriculture*, 32, 1955, pp. 210–40: Gray, J. T. S., *A report on the survey of the cola trade in Ashanti*, Accra, Dept of Ag., 1951

17   Pélissier, P., *Les Paysans du Sénégal: les Civilisations Agraires du Cayor à la Casamance*, St. Yrieix, 1966: Mortimore, M. J. and Wilson, J., *Land and people in the Kano Close-Settled Zone*, Ahmadu Bello University, Dept of Geog., occ. paper 1, 1965

18   Economic Associates, *Report on the ports of Nigeria*, London, 1968 (mimeo)

19   Pélissier, P., '*Les Paysans Sérères*', *Cahiers d'Outre-Mer*, 6, 1955, pp. 105–27

20   Jarrett, H. R., *op cit.*

21   Little has been written on cotton in recent years. For recent trends in Nigeria see Economic Associates *op cit.*

22   White, H. P., *Some Aspects of food crop production in the Gold Coast* International Geog. Union, *Natural Resources and population in intertropical Africa*, Makere Symposium, 1956, pp. 37–42

23   White, H. P., '*Movement of Staple Foods in the Gold Coast*', *Econ. Geog.*, 32, 1956, pp. 115–125

24   Gould, P. R., *Transportation in Ghana*, Evanston, North Western University, Studies in Geog. 5, 1960

25   Tricart, J., '*Les échanges entre la Zone Forestière du Côte d'Ivoire et les Savanes Soudaniennes*', *Cahiers d'Outre Mer*, 17, 1956. pp. 209–238

26   Hunter, J. M., *op cit.* No. 9

27   Morgan, W. B., '*Food imports of West Africa*', *Econ. Geog.*, 39, 1963. pp. 351–362

28   Lewis, W. A., *Report on industrialisation and the Gold Coast*, Accra, 1953

29   White, H. P., '*Mechanised Cultivation of Peasant Holdings in West Africa*', *Geog.* 43, 1958, pp. 269–70

30   Fréchou, H., '*Les Plantations Européens en Côte d'Ivoire*', *Cahiers d'Outre Mer*, 8, 1958, pp. 269–70

31   Coppock, J. T., '*Agricultural developments in Nigeria*', *J. Trop Geog.*, 23, 1966, pp. 1–18

32   Baldwin, K. D. S., *The Niger Agricultural Project*, Oxford, 1957

33   Spitz, G., *Sansanding: Les Irrigations du Niger*, Paris, 1949. Harrison
     Church, R. J., *Observations on large scale irrigation development in Africa*,
     F.A.O. Agricultural Economic Bull. 4, 1963

34   Boutillier, J. L., *et al.*, *La Moyenne Vallée du Sénégal*, Inst. Nationale
     de la Statistique et des Études Economiques, Paris, 1962, Papy, L.,
     '*La vallée du Sénégal*,' *Études Séngalaises*, 2 1952

35   Floyd, B. and Adinole, A. M., '*Farm Settlements in Eastern Nigeria*',
     Econ. Geog., 43, 1967, pp. 189–230

CHAPTER 6

Other Primary Resources & their Exploitation

MINERALS

On the whole West Africa is not highly mineralised and large areas such as the Voltaian Basin (Ghana), the Bandiagra Plateau (Mali), and Upper Guinée are all areas of Primary sandstone barren of economic minerals. There are, however, some notable mineral concentrations, though none comparable with the Katanga-Zambia Copper Belt or the Witwatersrand. Distribution of economic minerals is thus irregular, and not all deposits can be commercially exploited because of the exploration and prospecting costs, shortage of capital, the absence of or the high cost of transport facilities and labour costs, particularly of the necessary expatriate labour.

Nevertheless West Africa is an important world source for certain minerals, notably iron ore, bauxite, phosphates, manganese, diamonds and gold. Nigeria is rapidly becoming a major source of petroleum, although development was recently hindered by the civil war.

IRON ORE

Iron ore deposits are widespread thoughout West Africa commonly occurring as a lateritic capping on hills. In the west, notably in Guinée, Sierra Leone and Liberia, deposits are usually associated with the schists and ultra-basic rocks of the Pre-Cambrian Basement Complex. In the east, however, particularly in Nigeria, large amounts of low grade ore are contained in Cretaceous rocks. In many places surface working by modern mechanical techniques is possible.

Output of iron ore, exploited mainly in Liberia, Sierra Leone, and Mauritanie, has risen quickly recently, from 5·04

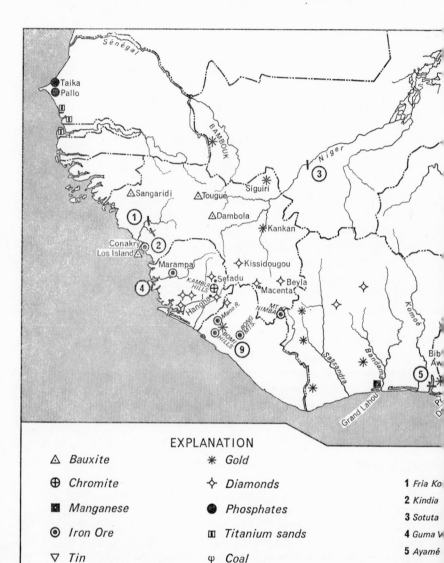

EXPLANATION

△ Bauxite	✳ Gold
⊕ Chromite	✧ Diamonds
▧ Manganese	● Phosphates
◉ Iron Ore	▥ Titanium sands
▽ Tin	φ Coal
☐ Lead, Zinc and Silver	▨ Oil and Gas

1 Fria Ko
2 Kindia
3 Sotuta
4 Guma V
5 Ayamé
6 Bui Gor
7 Volta H

Figure 6.1.

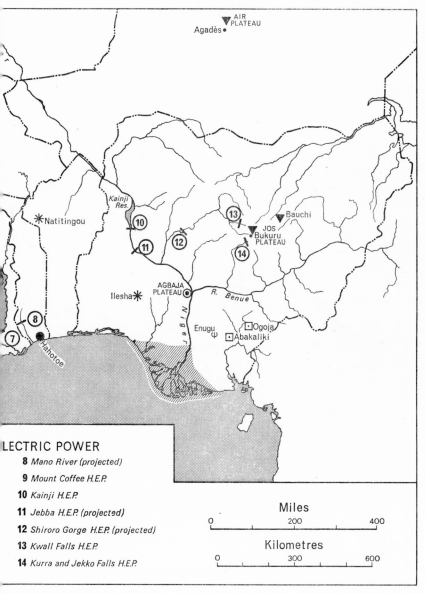

ELECTRIC POWER

8 *Mano River (projected)*

9 *Mount Coffee H.E.P.*

10 *Kainji H.E.P.*

11 *Jebba H.E.P. (projected)*

12 *Shiroro Gorge H.E.P. (projected)*

13 *Kwall Falls H.E.P.*

14 *Kurra and Jekko Falls H.E.P.*

Miles

```
0          200          400
```

Kilometres

```
0          300          600
```

er resources

million tons in 1960 to 24·1 million tons in 1964. The principal developments have taken place in Liberia, where reserves of the deposits currently being worked have been conservatively estimated at 900 million tons. The largest operation is now at Mount Nimba, 165 miles from the newly constructed port of Buchanan. Here haematite with an iron content of 66 per cent. is being mined.[1] Production began in late 1963 and quickly rose to 8·2 million tons in 1965. The main market is the countries of the E.E.C. Capital invested in the mines and in associated transport and port developments amounted to 220 million dollars by 1965 and the enterprise provided employment for 3,000 workers.

The deposits in the Bomi Hills, 42 miles north of Monrovia, contain reserves of 50 million tons with an iron content of 66 per cent. and these are surrounded by deposits with a content of 43 per cent. and reserves exceeding 150 million tons. The lower grades require concentration prior to railing to Monrovia. In 1965 the labour force amounted to 2,300. Mining of a concession on the Mano River, 40 miles inland from the Bomi Hills, began in 1961. Reserves here are 165 million tons with an iron content of 54 per cent. Production in 1965 was 3·5 million tons. More recently exploitation of reserves in the Bong Hills, 50 miles east of Monrovia has begun. Reserves are 230 million tons with an ore content of 37 per cent., raised to 65 per cent. before railing to Monrovia. Mining began early in 1965 and production was 1·5 million tons in the first year.

Exploitation of ore began earlier in Sierra Leone, where the first shipment from the Marampa mines took place in 1933. The deposits occur in two hills and initially were worked by hand. Since 1938 they have been worked by mechanised techniques. The labour force has therefore fallen from 4,000 in 1946 to 2,400 in 1965, although output rose from 0·65 million tons to over 2·0 million tons per year. Investment to 1965 totalled 84 million dollars and the ore is exported to Great Britain and the E.E.C.

In Guinée the largest deposit of lateritic ores was worked in the Kaloum Peninsula between 1952 and 1966. Operations ceased partly because of the difficulties of purchasing equipment because of shortages of foreign exchange and partly because of the diversion of the world iron ore market to richer deposits.[2] Finally, surface deposits are being worked near Fort Gourand in Mauritanie. Reserves are 215 million tons of ore with 63 per cent. ore content and 8,000 million tons of 40–45 per cent. ore content. The costs of the project were increased by transport problems, notably the necessity of keeping the railway line to Port Etienne (now Nouadhibou) within the national frontiers and thus increasing its length.

BAUXITE

The major producer is Guinée, where the mineral has been mined since 1952 on the Iles de Los off Conakry. At Sangaridi inland from Boké there are reserves of 700 million tons of 45 per cent. bauxite. Exploitation has necessitated the building of a new port, Port Kakandé, and a connecting railway. But the major operation is at Fria, where a deposit with proven reserves of 300 million tons and 42–44 per cent. content is worked. An alumina plant with a capacity of 480,000 tons per year was opened in 1960 at Kimba near Fria. The alumina is exported to Edea in Cameroun, to Ghana and to Norway. The only other major bauxite producer is Ghana where resources are exploited at Kanayerebo, 50 miles from Dunkwa. There are, however, major reserves as yet unexploited at Yenahin, west of Kumasi.

PHOSPHATES

In Sénégal the deposit of phosphates in rock form at Pallo near Thiès has reserves of 100 million tons. The second is at Taïba, 70 miles from Dakar. The rock is concentrated before despatch to Dakar. In Togo, where production began in 1961 at Hahotoe, the rock is railed to Kpémé, where it is concentrated prior to export from a special wharf. Phosphate deposits in Togo and Dahomey have estimated reserves of 50,000 million tons.

GOLD

Ghana has long been associated with gold production, as its former name of Gold Coast implies. Modern mining began in the 1880s, working the 'banket' deposits of Tarkwa and the alluvial deposits of the Ankobra river. In 1969, however, only three mines survived, two in government ownership and the Obuasi mine in private ownership. Ghana is the only major producer of gold but alluvial gold is won by between 70 and 100,000 African panners in the Siguiri area of Guinée. It is also won as a by-product of copper mining near Akjout in Mauritanie.

TIN & COLUMBITE

Alluvial tin deposits are mined on and near the Jos Plateau in Nigeria.[3] Although primitive methods still survive most of the ore is now produced by large scale hydraulic methods. The tin ore is smelted at Makeni near Jos before export. Substantial reserves of columbite occur in association with the tin deposits. Sporadic demand for this mineral is thus satisfied as a by product of tin mining. Smaller workings occur at Lirnei-n-Kano and Nassarawa in the northern states of Nigeria and in the Aïr Plateau of Niger.

MANGANESE

Ghana is the main producer of manganese. Working of the Nsuta deposits began in 1916. The ore, with a metal content of 50–57 per cent., occurs in thick beds permitting low cost, open cast mining. It is also worked near Grand Lahou on the lagoon coast of Côte d'Ivoire. Exports began in 1960 and production is already in excess of 100,000 tons per year.

DIAMONDS

Ghana produces most diamonds by weight but these are mainly industrial stones. Sierra Leone's smaller output, because it contains more gem stones, is worth more. In addition both Liberia and Guinée are also significant producers and there is a small output from Côte d'Ivoire. All these are mainly stones of industrial quality. Normally the workings are in alluvial deposits, and while some are operated by modern large-scale methods many are operated by hand by large numbers of independent African diggers. In Ghana Birrim Valley gravels are worked mechanically by large foreign companies, whereas those in the Bonsa Valley near Tarkwa are worked by Africans using hand methods. Until 1959 the whole of Sierra Leone formed one concession leased to the Sierra Leone Selection Trust, but in that year the concession was reduced to an area of 450 square miles (1,365 sq. kms.) in Kenema and Kono Districts. A system of licensing African miners and the establishment of a government marketing office were attempts to reduce the illicit mining and illegal exports of stones, which had been widespread. In Guinée alluvial workings in the Kissidougou and Beyla areas in the south east of the country employ several thousand Africans organised by European companies. Liberia, like Sierra Leone, has an extensive area where diamonds can be won from surface deposits.

Commercial, as opposed to indigenous, mineral exploitation has had very important consequences upon economic development. It was for instance the trade in gold that first attracted European traders to the Guinea Coast and to permanent European settlements there,[4] while the exploitation of petroleum in the Niger Delta during the 1960s led to the unprecedented development in a hitherto underdeveloped area.[5] The reasons for this are not far to seek.

In the first place, risk capital is more easily attracted to mineral exploitation than to other economic activities in economically underdeveloped areas. Almost the first example of this trend was in the establishment of large scale gold mining in Ghana from 1880 onwards, so that by 1894 there were four mines employing 22 Europeans and 2,400 Africans.[6] Iron mining brought large scale investment to Guinée and Sierra Leone in the 1930s and to Liberia after 1945, phosphates to Togo in the late 1950s and petroleum to Nigeria in the 1960s.[7] It was estimated that oil companies had spent some $140 million in Nigeria during 1966.

In the second place these minerals provide a basic export for several West African countries. Prices may fluctuate and so do trends over long periods, but the annual variations due to indifferent harvests are absent. In 1961 phosphates accounted for 3·4 per cent. by value of Togo's exports, and the country was dependent essentially on the export of palm products, for which its climate is marginal. By 1965 phosphates accounted for 32·4 per cent. In 1967 iron ore accounted for 72·6 per cent. by value of Liberian exports, and in 1968 diamonds accounted for 57·0 per cent. of Sierra Leone's exports, and iron ore a further 12·9 per cent. Bauxite, alumina and iron ore are the main source of foreign exchange for Guinée, while gold and manganese account for about 12 per cent. of Ghana's exports, and petroleum a growing proportion of Nigeria's

Thirdly, the exploitation and utilisation of minerals has resulted in the provision and extension of the infrastructure, often used for the general development of the economy. Principally involved are transport facilities and the provision of electric power. Railway building in Ghana was initiated in 1898 to connect the Tarkwa goldfield with the port of Sekondi, while the extension to Kumasi, opened in 1903 was motivated by the need to serve Obuasi gold mine as much as the military garrison in the Ashanti capital. The railway from Port Harcourt to Enugu in Eastern Nigeria was opened in 1916 to evacuate the coal from Enugu. 316 miles (509 kilometres) of railway have been built in Liberia since the war to serve iron mines.[8] Other lines include the Dunkwa-Awaso line in Ghana, built in 1944 to serve bauxite deposits and now used for general traffic and a 13·6 mile (25 kilometre) line in Togo opened in 1959 to serve the phosphate deposits. It will be noticed in passing that minerals have led to more railway building in anglophone countries than francophone (see Chapter 9).

Port building has also resulted from mineral exploitation. Port Harcourt was established in 1915 for the shipment of Enugu coal. Piers have been built at Pepel (Sierra Leone River) to handle iron ore and at Kpémé (Togo) for phosphate export, a new port has been built at Buchanan (Liberia) at the terminus of an iron ore railway, while oil shipping facilities have been provided at the Escravos, Pennington and Brass Rivers of the Niger Delta. Specialised mineral berths have also been provided in general cargo ports at Dakar (phosphates) Conakry (bauxite, iron), Monrovia (iron), Takoradi (bauxite, manganese), Port Harcourt (coal). Finally it should be noted that to accommodate oil tankers the Bonny Bar, the entrance to Port Harcourt, has been dredged to 11·58 metres at a cost of $7·2 million (see Chapter 9). Road building has also been stimulated by mineral exploitation. Internal air traffic in Sierra Leone was initiated by the Selection Trust to serve the diamond fields at Yengema.

Conversely, it was the fortuitous proximity of an existing line of communication that sometimes permitted the exploitation of an otherwise suitable deposit. Thus the Nsuta manganese deposits in Ghana happened to lie on the Sekondi-Tarkwa railway, and this allowed exports to begin in 1917. Similarly, the chrome deposits in Sierra Leone at Kenema could be worked because they were on the railway to Pendembu and because the ore enjoyed special low rates to Freetown. Again, iron ore deposits of the Kaloum peninsula lay athwart the railway.

Minerals have also led to the development of power. Two small hydro-electric plants, the first in Nigeria, were installed in 1923 and 1929 to supply power to the tinfields of the Jos Plateau and several of the early power stations in Ghana were built by the mining companies. In these cases surplus power was sold to neighbouring towns. More recently, the Konkouré hydro-electric scheme in Guinée has been initiated to process bauxite, and this was likewise the primary object of the Volta River Project (see below).

Finally there are two further aspects of the link between mineral exploitation and economic development. The mines have provided much employment outside agriculture. It is estimated that 40,000 people are dependent on the Liberian iron mines. They also provided the opportunity for West Africans to become familiar with the operation and maintenance of machinery and of acquiring other skills. Mining has also given rise to ancillary industries and has thus contributed to industrialisation. The processing of minerals for export includes the extraction of gold, a complex industrial process, the benefi- ciation of iron ore and the concentration of phosphatic rock. Perhaps the most important industrial development, however, has been the utilisation of limestone deposits for cement manu- facture (see page 182). The petroleum deposits in Nigeria resulted in the establishment of an oil refinery at Port Harcourt, which went on stream in 1965, while another is planned at Ughelli in the Mid-West.

In general, it is the deposits that are nearer the coast which have been developed. The exceptions have been high value minerals which can withstand transport costs, e.g. the tin of northern Nigeria, or low value ones with a local market. One example of this is limestone for cement, for transport costs on the latter give a high level of natural protection. The establishment of the Sokoto plant should be seen in this light, though it is in a far from ideal place for local distribution. Thus most mining activity is to be found in the Forest and to the west of the Futa-Nimba highlands. So the economic opportunities of the Forest Zone are further reinforced. Many deposits have been proved in the Guinea Savana and the Sudan, but exploitation is costly in this area, where supplementary resources are badly needed.

On the basis of the value of minerals exploited, we can divide the history of investment and development into two main periods, from 1900 to 1930 and from 1950 to the present separated by the depression of the 1930s and the Second World War. In the earlier period the interest was mainly focussed on the higher value minerals, gold, diamonds and tin, a reflection of the poor and costly transport facilities, which before 1900 were virtually non-existent. Proximity to a port or the availability of rail transport, however, enabled some low-value deposits to be opened up. Thus the exploitation of Enugu coal and Ghana manganese started in 1915 and 1917 respectively. The working of iron ore in Sierra Leone can also be assigned to this period.

The depression of the 1930s brought development to a halt, and activity did not revive until about 1950 because of the war and its immediate aftermath, though the British Government concerned itself with opening up the bauxite of Ghana. Since 1950 the main emphasis has been on the bulkier, lower value minerals, iron, bauxite and petroleum. Perhaps the best example of recent development is the exploitation of Liberian iron ore. The first shipment was made from the Bomi Hills in 1951. By 1965 exports had reached an annual rate of 14·5 million tons from four deposits, worked by as many consortia, mainly representing American capital but including German and Swedish. By 1968 exports reached 21·3 million tons, 2·4 million tons more than the previous year. Iron ore has also become the economic mainstay of Mauritanie, and by 1966 exports exceeded 5 million tons.[8] Bauxite, too, has also become of great importance in Guinée and to a less extent in Ghana and Sierra Leone, while phosphates have been developed in Sénégal and

Togo. High value minerals are represented by the exploitation in recent years of the rutile deposits of southern Sierra Leone and the uranium of Arlit (near Agadès in Niger).

The organisation has been, with few exceptions, on a large scale by foreign firms. Mining concessions have been relatively easy to secure in both the British and the French areas as well as in Liberia, though chance has decreed that the francophone areas were much poorer in exploitable minerals. Since Independence mining has not been a usual target for state-inspired investment and organisation. This is probably because the ease of attracting foreign capital to mining has placed this activity low on the list of priorities for scarce government capital, and its speculative nature renders it unattractive for foreign aid programmes. State aid has been mainly in the form of financing geological surveys, charged with locating economic minerals. Thus it was A. E. Kitson of the Gold Coast Geological Survey who discovered the diamond deposits of the Birrim Basin in 1919,[9] while many finds of lead and other minerals were made in Mali by the *Direction Fédérale des Mines et de Géologie*.

In the francophone countries France has been the main source of capital and enterprise. The iron and bauxite of Guinée and the phosphates of Sénégal and Togo were developed by French consortia. On the other hand Britain has been a less exclusive source for activity in the anglophone countries. In Liberia the original investment in iron, the Bomi Hills deposits, was mainly American, but the more recent concessions have been given to consortia of U.S., German and Swedish interests. During the Nkrumah regime, many gold mines were taken over by the Ghana government to prevent their closure and preserve employment. Oddly, they were only the unprofitable ones, the Obuasi mine, which because of the exceptionally high gold content and therefore low operating costs remained profitable, being left in the hands of its British owners. High costs, however, generally forced the closure of a number of large gold mines in Ghana, such as Konongo (1965) and Bibiani (1967), and production has become concentrated on only three mines.

The exceptions to the large scale operations are the exploitation of alluvial deposits of tin on the Jos Plateau of Nigeria[10] and of the diamonds of Ghana and Sierra Leone. The tin was

L

initially exploited by Europeans working individually or in small partnerships. In later years, however, amalgamations produced larger firms.

About half the diamonds are produced by subsidiary companies of the Diamond Corporation, the other half by licensed African miners working in small groups. The experience of Sierra Leone shows the limitations of these latter methods. In the first place the small scale workings are wasteful in that the small individual pits in the alluvial gravels leave much of the ground unworked. Secondly, the 'diamond-rush' of the 1950s diverted so many agriculturalists that the cost of food rose sharply. Thirdly, there was a spate of smuggling, which deprived the Government of revenue from the export duties. In 1956 it was calculated that $30·8 million worth were smuggled (total legitimate exports of all products amounted to $33·93 million).[11] There is also a small production of gold and diamonds by individual miners from Upper Guinée, though prior to World War II up to 70,000 people obtained a regular living from the alluvial deposits of the river Bakhay basin. Another example of indigenous exploitation and distribution is that of salt from the shallow coastal lagoons, which dry out during the dry season.[12] This is marketed widely in competition with imported supplies.

It seems that the important consequences of minerals upon economic development will be maintained. As we have seen, the reserves of minerals currently exploited are considerable, and there are large proven reserves in deposits not yet worked. A brief examination of the position with regard to two minerals will suffice as illustration. There are reserves of iron ore in the Mount Nimba area of Guinée estimated at 150–200 million tons with an iron content of 60–65 per cent., and others two or three times as large in the neighbouring Suniandan range. The bulk of the estimated 2,000 million tons of ore on the Kaloum Peninsula are still intact, and there are other known bodies in Lower Guinée. Unworked deposits exist in Liberia in the Puta Mountains and Bassa Hill, and in Nigeria on the Agbaja Plateau (100 million tons estimated with an iron content of 45–51 per cent.) and near Enugu (45 million tons estimated with a 43 per cent. ore content). There are also deposits in Dahomey, Niger and Sénégal.

Unworked deposits of bauxite include those in the lower Konkouré valley near Kindia in Guinée, near Dabola on the eastern flanks of the Futa Djalon and in Ghana not only at Yenahin but at Mount Ejaunima and in the Kibi area. The exploitation of these and other minerals, such as rutile in the sands of southern Sierra Leone, will depend on world markets for individual minerals, the availability of capital and of infrastructure, the political situation in individual countries and upon the rate of industrial development in West Africa.

POWER

The link between mineral and power production is provided by the two mineral sources of energy, coal and petroleum. West Africa is poorly endowed with the former. In Nigeria workable coal seams were discovered in 1910 at the base of the escarpment of Udi Plateau in the neighbourhood of Enugu. Exploitation resulted in the establishment of Enugu town and of Port Harcourt and in the building of the railway southward to Port Harcourt and northward to Kaduna Junction. There were in 1967 four working drift mines operated by the State owned Coal Corporation.

The calorific value is low and the ash content very high. The main market was the Nigerian railway. The coal was also exported for the Ghana and Sierra Leone railways, though in the 1950s this market could not always be satisfied, because of the expansion in the demand for electricity. Quite large coal burning stations were erected at Lagos, Ibadan and at Oji River (near Enugu and adjacent to the coalfield), and at Tema Harbour in Ghana. Dieselisation of the railways and the exploitation of Nigerian oil, which led to new power stations being equipped for oil burning and to the conversion of some old stations, resulted in a catastrophic contraction of the markets. The Eastern Region fought a delaying action, ironically won just as their oil began to come into production. The Coal Corporation also attempted to prove the coal suitable for coking so that it could be used to establish a Nigerian steel industry. There seems, however, to be no future for Nigerian coal. The industry would probably have collapsed by 1960 if it had been privately owned, and the mines may not re-open after the civil war. Table 6.2 shows recent production trends.

In 1958 a long period of prospecting for oil was successfully completed by the first substantial production from the Niger Delta. Impetus to this had been given throughout West Africa by the closing of the Suez canal in 1956 and again in 1967. In 1958, 249,000 tons were exported. A condition of the original Shell-BP concessions was the erection of a refinery at Okrika near Port Harcourt, and this went on stream in 1965 with a capacity of about 1 million tons. It now supplies the internal market for petrol, kerosene, and diesel oil for road vehicles, railway locomotives and small power stations, together with fuel oil for large power stations and ships. Exports increased very rapidly until 1966, when they amounted to 19 million tons. It was only the political troubles of 1967 which prevented a very big increase in that year.

TABLE 6.1

COMPARATIVE COSTS OF PRODUCING ELECTRICITY
IN DIFFERENT PARTS OF NIGERIA, 1962

	Units generated (million)	Costs per unit (pence)
Lagos	138·0	3·245
Ibadan	30·5	4·512
Kano	29·9	4·342
Kaduna	18·5	4·495
Zaria	7·5	5·297
Oshogbo	4·8	7·397

Source: Ledger, op cit.

The original fields were in the eastern part of the Delta north-west of Port Harcourt, but soon fields in the Mid-West around Ughelli went into production, and by 1966 the offshore field at the mouth of the Escravos was producing some 2·5 million tons. Active development is continuing on the continental shelf over the rest of the Delta and the search is continuing throughout south eastern Nigeria and the Mid-West.[13] Exploration in the Lagos area has not yet yielded results. Other areas of exploration have been on the Continental Shelf of Sénégal, Liberia and Dahomey and in the structural basins of the middle Niger and southern Sahara in Mali and Niger. Finds have been made and in 1967 drilling was in progress 350 miles north of Gao in Mali and 19 miles north of Dakar.

Both coal and oil are used for the generation of electricity. Until recently power stations were small and market-oriented, being located in the larger towns or at mines. During the 1950s domestic demand, the main market outside mines, grew and new markets became available through the establishment of manufacturing industries. Market growth was, however, limited by the high cost of power, which in turn was the result of small scale production for limited markets (Table 6.1). For low cost power, an essential basis for the successful industrialisation of West Africa, this vicious circle must somehow be broken.

In 1955 the combined capacity of the generating stations in Ghana, then unquestionably the most economically advanced of West African countries, was about 60 megawatts (mw), but by 1963 this had grown to 143 mw, 75 mw being accounted for by the town stations and 68 mw by those at the mines. In Côte d'Ivoire total production in 1952 was 52 million kilowatt hours (kWh). By 1962 this had reached 120·2 million kWh and by 1970 is expected to reach 500 million kWh.[14]

Much of this increased output has been from large (by previous standards) stations, located at ports (themselves the main markets) for ease of import of fuel. The oil-burning stations at Abidjan have capacities of 28 and 30 mw and the Ijora A and B stations on Lagos Lagoon 13·75 mw and 86·25 mw respectively.[15] The former burns coal and the latter oil. A trunk transmission power line connects them with the station at Ibadan. There are also large stations at Tema and Dakar.

But some stations are being built close to the source of power. We have already mentioned the Oji River station (30 mw) which is connected to the Enugu coal mines by an overhead bucket conveyor. There is also a great potential for electricity generation from natural gas in the Niger Delta. In 1966 the Delta Power Station at Ughelli was completed, using most of the 10 million cubic feet of natural gas sold daily in December of that year. Governments have, however, increasingly turned their attention to hydro-electric power, especially if they have no indigenous alternative sources of power.

Unfortunately, West Africa is not particularly favoured by

water power potential. Rivers, with a few exceptions, are limited in volume and liable to extreme seasonal fluctuation. The nature of the terrain also means that sites are few in number and some of these are remote from markets. The first installations were two small ones at the edge of the Jos Plateau in Northern Nigeria, built to supply power for the tin field. In 1951 the Ayame I station on the Bia River in Côte d'Ivoire was inaugurated. Its capacity is 19·8 mw. The larger Ayame II, three miles away, was opened in 1965 with a capacity of 30 mw. In Guinée a rather similar sized station was built at the Kindia falls in the Futa Djalon and another on the Konkouré River. In Sierra Leone the Guma Valley Scheme, completed in 1966 to assure the Freetown water supply, included a small 2·8 mw station.[16] There are also plans for a station on the Mono River, the frontier between Togo and Dahomey, which will be jointly owned by the two countries, while a station has been built in Liberia at Mount Coffee (34 mw) near Monrovia and another near Buchanan. Mali has built one at Sotuta near Bamako.

All of these are small compared with two very large schemes, the Volta River Project in Ghana and the Kainji Project in Nigeria. The harnessing of the Volta was first recommended in 1917 by Sir Arthur Kitson, the Director of the Gold Coast Geological Survey, for processing the newly proved bauxite deposits. Over the following decades the idea was revived several times, culminating with the setting up of a Preparatory Commission, which reported in 1956[17] on the feasability of the Volta River Project, and in 1961 the Volta River Authority was established to implement the scheme. As now envisaged, the Project was far more than a power station and smelter. A considerable surplus of low cost power was to be made available for general industrialisation, a new town was to be built at Kpong for the smelter workers, railway extensions were to connect the Yenahin bauxite deposits with Kpong, and above all, massive 'social engineering' would be necessary consequent on the creation of the 9,000 square kilometre Lake Volta. It was hoped, in short, to provide the infra-structure to enable Ghana to reach a 'take off' level for economic development. This scheme, technically very attractive, was estimated by the Preparatory Commission to cost not less than $646 million, and was too ambitious for the available finance. It was therefore modified by transferring the smelter site to Tema to use alumina imported from Guinée. This eliminated the new town, the development of the Yenahin deposits and the railway extensions, permitting reduction of the estimated costs by 40 per cent.

On 22nd January, 1966, the Project was inaugurated. The dam at Akosombo, in the gorge of the Volta through the Akwapim Range, is over 60 metres high and the power station at the foot has an ultimate capacity of 768 mw. The smelter, which exported its first batch of 250 tons in March 1967, has a planned output of 103,000 tons of metal in 1969, rising to 145,000 tons by 1973. Excess power is fed into power lines to Accra, Kumasi and Takoradi. With the completion of a dam and power station at Bui on the Black Volta, 370 miles (595 kms.) upstream, and a projected station at Kpong, 1,000 mw should be available from the Volta, though work on these two schemes has for the time being been abandoned. The creation of Lake Volta involved the resettlement of 80,000 people from 700 villages at a cost of $22·4 million, together with the re-siting of several towns and the construction of many miles of road. There is also considerable potential for irrigation, especially of the Accra Plains, for fisheries and for water transport.[18] It is now hoped to build an alumina plant to enable Ghana bauxite to be used.

The Kainji dam is on the Niger above Jebba. Completed in 1967, at a cost of $238 million, its associated power station will have a capacity of 960 mw. The current is to be distributed throughout northern and much of western Nigeria, but, unlike the Volta Project, it has no guaranteed base-load market. Preliminary investigations suggested that there was little difference between the profitability of the Kainji scheme and alternatives using natural-gas fired thermal stations for the provision of power. The dam was chosen because of the added advantage of providing agricultural, navigational and other benefits at little extra cost. The principal by-products hoped for are that navigation will be improved and that greater agricultural use can be made of the flood plain. Full realisation of projected improvement to navigation is unlikely until further works at Jebba, not yet started, are completed. Regulation of flooding is, however, making new land available for cultivation on the flood plain. In addition it is also possible to develop irrigation agriculture of both cash and food crops on parts of the plain. Indeed, the sugar plantation at Bacita may be a forerunner of development in the area. Furthermore, the lake, 80 by 4 miles (129 by 6·5 kilo-metres), will provide an important fishing ground, and the dam will provide a crossing of the Niger alternative to the overloaded Jebba bridge.[19]

Because of the nature of the sites, the need for large scale associated works, and the cost of power distribution over long distances, all these hydro-electric projects represent a very large investment in relation to unit production. To get the scale of the projects mentioned into focus, it is worth recalling that the capacity of a single generating set in a modern British power station is 500 mw or more. Although power costs will be lower than from the small diesel stations, it is by no means certain that power costs will be low by world standards, especially if the capital redemption is at commercial rates. However this may be, it is clear that adequate supplies of energy at reasonable cost are a pre-requisite for economic development in West Africa, and these recent developments are to be viewed as the beginnings of a real attack on the general deficiency of energy supplies.

FOREST RESOURCES[20]

A very important primary resource is provided by areas of uncleared Forest. In the past various products such as gum copal and rubber were collected, but since World War I commercial exploitation has been virtually only for timber. Prior to 1939 this was almost solely confined to the mahoganies, and in 1937, 95 per cent. of the logs shipped from Ghana were from these species. After the war, because of exhaustion of mahogany supplies and of the world timber shortage, it became possible to market a much wider range of species, and by 1954 only 24 per cent. by value of Ghana's timber exports were of mahogany, and this was exceeded in value by shipments of *Wawa* (*Triplochiton scleroxylon*), a softwood.

The Nigerian Forest Research Departments list 57 species of economically useful timbers,[21] predominantly, but by no means exclusively, hardwoods. They include highly decorative species suitable for furniture and panelling, species resistant to damp and decay and suitable for yacht hulls, decking, and wharf and structural timbers, and others suitable for veneers, plywood, chipboard and concrete shuttering.

The first problem connected with exploitation is the floristic composition of the forest, for though trees grow close together, the stands are extremely mixed in variety and age. No single 400 hectare block will include all the principal economic species. Even in areas most favourable to their growth, the density of mature *Khaya ivorensis* (the most common mahogany) will be less than one per 4 hectares, of *Chlorophera excelsa* (*Odum*) less than one per 8 hectares, and of *Entandrophragma cylindricum* (*Sapele*) less than one per 2 hectares.[22] This increases the difficulty of extraction, and therefore increases costs. Time is consumed in locating suitable trees; a considerable mileage of tracks must be cleared and bridges must be built for the removal of a comparatively small number of trees; heavy equipment must be moved frequently and camps can rarely be permanent.

Movement of the logs to sawmill or port presents the next problem. The use of natural waterways is best where possible. Much timber is moved on the waters of the Niger Delta to the sawmills at Sapele or to the ports, or through the lagoons of western Nigeria to Apapa. The rivers of Ghana are no longer of much use, but in Côte d'Ivoire the Bandama, Melorel, and Camoé are of considerable value, as are the lagoons of the south-east, now inter-connected by canals. Unfortunately the Nigerian railways do not serve the principal working areas, though those of Ghana and Côte d'Ivoire do. When, through lack of alternatives, the main roads are used, extensive damage is done as the road foundations are inadequate for the constant passage of heavy vehicles.[23] This is a cost borne by the country and not by the industry.

A third problem is the ensuring of a sustained supply. High forest is a wasting asset, and is being cleared rapidly through population increase and the spread of cash crops. In Ghana it has been estimated that about 31,000 square miles (80,300 square kilometres) are capable under natural conditions of supporting forest, but that by the mid-1950s less than half this was under closed forest, while the latter was being cleared for agriculture at the rate of 300 square miles (775 square kilometres) a year.[24]

Each country is therefore concerned with establishing a sufficient area of forest reserve to enable a sustained yield of timber to be extracted, and at the same time to ensure regeneration. Concessions are freely allocated outside the reserves so that economic timber can be extracted in advance of clearance by agriculturalists. In theory at least, concessions in reserves are less easily granted and under conditions which will ensure regeneration. Unfortunately this has not always been so. In Nigeria policy towards the reserves varied from one region to another. During the late 1950s and the early 1960s the Western Region hurried into leases for quick returns, and large areas were ruined. The Mid-West was saved from the consequences of this short sightedness by the vast concessions to the African Timber and Plywood Company which was able to exploit only part of the area. While the Eastern Region neglected its reserves, they remained largely uncut, and it is to be hoped that they will be better managed.

Three countries are concerned with large scale timber production, Côte d'Ivoire, Ghana and Nigeria. Concessionaries include expatriate and African companies, both large and small. The tendency in recent years has been to encourage as much processing before export as possible. While a high proportion is still exported in the form of logs, an increasing proportion is as sawn timber, plywood and chipboard. The location of sawmills and other plants is dealt with in Chapter 8.

In Côte d'Ivoire the main areas are the eastern and central parts of the Forest belt. Tricart's survey of 1955[25] showed 42,000 cubic metres of logs floated down the Bandama and 33,700 down the Mé and Camoé, all eastern rivers. 28,100 cubic metres reached the lagoon at Dabou via the Tiassalé road, and 48,700 were railed, mainly from Agboville and neighbouring stations. In contrast only 6,400 cubic metres reached Sassandra from the west. Exports of timber, logs and sawn, amounted to 81,019 tons in 1949, rising to 214,576 tons in 1956 and to 915,110 in 1962.

Exports from Ghana show the increasing importance of sawn timber, In 1950 360,000 cubic metres were exported, 290,000 as logs and 70,000 sawn. In 1956, of the 800,000 cubic metres exported, 544,000 were logs and 256,000 sawn. By 1963 total exports had fallen back to 446,000 cubic metres, but sawn timber had remained at 256,000 cubic metres and logs had fallen to 288,000

Extraction is mainly from the wetter western parts of the forest from the areas around Goaso and Wiawso. Evacuation routes converge on Kumasi for railing to Takoradi, on Takoradi itself or on the large sawmills at Samreboi. Less important foci, because the surrounding areas are more nearly worked out, are around Kade and on the Kwahu plateau.

From Nigeria, exports, though fluctuating, showed a rising trend from 300,000 tons in 1954 to 623,000 in 1964. Log exports rose from 256,000 to 536,000 tons, while sawn timber tonnage increased from 32,000 to 67,000 a fairly constant proportion of the total. Plywoods and veneers rose from 12,000 to 20,000 tons.

The main extraction areas in the West and Mid-West are the uncleared forest and the reserves south of the cocoa crescent and aligned along the Ijebu Ode-Benin road through Ore. The second great area is the Niger Delta and surrounding lowlands. Production now seems to be stationary, due more to difficulties of transport than to decline of reserves. Finally, the largest area of unexploited resources is the East Cross River Basin, where most of the reserves in the East are located.

The home market for timber is gradually expanding for furniture, flooring and construction. Some wood is also used in match industries established in Nigeria, Ghana and Côte d'Ivoire. The greatest future, however, probably lies in the production of pulp and paper. The scattered nature of suitable species in the rainforest makes exploitation for pulp difficult, but if the mangrove forests can be exploited for pulp there is a vast potential resource.

Forest products also enter the internal exchange as firewood and charcoal, a very large tonnage of both being produced. In the Western Region of Nigeria it was estimated that 12,000 cubic metres were used for these purposes in 1963–64. An estimate for Nigeria as a whole during the 1950s was an annual consumption of 50 million tons of firewood for a population of 30 million. It is in this way, too, that most wood cut in the Guinea Savana and Sudan is used. So great is the demand that plantations have been established in the neighbourhood of large towns to ensure supplies. There is probably a considerable potential for pulp and for timber from the Savana woodlands, but as yet this has been scarcely realised, though there are extensive teak plantations in Dahomey.

FISHERIES (see page 100)

Protein is deficient in the West African diet and an important social problem is how this may be remedied. Because of social and economic problems of stock rearing and even more of meat distribution, meat supplies have not expanded very much, in spite of an enormous unsatisfied demand. Fish, however, is a popular and low priced substitute that can be dried, canned or made into meal. The trade between Norway and West Africa in 'stockfish' (dried cod) is of long standing, while sea fish landed by Ga and Fanti fishermen, and river fish from the Niger are widely distributed.

Many governments have therefore concerned themselves with developing sea fishing by means of power vessels. This has been aided in recent years by the building of harbours (see Chapter 9), many of which include facilities for fishing vessels. Among them are Tema, Cotonou and Abidjan. Perhaps the most successful of the countries has been Ghana, where there are now numerous power vessels at work, operated by fishermen's co-operatives with the active encouragement of the Fisheries Department. In addition several hundred of the traditional dugout canoes have been equipped with outboard motors.

There is also considerable potential for increasing the productivity of the Niger, the Volta and the coastal lagoons by fish farming and other methods. But this and improvement of the sea fisheries depends on simultaneous establishment of processing plants and improvement of the marketing system, which at present involves a long chain of small middlemen.

The exploitation of primary resources thus has an important place in the economy for a number of reasons, including the contribution of the production to exports, the attraction of capital from overseas, the provision of infrastructure which can be used for other purposes and the possibility of skilled employment. Not least, however, is the provision of raw materials and energy, which form a basis for the development of manufacturing industry, which is dealt with in the next chapter.

TABLE 6.2

COAL PRODUCTION, NIGERIA, 1954–64

	Long tons
1954	643,000
1955	749,000
1956	787,212
1957	815,271
1958	924,419
1959	741,753
1960	565,681
1961	595,502
1962	622,504
1963	582,989
1964	688,207

Source: Handbook of commerce and Industry in Nigeria

REFERENCES

1 Swindell, K., 'Iron Ore Mining in West Africa', Econ. Geog., 43, 1967, pp. 333–346

2 ibid., 'Industrialization in Guinea', Geog., 54, 1969, pp. 456–458

3 Hodder, B. W., 'Tin mining in the Jos Plateau of Nigeria', Econ. Geog., 35, 1959, pp. 109–122

4 Bovill, E. W., The Golden Trade of the Moors, London, 1958. Junner, N. R., The geology and mineral resources of the Gold Coast, Accra, 1938. The latter contains an excellent essay on the early development of gold mining in Ghana

5 Melamid, A.. 'The Geography of the Nigerian Petroleum Industry', Econ. Geog., 43, 1967, pp. 37–56

6 Burton, R. F. and Cameron, V. L., To the Gold Coast for Gold, London, 1883

7 Swindell, K., 'Iron ore Mining in Liberia', Geography, 50, 1965, pp. 75–78. Ibid. op cit., 1967. Melamid, op cit.

8 Swindell, K., op cit., 1967

9 Junner, N. R., 'Diamond deposits of the Gold Coast', Bull. Gold Coast Geog. Survey, 12, 1943

10 Hodder, B. W., op cit.

11 See also Jack, D. T., *Economic Survey of Sierra Leone*, Freetown, 1958: note also Williams, G. J., *'Sierra Leone stakes its mineral claims'*, *Geographical Magazine*, 42, 1970, pp. 392–402 estimates diamonds worth $450·4 million were illegally exported 1955–59

12 Morgan, W. B. and Pugh, J. C., *West Africa*, London 1969, p. 163

13 Melamid, A., *op cit.*

14 Hilton, T. E., *'The Changing Ivory Coast'*, *Geography*, 50, 1965, pp. 291–295

15 Simpson, E. S., *'Electricity Production in Nigeria'*, *Econ. Geog.* 45, 1969, pp. 239–257

16 Williams, G. J., *'The Guma Valley Scheme, Sierra Leone'*, *Geography* 50, 1965, pp. 163–168

17 *The Volta River Project*, Report of the Preparatory Commission, London, 1956

18 For accounts of the Volta River Project *see*: Jackson, Sir R., *'The Volta River Project'*, *Progress* (Unilever Quarterly) 50, 1964, pp. 146–161: Phillips, J., *Agriculture and Ecology in Africa*, London, 1959: Hilton, T. E., *'Akosombo Dam and the Volta River Project'*, *Geography*, 51, 1966, pp. 251–254

19 Ledger, D. C., *'The Niger Dams Project of Nigeria'*, *Tijdschrift voor Econ. en. Soc. Geografie*, 54, 1963, *pp.* 242–247: Wagland, P. J., *'Kainji and the Niger Dams Project'*, *Geography*, 54, 1969, pp. 459–463

20 *See* especially: United Africa Co., *'Timber in West Africa'*, *Statistical and Economic Review*, 10, 1952, pp. 1–61: Jay, B. A., *Timbers of West Africa*, London, Timber Development Assoc., 1951

21 *Some Nigerian Woods*, Lagos, Federal Ministry of Information, 1966

22 Marshall, R. C., *Gold Coast Timbers*, Accra, 1942

23 Bonavia, M. R., *Report on Transport in the Gold Coast*, Accra 1951

24 Charter, C. F., *The Nutrient Status of Gold Coast Forest Soils*, Report of Cocoa Conference, London, 1955, pp. 40–48

25 Tricart, J., *Etude Géographique de Problèmes de Transport en Côte d'Ivoire*, Strasbourg, Université, Centre de Géog. Appliquée, 1955 (mimeo)

CHAPTER 7

Manufacturing Industry

In Chapter 5 the difficulties to be overcome in developing agriculture, one of the keys to economic and social progress, were examined. Industrial development is another key. In 1950, however, industry provided only 5 per cent. of gross domestic product in West Africa. By 1963 this contribution to gross domestic product had risen to 7 per cent. but West Africa still lagged behind the remainder of the continent.[1] There is, however, considerable variation in the level of industrial development among the West African countries, which can be divided into two groups. In the first one are the countries which already have a range of industry, Ghana, Côte d'Ivoire, Nigeria and Sénégal. The second consists of the other countries, in which industrialisation has hardly begun.

Though industry as yet provides only a small percentage of g.d.p., industrial growth has been proceeding rapidly during the last two decades. Between 1950 and 1963 manufacturing industry in West Africa grew at a compound annual rate of 8·8 per cent. The economy as a whole grew at 4·4 per cent. per annum in the same period and in some countries, notably Côte d'Ivoire, industry was the most rapidly growing sector of the economy.[2] Further, it appears that the pace of industrialisation is quickening. Of the manufacturing and construction firms operating in Ghana in 1959 some 80 per cent. had begun operations since 1940 and well over half since 1950.[3] Similarly, total gross revenues of industrial firms in Côte d'Ivoire were nearly six times as great in 1964 as in 1954, and in Nigeria industry grew at 17 per cent. per year through the 1950s.[4]

Impressive though these growth rates are, it should be remembered that the bases were small, so they can be accounted for by one or two new plants commissioned each year. But it is the policy of all West African governments to sustain or accelerate rates of industrialisation by means of economic development planning. It is pertinent, then, to consider the factors upon which industrial growth has been based and which will become increasingly significant as industrialisation proceeds.

FACTORS IN INDUSTRIAL LOCATION & DEVELOPMENT

1. RAW MATERIALS. West Africa has an abundant supply of certain raw materials which form the basis of industrial development. These have been considered in some detail in previous chapters. Amongst these raw materials are minerals, such as oil, bauxite, iron ore and limestone; forest products, notably timber; fish and agricultural produce, of which oil seeds, fibres, starches and sugar are particularly important.

2. POWER SUPPLIES. It has already been indicated (page 151) that energy supplies are both limited and costly. This underlies the importance of the petroleum resources of the Niger Delta and the large scale hydro-electric plants.

3. CAPITAL SUPPLIES. This is a convenient place to discuss capital supply for all economic activities rather than for manufacturing alone. It is generally held that shortage of capital is a major barrier to development, and discovering ways to increase supply at reasonable cost is a first priority. Certainly the West African countries are under-equipped with capital in relation to their populations and natural resources. This can be partly explained by a 'vicious circle of poverty', in which low real income leads to low buying power and low savings capacity, which in turn leads to a low rate of capital formation. This in turn leads to lack of capital resulting in low productivity and low real income. S. P. Schatz[5], however, has challenged this widely held view, basing his argument on the experience of the Nigerian Federal Loans Board. The Board is a development bank which makes loans to Nigerian entrepreneurs in fields other than agriculture or trade. Between 1956 and 1962 there were 290 applications to the Board for loans, of which 79 per cent. were rejected. Of the 61 approved applications only 54 had acceptable security,

whilst the remainder did not. Thus it appeared that there was more a shortage of viable projects than of capital. Reference was also made to the subsequent performance of firms which had received loans. Almost half proved to be unsuccessful and a further quarter were described as shaky in spite of guidance and help from the Board. Schatz concludes, therefore, that in Nigeria capital has been vainly seeking viable private projects rather than the reverse and suggests that this is also true elsewhere. It must be stressed, however, that Schatz is looking only at small scale manufacturing enterprise.

Capital employed in West Africa stems from several sources, of which three are particularly important. The first is the large expatriate merchant firms, which in the past decade have been diversifying their activities into manufacturing by investing the profits of trade in industrial plants. The second major source is investment by foreign manufacturers. Many of the larger European and American firms, including ENI, Shell, ICI, l'Air Liquide, Guiness, Glaxo, Raleigh, Brasseries Alsaciennes, Nestlé, have established plants in West Africa. Many firms would doubtless have preferred to continue supplying from their home plants at lower unit costs because of economies of scale, and minimising the amount of capital at risk overseas. The pressure from West African governments to set up local plants, however, was strong and was reinforced by practical measures of tariff protection and tax concessions. To have opted out of local manufacture would not only have meant the immediate loss of export markets, but would also have made it difficult to re-enter the field when the market had developed.

The third major source of capital is West African governments, who provide capital from taxation and by borrowing abroad. This capital is usually administered by Development Corporations, which enter into partnership with expatriate enterprises. The former provide much of the capital, the latter some capital together with managerial and technical expertise. Thus in all countries government participation in industrial development is much greater than in Western Europe. Some governments, however, have gone further than others. In the Ghana of Nkrumah the 'State Enterprises' were in some cases partnerships between public and private

M

investors, but in others were entirely publicly owned. They numbered 47 and engaged in an impressive range of activities in all sectors of the economy. Manufacturing included canning, distilling, tanning, the manufacture of jute bags, toilet rolls, furniture, paint, matches, nails, and metal sheets, whilst there are also an Electronics Corporation and a Tobacco Products Corporation. The trading deficits of most of these State Enterprises, however, are as impressive as their range of activities. Guineé and Mali have also founded most new industries through state enterprise. Joint enterprises have performed more effectively than those which were wholly government owned and those in the secondary sector better than their counterparts in the other sectors. Accordingly the post-Nkrumah government adopted a policy of transferring the whole of some corporations and an interest in others to private enterprise, maintaining complete control of the remainder. Capital from government sources is also made available to local entrepreneurs in most West African countries through loan organisations, of which the Federal Loans Board of Nigeria is an example.

In addition to these major sources of funds there are others individually less important. Some are quasi-government bodies, such as the Commonwealth Development Corporation, the Commonwealth Development Finance Company, the *Caisse Centrale de Co-opération Économique* and the U.S. Agency for International Development. Communist governments have also provided the capital and expertise for specific projects, including industrial plants. This aid went mainly, but not exclusively to Ghana, Mali and Guinée. There are also specialised agencies of the U.N., although these tend to concentrate on projects to develop the infrastructure rather than on manufacturing. Of the many U.N. bodies, the International Bank for Reconstruction and Development (World Bank), the International Development Association and the International Finance Corporation are most concerned with industrial projects. Similarly, the European Development Fund provides capital from the Common Market countries for development projects, some of which are of an industrial nature. The capital for some industrial projects is provided by 'contractor finance', whereby the supplier of plant and machinery makes short-term loans at market interest rates to cover the cost.

Apart from retained profits of firms and the proceeds of taxation the sources of capital so far reviewed are external. As yet these contributions are not matched by indigenous private capital. Low *per capita* incomes partly explain this paucity, but such local investment as there is takes place in activities in which returns are greater, such as trade, houses for rent and taxis. Further, such capital as exists can be only partially mobilised in view of the embryonic nature of the capital market and the imperfect state of company law. Only Lagos has a stock exchange, opened in September, 1960, although other means of raising capital, such as the issue of development bonds, have been adopted. Finally short term capital is also provided by the commercial banks, both expatriate and indigenous, although it should be noted that the network of branches is not dense and closely follows the distribution of commercial production.

4. LABOUR SUPPLIES. While the assembling of a labour force presents no problem, there are acute shortages of technical skills at all levels from factory-floor to boardroom. This is partly because of incomplete schooling and lack of training facilities. There is also a strong migratory element which increases the problem of in-service training and promotion.

There are several consequences of this. Firstly, industry relies to a considerable, though diminishing, extent on expatriate managers and technicians, who are able to command salaries and fringe benefits far in excess of their counterparts at home. Secondly, the productivity of the work force is lower than in the industrialised nations. To some extent low wage rates compensate for low productivity, although union activity is pushing up wages. The large firms also incur high costs in providing health and welfare services and training schemes for workers. Thus the overall effect is to produce a low wage-cost but high labour-cost economy. Finally, there are problems of mistrust and misunderstanding between indigenous workers and expatriate management; of the strong tribal loyalties which complicate management-worker relations and often influence recruitment and promotion; and of premature 'africanisation'.

Nevertheless, the long term prospects are bright. Kilby[6] found in a study of 29 establishments in Nigeria that, contrary to popular belief, voluntary absence and labour turnover were low, that the workforce had a good capacity for sustained work and that productivity was high in work involving simple repetitive motions, although lower where co-ordination of various operations was required. Africans are thirsty for education and the education system is expanding rapidly throughout West Africa in the general sphere, though to a more limited extent in technical and vocational spheres. Industrial research in universities, commercial firms and research institutes is beginning to bear fruit. With progress in medical services and increasing wealth, the labour force may be expected gradually to become more healthy, better fed and better housed.

5. MARKETS. Potentially the 90 million inhabitants of West Africa form a considerable market for industrial products. Currently, however, the market is limited by low purchasing power, the average per capita income in 1960 being only $89·6. When incomes are low, food represents a high proportion of total purchases, leaving little surplus for goods and services. This has been demonstrated for Nigerian conditions by surveys carried out between 1953 and 1955.[7] In Kaduna and Zaria the lowest income group, with less than $14 per month, spent 61·6 per cent. on food. As incomes increased the percentage fell to 43·2 for households with between $35 and $39 per month.

West Africa is also fragmented by political boundaries within which only Nigeria with its 55·6 million people represents a sizeable market in terms of population. Most of the states by comparison have small populations generally tied to low per capita incomes. Each state pursues its own programme of industrial development in isolation and is reluctant to rely upon neighbours for manufactured goods. There is also some jealousy between the landlocked states and the usually richer coastal states. Finally the division between anglo- and francophone countries with differing economic systems and external ties, not to mention the American-oriented Liberia and the colony of Portuguese Guinea, further breaks up the West African market.

The limited markets mean that for many industries optimum plant capacities are not attainable, particularly for those producing capital and intermediate goods. An integrated iron and steel works requires a minimum output of half a million ingot tons even if it concentrates on light steel products, and the optimum size is even larger. Similarly ammonia, used for the production of nitrogen fertilizer, can be economically produced by plants with an annual capacity of 50,000 tons, although costs fall rapidly as capacity increases above this level. But no individual West African market can currently absorb these levels of output,[8] though that of the whole subcontinent probably could. So far this problem has not been a pressing one because the emphasis has been on the establishment of industries producing import-substitution consumer goods, for which minimum economic plant capacities are generally lower.

The point is approaching, however, particularly in Sénégal, Côte d'Ivoire, Ghana, and Nigeria, where further progress depends on development of intermediate and capital goods industries. To make such industries feasible, it is necessary to increase the size of markets, which can best be achieved by grouping economies into common markets. This pre-supposes international specialisation and the co-ordination of industrial development plans. To this end conferences have been held under the auspices of the Economic Commission for Africa (ECA), a U.N. body, which has undertaken many studies and produced plans for integrated development notably in iron and steel, rubber, synthetic fibres, fertilisers, flat glass, textile products, cement and forest products industries. While ECA plans, however, there have been few signs that Governments have the will to proceed from planning to action.[9]

6. OTHER ASPECTS OF THE INFRASTRUCTURE. Production and distribution costs are increased by the inadequacies of the infrastructure, and cost reductions, which improve the competitive position of West African industry and increase the potential market, depend partly on an improved infrastructure. Most aspects of the latter are dealt with elsewhere, but two others, water supply and sewage and effluent disposal should be briefly considered. Piped water supply is available only

in the larger towns. Supplies in the Forest Zone are generally adequate, though liable to interruption in the dry season, and 1961 consumption level in Ibadan equalled that of maximum yield from the reservoir. In the Sudan zone, however, water supply is generally problematical and may act as a check to the development of large industrial users. The effect of water supply on location is therefore three-fold. First, it restricts industrialisation to the larger urban settlements; secondly, it favours the south; and, thirdly, it favours those urban centres which have good supplies, spare capacity and plans for enlargement.

Sewage and effluent disposal is more a potential than an actual problem. No West African city is fully sewered and in most countries there is no effective legislation on effluents and trade wastes. As industrial development proceeds and heavy industry spreads with its greater effluent problem, legislation can be expected to place a premium on sites where disposal is easiest. This will again favour the larger urban centres as they will be sewered first and particularly those on river banks, at the coast or sited on porous rocks.

7. GOVERNMENT POLICY. All West African governments have adopted policies of industrial development as a means of fostering economic growth. But they differ in the emphasis placed on industrialisation relative to other sectors of the economy and in the means of achieving this end. Gambia, Mauretanie and Liberia are currently concentrating development efforts on the primary sector, whereas Côte d'Ivoire, Sénégal, Ghana and Nigeria anticipate a more balanced development with industry playing an increasingly important role. Guinée and Mali pursue socialist policies and all industries are state owned. Ghana in the Nkrumah era followed similar though less extreme policies, but the policy of the subsequent military government aimed at encouraging private investment from overseas, both in new enterprises and in those disposed of by the state. Côte d'Ivoire, on the other hand, like Nigeria, has since independence consistently tried to attract private foreign capital. Its attitude is summed up by President-Houphouet-Boigny in 1962. 'We have no factories to nationalise, only to create; we have no commerce to take over, only to organise better; no land to distribute, only to bring into

production.' And the Finance Minister has said more recently, 'We are practical men, not madmen or theoreticians,' an implied rebuke to certain neighbouring governments.[10]

Perhaps the most important factor in creating a favourable investment climate is freedom to repatriate profits. In Côte d'Ivoire and Dahomey there is virtually no restriction and the same was true of Nigeria until exchange control was introduced with a deteriorating balance of payments arising from the civil war. Firms with 'approved status' have now priority over those without.

Tariff protection for new industries is also important. Relief from duty is also afforded on materials needed for additional processing and manufacture in West Africa. Another common device is the granting of 'tax holidays' of various kinds to approved enterprises. Dahomey, for instance, confers tax holidays of 5, 8 and 25 years for small, medium and large enterprises respectively. The regulations provide for exemption from import duties on equipment, raw materials and materials needed for production: reduction on export taxes on finished and semi-finished goods produced by the enterprise. Medium and large firms are also exempt from certain other taxes; and for large enterprises stable fiscal advantages over a maximum period of 25 years are granted in addition. Similar, but more complex and comprehensive, measures, have been built into the investment code of Côte d'Ivoire. Nigeria, too, refunds import duty for up to 10 years. In addition some industries are granted 'pioneer status', which affords exemption from company income tax for up to five years, and if the firm makes losses during the tax holiday the time of exemption is extended. Additional policies widely adopted include accelerated depreciation of machinery and industrial buildings, while most countries have commercial and industrial advisory services aimed at providing guidance and assistance to would-be investors.

Finally, it is generally held that political stability is a prerequisite for the attraction of private foreign capital as of overseas investment as a whole. West Africa has suffered its share of political instability in the Independence Era, several governments having been replaced in *coups d'état*. But it appears that businessmen are not inclined to panic at the first sign of disturbance and have considerable confidence which has been maintained through recent political disturbances, even during the Nigerian civil war.

THE ORGANISATION OF INDUSTRY

Three forms of manufacturing can be distinguished, craft industries, modern workshop industries and large-scale industries.

CRAFT INDUSTRIES form part of the indigenous economy which survives alongside the modern economy (page 102). They have often changed little in terms of methods and organisation. Their importance continues to decline both absolutely and relatively. Absolute decline of some craft industries results from the import of cheaper and better articles. Relative decline of apparently thriving crafts stems from the more rapid growth of employment in factory industry in West Africa. Craft industries are commonly organised on a compound or family basis, and are located within the compound or in the home. Originally raw materials were of local origin, but now many are either imported or produced by large scale industries in West Africa. Jennifer Bray, for example, has shown[11] how Yoruba weavers in Iseyin use yarn produced in factories at Apapa and Kaduna or locally spun yarn and imported coloured yarn. The production of the magnificent *kenti* cloth of Ghana also depends on imported yarn. Similarly the *adire* dyeing industry in Ibadan now relies on imported dye as well as on local indigo. Craft industries are small scale, depending upon family labour and to a lesser extent upon hired employees. Some are still organised on a guild basis. Fixed-capital investment is small as power-driven machinery and expensive equipment are not required.

There is no generally accepted definition of MODERN WORKSHOP INDUSTRY in West Africa. It differs from craft industry in organisation and capital requirements, if not in the scale of operations. Some form of power driven machinery, be it sewing machine, electric tools or small corn grinders, is generally used. Employees and apprentices are not necessarily related by blood ties. Such industries produce a wide variety of goods, ranging from underwear, footwear, mattresses, travelling bags, jewellery, bread, biscuits and soft drinks, to household utensils, furniture (of both wood and wrought iron), bus and lorry bodies, agricultural tools, nails and simple machinery.

The workshop industries, together with craft industries, are much more important than large-scale modern industry measured by employment and by number of enterprises. For instance, the 1962 industrial census of Ghana revealed that 92 per cent. of the 95,167 manufacturing establishments were based on self-employment and family labour only. It was estimated that in Eastern Nigeria in 1964 small-scale industry provided employment for approximately three times the number employed in large-scale manufacturing. But craft and workshop industries are discriminated against by some governments and are only rarely encouraged. Indeed, little is known of them, since in collecting industrial statistics a cut-off point of 10 employees is commonly adopted.

Small-scale industries are not without their disadvantages. Technical and management skills are lacking, as demonstrated by Schatz. Further, although the small industrialist produces the lowest-cost goods to satisfy an extremely competitive market, this low cost is based on low-paid labour, lack of modern equipment and very small profit margins. It is therefore difficult to accumulate the capital needed for the introduction of more advanced production techniques, which permit higher productivity, better quality and greater range of output.

Small-scale industry, however, has certain advantages at the present stage of development. These include a large and growing market for processed foodstuffs and consumer goods, employment possibilities for an abundance of low-cost, semi-skilled labour, and extensive possibilities for import substitution. In addition, capital investment per unit of output is less because tools and equipment costs are low, while expensive new buildings are unnecessary. Management costs are also lower because expatriate skills are not necessary, although in Sénégal and other former French Territories even small enterprises tend to have expatriate management.

An indigenous enterpreneurial class is thus emerging, especially in Ghana and Nigeria.

It is for reasons such as these that ECA is actively encouraging governments to foster small-scale industries. They are considered more suited to African needs because it is possible to disperse them widely through a country. In this way unemployment in rural areas and small towns can be allieviated over a wider area than is possible when fewer and larger industrial enterprises are established. They are therefore viewed as a means of staunching the continual migration to the larger towns.

LARGE-SCALE MODERN INDUSTRY is, on the other hand, encouraged by governments. Although large by West African standards, many plants are small in world terms, a reflection partly of the size of local markets, but also of their status. Most of these are branch plants of large international manufacturing or trading companies, some of which have invested in more than one plant in West Africa. Many of the remainder are small because of intense competition in the local markets they serve and because of limited capital available to local entrepreneurs. The baking of bread in Lagos and Ibadan can be cited as an example.[12] Nevertheless capital investment in land, buildings and plant is high and labour forces vary from small to large, the lower level depending upon the country definition of 'Large-scale'.

Most large-scale industries are 'light', only a few being concerned with either capital or intermediate goods. Thus linkages between firms, industries and other sectors of the economy are few, although with the development of certain branches of the chemical industry, aluminium smelting, cement manufacture and processing of agricultural products, this situation is changing. The rate of industrial growth in Ghana and Sénégal has eased because of early development of consumer good industries, further growth being increasingly dependent on the development of capital and intermediate goods industries. It has been suggested Côte d'Ivoire and Nigeria are also approaching this point. It must be remembered that the existence of a large-scale industry in West Africa does not necessarily indicate financial viability or guarantee survival. Several are in need of financial rehabilitation only a few years after inauguration, especially if the capital was not invested on a purely commercial basis.

THE DISTRIBUTION OF INDUSTRY

When considering the distribution of industry, a classification based on the major factors influencing location has been used. Hance[13] has used a four-fold classification: orientation to (i) raw materials (ii) labour (iii) market (iv) power. At the present time it is more realistic to adopt a classification also based on orientation, but refined by taking more account of the market. Thus five classes can be identified.

1. Primary processing industries.
2. Raw material oriented secondary industries producing mainly for the home market.
3. Market oriented industries based on local raw materials.
4. Market oriented industries using imported raw materials.
5. Miscellaneous industries.

1. PRIMARY PROCESSING INDUSTRIES. This group of industries was the earliest to emerge and is still the most important. Processing of primary products prior to export takes place to lessen perishability, as in canning or the extraction of pericarp-oil; to reduce bulk and thereby save transport costs, as in the processing of meat and the squaring of logs; to reduce the weight of material shipped as in the sawing of timber, the decortication of groundnuts and the concentration of minerals; or to achieve all three. It also increases the value of exported products, provides employment and keeps within the West African country a little of the value added by manufacture. Processing industries deal with the produce of farm, fishing, forest and mine.

The extraction of vegetable oils is the most important industry based on agricultural raw materials. The extraction of groundnut-oil is the most important industry in Sénégal, measured either in employment or in value of production. The first mills were built after the 1914–18 war in the producing districts of Kaolack, Diourbel, Ziguinchor and Louga to satisfy local demand. The first in Dakar, where there are now eight, was built in 1924. Large-scale operations, however, began only during the 1935–45 war through shortage of cargo-space. By-products, including cattle-cake and otherwise wasted materials sold to soap factories, are disposed of locally and shells are used as fuel in the mills. The market for cake is limited and this raises total costs. Sales of oil are regulated in agreement with metropolitan processers. Mills were built in Mali at Koulikoro in 1941 and later at Bamako, in Haute Volta at Bobo Dioulasso in 1942 and in Niger at Maradi in 1943 and Matamye in 1956.

In anglophone West Africa development has been more recent, as nuts in shell were generally preferred by the British market. Decorticating mills have, however, been built in Gambia and Nigeria, and in the latter a crushing industry has grown up since 1950. Kano, the main centre, has four large mills and one small mill, and a further mill was opened at Maiduguri in 1964. In 1965–66 351,000 tons of groundnuts, 35·6 per cent. of the tonnage bought by the Marketing Board, went to the crushers, which produced 154,500 tons of oil and 193,900 of cake.

In anglophone West Africa much effort has been devoted to the improvement of palm-oil extraction, but primitive methods still account for more than half the output. These express only 45–55 per cent. of the pericarp-oil and this has a high 'free-fatty-acid' content. This 'hard' oil, though its flavour is more acceptable in the local market, is less acceptable to the manufacturer, so that higher prices are obtainable in the export market for 'soft' oil.

From an early date hand presses, with a 45–60 per cent. extraction rate were encouraged, supplemented by the more recent Duscher hydraulic hand press, raising the rate to 80 per cent. This is only a slightly lower extraction rate than that of the 'pioneer' oil mills established from 1945 onwards. These were small-scale industrial plants capable of producing high quality oil. In Nigeria there were 110 in the Eastern Provinces and 15 elsewhere, reflecting the high proportion of oil exported from the East. There were nine pioneer mills in Sierra Leone and several in Ghana.

Their share in production has fallen and many are out of use (only one survives in Sierra Leone), because of the fluctuating and inadequate supply of fruit, which to arrest fermentation must be sterilised in the mill boilers as soon as possible after cutting, and because of opposition from those who see in them a threat to their own livelihood. Large-scale plants, in association with plantations, have been erected in Sapele, Calabar, and elsewhere in Nigeria. There are also large-scale mills in southern Côte d'Ivoire at Dabou, Mopoyem, la Mé and Grand Drewin, and in Togo. In Dahomey nearly the whole crop is processed in the large mills at Avrankon, Gboda, Ahozon and Bohican.

Palm-kernels are still mainly exported unprocessed, but the trend is now towards crushing before export. In Nigeria a kernel-oil mill was opened in 1965 near Ikeja on the outskirts of Lagos, with a capacity of 121,000 tons per annum, about equal to the previous exports from the Western Provinces. Most of the output is exported, though a soap works at Apapa is also supplied. It is anticipated that other linkages will develop, such as with the Ikeja cocoa processing plant and by the supply of cake to agriculture. A much larger plant is nearing completion at Port Harcourt. In Sierra Leone one went into production in 1968 at Wellington near Freetown.[14]

As the textile industry develops in West Africa, exports of cotton lint are tending to fall but cottonseed exports are being maintained. A plant for seed crushing is in operation at Zaria and others are planned in several countries. The processing of rubber is another growing activity, in Liberia, particularly at Harbel, in Côte d'Ivoire at Bingerville and Pakidié and in Nigeria at Sapele (17 plants), Calabar (4), Benin City (13), Warri (2) and Hagbo-Uno in Mid-Western Nigeria and at Owerri and Elele in the Eastern Provinces. Rice milling is also important, particularly along the Niger valley in Mali and Guinée.

Of lesser importance are tanning, found in Northern Nigeria and westwards through the Sudan Zone, kapok cleaning and sisal preparation. The processing of manioc at Ganavé ranks second only to phosphate beneficiation among manu-facturing industries in Togo.

Vivid contrasts between traditional and modern enterprises persist in many processing activities based on agricultural produce and this is equally true of fish processing. Traditional methods of processing include sun drying, charring and smoking. In addition, however, modern processing takes place in larger ports, where it becomes a secondary industry, although it is convenient to consider it here. There are two freezing plants and two tuna canneries at Abidjan, there are freezing plants and cold stores in Lagos to handle frozen fish landed by foreign trawlers, there are freezing plants and canneries at Dakar, Port Etienne, Monrovia and Tema, whilst further developments are planned or under construction at these and other ports, such as Elmina (Ghana) and Cotonou.

The processing of timber is an expanding activity. An increasing percentage of timber is exported as sawn lumber, plywood and veneer (page 158). Nigeria exported no sawn wood prior to the last war but by 1961 the value of sawn timber was 22·7 per cent. of logs and by 1965 this had increased to 30·0 per cent., and Ghana shows a similar trend. Exports of logs from Côte d'Ivoire, however, increased 250 per cent. between 1956 and 1961, while sawn timber only increased by 50 per cent. But by 1966 the value of sawn timber exports had reached 22·4 per cent. by value that for logs.

Saw-mills have greatly increased in number since 1945. A few plants are large and highly capitalised and also produce plywood and veneers. The majority, however, are small and, along with hand-sawing, cater mainly for the home market. In Côte d'Ivoire there are 40 saw mills, but the 4 at Grand Bassam account for over half the output. In Ghana the U.A.C. sawmill and plywood plant at Samreboi is much the largest of the numerous establishments. In Nigeria there were 80 plants in 1964, of which only 12 sell in the export market. The African Timber and Plywood plant at Sapele is the largest in West Africa, and there are also large plants at Ijora, Lagos (operated by the Public Works Department) and Ijebu-Ode. In Liberia there were 12 mills in the early 1960s, while new plants, including producers of plywood and veneers, have been established with the granting of large forest concessions.

Primary processing industry is also based on minerals. The metal content of most mineral ores is low, so that concentration by removal of waste to minimise transport costs should be carried on as close as possible to the mines. Examples of such industries include the separation and washing of tin and columbite at Bukuru, which permitted concentrates of 74 per cent. to be exported. This was partially superseded by the opening in 1961 and 1962 of two tin smelters at Jos, one of which has subsequently closed down. Similarly iron ore is concentrated at the four mines in Liberia and at Marampa in Sierra Leone, alumina is produced at the Fria plant and on the Los Islands in Guinée, phosphates are concentrated in Sénégal and Togo and gold is extracted at Tarkwa, Dunkwa and Obuasi in Ghana.

2. RAW MATERIAL ORIENTED SECONDARY INDUSTRIES. This is a diverse group of activities, usually established to cater for the home market but with the possibility of export to neighbouring countries and even beyond West Africa. Fish canning has already been mentioned. Meat canning is found in Kano and eslewhere in the Sudan Zone. Similarly the canning and bottling industry, using local fruit and fruit juices, has developed widely but mainly in the forest zone in Nigeria between Ibadan and Lagos, at Umuahia and Aba, and in other countries round Accra, Abidjan and Conakry. Many of the larger plants, such as the Lafia factory in Ibadan, suffer from inadequate and irregular supplies of fruit. This plant was established to provide a market for citrus fruits and pineapples planted to replace cocoa devastated by swollen shoot. It has a capacity of 20,000 tons of fruit per year but has never processed more than 3,000 tons in spite of pineapple plantation development to increase supplies. But the home market cannot absorb more than five per cent. of total capacity, while in export markets the product cannot compete successfully with products from the U.S., Australia, South Africa and Israel. Further, cans and sugar had initially to be imported. Similar problems beset the meat canning plant in Kano. A more successful venture is the Nescafé plant in Abidjan, which exports some of its output throughout West Africa.

In recent years the manufacture of jute and kenaf bags has been established. Development of the Badagry plant in western Nigeria and of the Jema'a plant near Kafanchan was associated with plantations, followed by encouragement of peasant farmers. Other plants in this and associated industries, such as sisal rope making, are located at Dabai and Bouaké (Côte d'Ivoire), Kumasi (Ghana), Kankan (Guinée) and Jos (Nigeria).

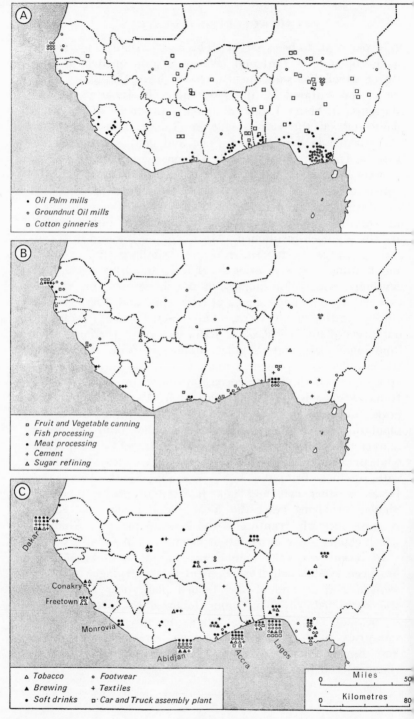

A

- Oil Palm mills
- Groundnut Oil mills
- Cotton ginneries

B

- Fruit and Vegetable canning
- Fish processing
- Meat processing
- Cement
- Sugar refining

C

Dakar
Conakry
Freetown
Monrovia
Abidjan
Accra
Lagos

- Tobacco
- Brewing
- Soft drinks
- Footwear
- Textiles
- Car and Truck assembly plant

Miles 50
Kilometres 80

Figure 7.1

Sugar refining is a growing industry also associated with plantation development. A Chinese-built factory at Dougabougou in Mali, about 19 kilometres from Markala, is associated with an irrigated area of 2,498 hectares, of which 1,984 are under cane. The annual production target of the factory is 13,000 tons. In Ghana the Asutuare factory is served by a plantation of 3,237 hectares on irrigated land made available by the Akosombo Dam. It has a capacity of 24,000 tons of refined sugar, and the plantation is being expanded to make such a level of output possible. A second refinery is located at Komenda to process sugar produced on a 810 hectare plantation and by a farmers' co-operative on 81 hectares drawing irrigation water from the Pra river. Ultimate output is 12,000 tons, although suggested extensions might raise this to 18,000. In Nigeria there is some traditional processing of about 10,000 tons of crude sugar produced on 8–12,000 hectares of small plots around Kano, Zaria and Katsina. At Bacita on the Niger about 10 miles downstream from Jebba is a plantation extending to 5,000 acres with a refinery. The capacity of the plant is 30,000 tons and projected extensions will double this. The only plant not associated with a plantation is at Dakar and uses imported raw material.

The combined output of the plants will eventually reach about 100,000 tons. Consumption of sugar in West Africa however is about 300,000 tons, and in 1965 imports were between 250 and 280,000 tons valued at $131·6 million. There is thus considerable scope for further expansion of this import-substitution industry and, in spite of low world-prices, developments are projected in Mali in the Sikasso area, in Togo and Dahomey on the Mono River, in Côte d'Ivoire as part of the Bandama Dam project, at Torualsum on the Suva river in Sierra Leone, near Mediné Oula on the Kolenta River in Guinée, on the Richard Toll project in Sénégal and at Diarabakoko in Haute Volta.

Figure 7.1. Manufacturing industry

(A) Primary processing industries
(B) Raw material oriented secondary industries
(C) Market oriented industries

Another important import-substitution industry is that of cement manufacture. Transport charges on imports of this low value-weight ratio commodity are high and this provides a natural protection for the establishment of a home industry. Cement manufacture enjoys considerable economies of scale and large capital inputs are necessary. In West Africa limestone outcrops are restricted. These factors, together with the need for fuel at reasonable prices and adequate transport for distribution, result in the establishing of a few plants in the most favourable location. These locations must also take into account proximity to markets so that total transport costs can be minimised. To this extent cement manufacture is also market oriented. In Nigeria there are four plants operating, at Nkalagu near Enugu (capacity 300,000 tons) and at Calabar (200,000 tons) in the Eastern States, at Ewekoro (400,000 tons) near Abeokuta in the Western State, at Kalambaisa (100,000 tons) near Sokoto in the Northern, and another under construction at Ukpilla (100,000 tons) in the Mid-West. In 1961 450,000 tons of cement were imported into Nigeria, but by 1965 imports had fallen to 171,700, mainly for the Kainji Dam, while home production reached, 977,700 tons.

By 1967 there were plants at Nauli in Brong-Ahafo (Ghana), at Malbaza in Niger, at Rufisque in Sénégal, and two at Abidjan. In addition there are plants using imported clinker at Takoradi and Tema in Ghana, Wellington in Sierra Leone, and at Cotonou, Abidjan, Lagos and Port Harcourt.

Petroleum refining in West Africa normally uses imported raw materials but Nigeria uses local crude. Here the refinery was located near the village of Alesa-Eleme, about 20 miles from Port Harcourt. It refines about 10 per cent. of Nigerian output and produces virtually all the country's needs of petrol, kerosine, diesel and fuel oils. It also produces liquified gas. In normal times, products for Lagos and the Western State are shipped coastwise from the refinery jetty, those for the Mid-Western State by barge along the creeks, those for the Eastern States by road tankers and those for the Northern States by rail. Other refineries, using imported crude, are in the ports of Takoradi, Abidjan and Freetown.

3. MARKET ORIENTED INDUSTRIES BASED ON LOCAL RAW

MATERIALS. Industries become market oriented if as a result of the manufacturing process the product becomes more perishable, bulkier, or more fragile than the raw materials. The oldest and best developed secondary industry is the manufacture of textiles. As a craft industry it still flourishes (indeed independence, with the consequential trend toward national dress, gave it a boost) and attempts have been made to modernise, through producer co-operatives. It is widespread and serves a market throughout West Africa accounting for about 30 per cent. of locally produced cloth in 1964. All but four countries (Sierra Leone, Liberia, Gambia and Mauritanie) now have modern industries in addition to craft enterprises. Of these Sierra Leone has firm plans to establish the spinning and weaving branches of the industry and already has a clothing factory at Wellington. The industry is best developed in Nigeria, where the area in which cotton is grown is extensive. There are 13 ginneries scattered through the producing area which supply lint to the mills. In Nigeria most of these are integrated, preparation, spinning, weaving and finishing all being carried on in the same plant. The main centre is Kaduna with 117,000 spindles installed in five modern plants, all built since 1957. One specialises in industrial yarn and supplies a tyre factory at Ikeja and a thread factory at Apapa in addition to handloom weavers. The remainder also weave and have 2,450 looms installed. Another plant has 360 looms installed for synthetic fibre weaving. A second concentration is in the Lagos area. Here there are 29,200 spindles in two plants, the large thread plant already mentioned and 1,070 looms installed in five plants. Outside the two major concentrations there is a small, specialist weaving and finishing firm and two firms weaving blankets at Kano. There are large integrated mills at Aba and Asaba with a third being built at Ado Ekiti and there is a large printing mill at Onitsha. Finally there are six knitted textile plants in the Greater Lagos area and one each in Kano and Enugu. Most of Nigerian textile output is sold on the home market and in cotton piece goods the industry is able to supply much of the market. Though imports have remained stationary, due to increasing demand, by 1967 the home industry was supplying 45 per cent. of the market.

Nigeria is the largest producer of cotton cloth in West

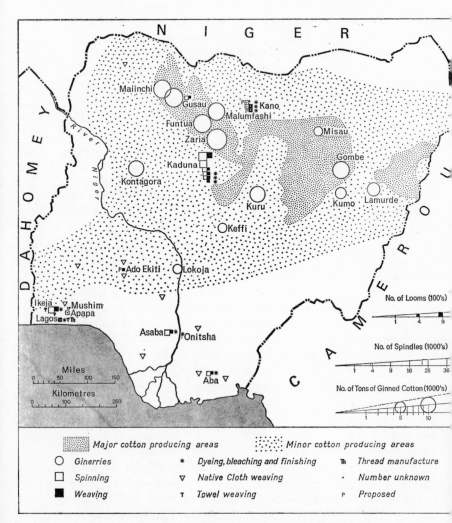

Figure 7.2. The cotton industries of Nigeria

Africa and accounts for about half of West Africa's output. Ghana produces only one quarter as much as Nigeria. There are two important integrated plants at Tema and other plants at Juapong and Accra. The major concentration of the industry in Sénégal is at Dakar and Rufisque, where there are 11 mills, none of which is integrated. The industry, which exports a large part of its output, satisfies about half the Senegalese market. The oldest textile mill in West Africa was established in 1922 near Bouaké in Côte d'Ivoire. It has since been expanded several times both by increasing existing capacity and by adding new activities. In addition there are two printing works and three hosiery and clothing factories in Abidjan. There are also new integrated plants at Dadja in Togo, Ségou in Mali and Parakou in Dahomey, with plants under construction in Niger, Dahomey and at Ouagadougou in Haute Volta. The integrated plant at Coyah in Guinée, inaugurated in 1966, produces about half the country's requirements (imports were at about $12 million a year), but it uses cotton imported from the U.S.A.[15]

The manufacturing of tobacco is also expanding rapidly. The first cigarette factory was established at Oshogbo in western Nigeria in 1935 to use imported leaf and a second in Ibadan two years later. These, and other plants at Port Harcourt, Zaria and Ilorin, now use a high proportion of locally produced tobacco and satisfy about 80 per cent. of the Nigerian market. In Ghana there are plants at Takoradi and Tema, which produce a large proportion of the country's needs. In Sierra Leone there is a factory at Wellington, in Côte d'Ivoire at Bouaké, in Sénégal at Dakar, and in Mali at Bamako. Their establishment has encouraged the growing of improved tobacco and thus the saving of precious foreign exchange. Some, such as the Bouaké plant, export to neighbouring countries.

Industries using mineral raw materials include brick and tile making. Unlike cement, the industry tends to be widespread, as clay is common and small scale enterprises can be competitive. Concrete blocks are manufactured in several centres using home produced cement and the making of pre-stressed posts, poles and beams, as at Abeokuta, is likely to expand. There are also factories producing asbestos cement sheets and pipes at Ikeja and at Emene near Enugu.

The chemical industry has hitherto been based on imported raw materials and is accordingly discussed later. Fertilizer manufacture, however, is based on local raw materials. A plant, the first in francophone West Africa, was opened early in 1968 at M'bao near Dakar, using phosphate from Taiba and Thiès. Plans are well advanced for a plant in Côte d'Ivoire and feasibility studies for one in Togo have been undertaken.

Finally, in this category are industries using local forest products as raw materials, notably furniture and paper making, though strictly the latter is more raw material oriented. Furniture making on a semi-handicraft basis is an industry of long standing in almost every large city in West Africa. More recently factory enterprises, both indigenous and expatriate, have entered the industry to produce not only furniture but also other joinery products. The paper industry has a great potential and, according to the ECA, import-substitution possibilities and growth prospects warrant each country endeavouring to satisfy its own needs. A paper mill was erected in 1949 at Bruibesso, west of Abidjan, but it soon closed down. It was not until 1965 that another was built, in Takoradi. At the time of writing three more are under construction. Those at Jebba and Akure in Nigeria will use *bagasse* from sugar factories, whereas that at Yaou in Côte d'Ivoire will use hardwood.

4. MARKET ORIENTED INDUSTRIES USING IMPORTED RAW MATERIALS. These import-substitution industries are encouraged, as the value added to raw materials by manufacture is gained for the West African country. The use of tariff protection and the structure of freight rates also make it less costly to import raw materials and semi-finished goods. Already a wide variety of commodities is produced and the range is extending year by year. Plant size varies from large, highly capitalised plants to small workshops.

Flour-milling, sheltered by tariff barriers, is a port industry found at Dakar, Freetown, Abidjan, Apapa and Port Harcourt. Baking is carried on in small enterprises in many towns and cities, whilst large mechanised bakeries and biscuit factories are found in the larger towns.   Ice-cream making is also carried on in several centres.   Perhaps the most important of this group based on imported agricultural raw materials is, however, brewing and soft drink bottling.   These products, because of their large water content, permit considerable savings by local manufacture when a good water supply is available in the market area.   For long the brewing industry had to rely on re-using empty bottles of imported beer.   Now bottles are made in Port Harcourt and cans in Abidjan, but 'empties' still forms a minor, but widespread item of internal trade.   Breweries producing lager-type beer are located in most of the major cities, at Dakar, Wellington near Free-town, Monrovia, Abidjan, Kumasi, Accra, Tema, Lomé, Cotonou, Lagos, Abeokuta, Umuahia, Aba, Kaduna, and Kano. Stout is brewed at Ikeja.   Carbon dioxide is produced as a by-product and has given rise to associated production of soft drinks.   But the lower capital inputs, lower level of skill required in producing soft drinks and lower value per bottle compared with beer result in their more widespread production.

In this group the chemical industry, as yet, concentrates on lighter products, semi-finished and finished, including industrial gases, dyes, paint and varnishes, pharmaceuticals, insecticides, matches and storage batteries.   The semi-finished products, together with the newly introduced fertiliser industry provide inputs for other activities and are establishing industrial links and sectoral interdependence in the economy.   The major centres are Dakar-Rufisque and Greater Lagos, while other coastal cities, Abidjan, Accra-Tema and Port Harcourt are growing in importance.

There are no plastics plants, but consumer goods are produced from imported polythene, polystyrene and polyvinyl chloride.   These can be easily imported, while initial installations can be small, and so capital requirements can be modest and labour costs are not high.   Plants are found in Abidjan, Ibadan, Apapa, Enugu, Takoradi and Conakry, producing such items as bowls, beakers, combs, pipes and packing materials.   At Abeokuta a plant produces fibre-glass reinforced plastic goods, such as corrugated translucent roofing sheet, small boats, and insulation material.   Perhaps the most rapidly expanding use of plastic, however, is in the shoe industry. Plastic shoes are cheap and colourful, appealing to West African pockets and taste, and are bought in increasingly large numbers. Rubber, canvas and leather footwear is also manufactured. The widespread distribution of the industry suggests that the market is the dominant location factor.

A problem of using raw material orientation as a means of classification, that of changing orientation, is illustrated by the rubber goods industry. The earliest activity was tyre-retreading using imported raw materials. Plants were established, usually by local entrepreneurs, in the major Nigerian towns. There are two each in Ibadan and Onitsha and others in Lagos, Ijebu-Ode, Aba, Kano and Jos. With the expansion of rubber growing and primary processing, these now use increasing amounts of local rubber. In addition expansion of the market and of the textile industry has encouraged development of tyre and inner-tube making at Ikeja and Port Harcourt. This pattern appears to be repeating itself in Ghana and Côte d'Ivoire. Tyre-retreading at Accra is to be supplemented by manufacture using local rubber at Bonsaso by a partnership of the Government and Firestone. At Abidjan there has been a retreading plant since 1961, which is now expanding, and there are firm plans to establish a tyre plant.

The final two groups of industry based in imported raw material are the assembly industries and the engineering and metal industries. Considerable savings in transport costs are affected by locating both groups in the market area as the finished products are bulkier than their component parts. They also provide employment and some value by manufacture accrues in West Africa.

The assembly industries tend to be located in the major ports although this tendency weakens as the product gets less bulky. Thus motor vehicle assembly plants are to be found in Abidjan, Tema, Apapa, Port Harcourt and Cotonou. Bicycle assembly plants, however, are also located in inland centres as at Zaria and lesser ports as at Warri. Sewing machines are assembled at Apapa and pumps at Jos. Radio and television assembly plants are located in Abidjan, Tema,

Apapa, Lagos and nearby Ikorodu, Kano, Port Harcourt and in Mali at Bamako. Assembly plants are also useful through linkage with other local industries, for they provide a market for industrial gases and paints, while radio assembly works depend on local cabinet makers and plastics manufacturers for cabinets.

Engineering and metal industries depend upon imported raw materials, as there is no iron and steel industry in West Africa apart from steel rolling mills using local scrap at Tema and Emene near Enugu. The metal fabricating industries produce a wide variety of products large and small, including constructional steelwork, window-frames, furniture, truck bodies, railway wagons, oil storage tanks, cans, and bottle tops. They are closely tied either to the ports such as Dakar, Abidjan, Greater Lagos and Port Harcourt, or to large interior cities such as Ibadan, Kano and Enugu. The engineering industries also tend to be coastal for in the ports there are not only the requirements of shipping but the chief centres of manufacturing and the major railway workshops.

5. MISCELLANEOUS INDUSTRIES. Some industries do not fall easily into the categories adopted. These include the packaging industry, stationery manufacture, gramophone record making, printing and the glass plants making bottles, tumblers and sheets at Tarkwa and Port Harcourt (based on natural gas fuel). But most important is the aluminium smelter at Tema. This, and the glass factory at Port Harcourt, are the only power-oriented industries currently operating in West Africa. The smelter is an integral part of the Volta scheme (page 154).

The maps indicate the irregular distribution pattern of industry in West Africa.[16] Theoretically manufacturing should be concentrated in the interior where additional transport costs act as a protective barrier in the same way as tariffs. In fact, industry is markedly coastal and southern in its distribution and the major ports are the chief industrial centres. Closer examination reveals a clear distinction between the patterns of primary processing and market oriented industries. Primary processing tends to be dispersed through the areas of primary production. But as we have seen these are mainly in the Forest Zone, apart from the groundnuts and cotton produced in the Sudan. Modern fish processing is a coastal activity. Similarly mineral processing takes place close to the coast as the most accessible deposits are worked, first. Futhermore, the northward bend of the coast brings the groundnut and cotton producing areas of the Sudan Zone in Sénégal in proximity to it. Thus, whilst the pattern is very open, it is markedly concentrated in a belt within about 100 miles of the coast.

Raw material-oriented secondary industries display a similar pattern, although the association of some of these industries with irrigated plantations is resulting in occasional developments in the Guinea Savana Zone. But more significant than this tendency is for such industries to locate in the cities within the raw material producing areas. In such a location they reinforce the distribution pattern of market-oriented industries.

The market-oriented industries are concentrated in the major cities, which are commonly ports and capitals. In the most industrialised group of countries Dakar is the main industrial centre of Sénégal and Abidjan of Côte d'Ivoire. In Ghana Accra is the main centre of consumer goods industries although nearby Tema has been receiving many of the new developments and increasingly is assuming the role of port and industrial satellite to the capital. Outside these main centres lesser centres are developing, such as Rufisque, increasingly a part of Greater Dakar, Bouaké, Takoradi and Kumasi, but these are growing less rapidly than the major centres. Nigeria with its federal constitution is a special case. Greater Lagos, including Apapa, Ebute Metta, Mushin and Ikeja contains the largest industrial concentration in the country. But the four former Regions enjoyed considerable autonomy over internal policy and, from the point of view of industrial development and location acted as separate states. There has been duplication of plants in several industries such as textiles, cement and metal fabrication. This has resulted in more industrial dispersion than might otherwise have happened. Each former Region had its rising industrial centres, Port Harcourt, Enugu, Aba and Onitsha in the East, Ibadan, Abeokuta and Ikeja (actually in Greater Lagos) in the West, Benin in the Mid-West and Kaduna and Kano in the North. The country has now been reorganised into

12 states which enjoy similar autonomy. The effects on industrial patterns of this recasting of political divisions is a matter for speculation and lends further interest to the subject.

In the smaller countries the capital city usually has the great majority of market-oriented plants. Thus Conakry, Freetown, Monrovia, Lomé and Cotonou, which are the leading ports in their countries as well as the capital cities, in spite of having fewer plants and a more restricted range of this type of industry than their counterparts in the more industrialised countries, enjoy a greater degree of primacy. In the landlocked countries, where levels of industrialisation are even lower, Bamako, Ouagadougou and Niamey enjoy similar primacy.

TABLE 7.1

NUMBER OF INDUSTRIAL PLANTS IN NIGERIA

REGIONS

	Lagos	West	Mid-West	East	North
pre-1959	103	70	39	103	68
1960	28	9	2	8	4
1961	12	16	5	10	7
1962	12	13	3	17	5
1963	14	8	3	14	16

The present distributional pattern is the result of recent growth and present trends can be expected to continue. Primary processing is levelling off, while consumer goods industries, based on both local and imported raw materials, are expanding. Expansion of intermediate goods, often market oriented, has also begun, particularly in the four most industrialised countries. In this situation the existing major industrial centres will continue to attract most of the new manufacturing industry. Recent experience in Nigeria illustrates this point, although in a less extreme way than elsewhere. The number of industrial enterprises, excluding pioneer oil-mills in the East, established up to and including 1959 and post-1959 experience are indicated in Table 7.1. Sixteen of the establishments recorded in 1959[17] as in the West were in fact within Greater Lagos, as they were located on the Ikeja industrial estate, and of the 46 industries subsequently located in the

Region at least 25 are in the metropolitan area. Thus metropolitan Lagos had 129 of 383 (33 per cent.) plants of all kinds in 1959 and between then and 1963 has attracted 91 of 206 (44·17 per cent.) plants of all types in spite of active promotional efforts by the Regional Governments.[18]

Location in the port-capital cities is attractive to manufacturing industry because they possess much of the market, the best facilities for import of machinery, plant and raw materials, the best transport links with inland centres, a considerable labour force, the best developed infrastructure and proximity to government departments. Further, industries are now at the stage where linkages are developing which will further encourage concentration.

REFERENCES

1 United Nations, *Industrial Development in Africa*, New York, 1967, Table 23, p. 25

2 *ibid.*, table 25, p. 26

3 Killisle A. and Syeresyewski, R., *The Economy of Ghana* in Robson, P. and Lury, D. A. (Edts.), *The Economies of Africa*, London, 1969, p. 113

4 Miracle, M., *The Economy of Ivory Coast, ibid* p. 219 and Aboyade, A., *The Economy of Nigeria, ibid* p. 176

5 Schatz, S. P., *The Capital Shortage Illusion: Government Lending in Nigeria*. Oxford Economic Papers 17, 1965 pp. 309–16. Reprinted in Whetham, E. H. and Currie, J. I. (Edts.). *Readings in the Applied Economics of Africa*. Vol. I: Micro-economics, London, 1967

6 Kilby, P., *'African Labour Productivity Reconsidered'*, Econ. Jour., 1961, pp. 273–91

7 Oluwasanmi, H. A., *'Agriculture in a Developing Economy'*, Jour. Agric. Economics, *14*, 1960 pp. 234–41. Reprinted in Whetham and Currie, *op cit.*

8 Ewing, A. F., *Industry in Africa*, London, 1968, Chapter 1.

9 Hodder, B. W., *West Africa*, Chapter 4 in Hodder, B. W. and Harris, D. R. (Edts.), *Africa in Transition—Geographical Essays*, London, 1967, pp. 249–253

10 Reported in *West Africa*, June 26, 1965

11 Bray, J., '*The Craft Structure of a Traditional Yoruba Town*', Trans. Inst. Br. Geog. *46*, 1969, pp. 179–193

12 Kilby, P., *Competition in the Nigerian Bread Industry*, reprinted in Whetham and Currie, *op cit.*

13 Hance, W. A., *The Geography of Modern Africa*, New York, 1964. Chap. 13. *See* also Sokolski, A., *The Establishment of Manufacturing in Nigeria*, New York, 1965

14 Clarke, J. I. (Ed.), *Sierra Leone in Maps*, London, 1966, p. 78

15 Swindell, K., '*Industrialisation in Guinea*', *Geography*, *54*, 1969, pp. 456–458

16 Information on individual plants has been culled from the following sources: *Nigeria Trade Journal*, *West Africa*, *Marchés Tropicaux et Meditérranéens* and *Africa Research Bulletin*.

17 Data from *Industrial Directory*, 1964, Lagos, 1964. Not all dates for commencement of production are listed. Those plants for which no date is given have been ignored here

18 For example, there was an impressive brochure: *Investment Opportunities in Eastern Nigeria*, Enugu, Ministry of Commerce, 1966

CHAPTER 8

Trade & Commerce

Great changes have taken place in West African trade and commerce since 1885. These can be summarised as increasing commercialisation (i.e. the exchange economy growing at the expense of a purely subsistence one), increasing complexity of trade patterns, and an increasing role of full-time professional traders. There have been other, consequential changes. Traditionally marketless societies now have markets, at least in the towns. Cash transactions came to predominate over barter, while currency has superseded the more primitive exchange media (page 71). Control of the markets is passing, or has passed, from chiefs and elders to Local Authorities, while the market places are evolving from crude shelters of bamboo and thatch to concrete structures with 'pan'[1] roofs on planned layouts. Outside the market places stores and shops are now common, even in villages.

Trade and commerce have expanded greatly in volume and value. This and everything else has been stimulated by increased cash cropping and by increasing urbanisation, trends which provide money incomes and a demand for foodstuffs and consumer goods; by more settled conditions, fostering inter-tribal and long-distance trade; by the influence of expatriate mercantile firms, which made a range of hitherto unknown goods available; and by the increasing sophistication of West African merchants.

The impact of these changes varies from area to area. In the prosperous, densely peopled areas of most intense cash cropping, modernisation has proceeded farthest. Here the traditional institutions and methods have evolved along with newly introduced ones to produce a characteristically rich blending. On the other hand, in the remoter, sparsely populated, least prosperous areas traditional institutions and methods, comparatively unchanged, reign supreme. A distinction must consequently be made in the speed of modernisation between the large city, the town, the more accessible rural areas, and the remoter ones.

It is usual to treat import, export and internal trade separately.[2] But this tripartite division, always somewhat artificial, is becoming increasingly unrealistic as local production increases and as the home market absorbs more of the local output. It is accidental whether a given sample of palm oil sold by a farmer is consumed locally, enters internal trade or eventually enters export trade. The distributional chain through which it passes is the same at the local level regardless of its final destination. Similarly, no distinction can be made in marketing between crates of imported and of locally brewed beer.

Such an approach also leads to over-simplification of the nature of trade. The situation in this area of sub-continental size is complex and, as B. W. Hodder reminds us, 'our knowledge of the forms, mechanisms, and institutions of indigenous trading and marketing in most tropical countries is very scanty and uneven'.[3] Considerable research effort has recently been expended on this subject in West Africa, compared with other parts of the tropical world. Nevertheless, it is still dangerous to generalise about the functioning of West African market institutions.[4]

We have, therefore, expressed the exchange economy as an open system (Figure 8.1). The *local* exchange sector is defined as exchange within a village or a town and its hinterland, the *internal* as that between regions within a country such as between forest and savana, the *intra-continental* as export/import between West African countries, and the *inter-continental* as overseas trade. In general, goods moving up the system are increasingly bulked. Palm-oil enters the local exchange in kerosine tins and leaves the ports in hold-tanks of ships. Conversely, goods moving downward through the system are involved in successive processes of bulk-breaking. Matches are landed from ships or leave factories in wooden crates of cartons. They are finally sold at the street corner not by the box, but in tens with a small part of the striking surface of the box.

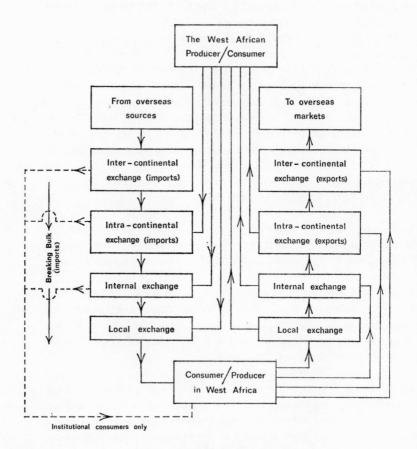

Figure 8.1. The exchange economy

The system is operated by various types of trading organisation which may be classed as (i) small West African traders; (ii) co-operatives; (iii) small expatriate traders; (iv) expatriate firms; (v) state corporations.

Such a classification must not obscure the fact that, though operating at different levels they are links in a chain, and goods moving within the system pass through the hands of several types of organisation. At the higher levels, those more remote from the individual producer/consumer, are found the expatriate firms and state corporations, at the lowest levels the individual West African trader. Interposed are the expatriate individual or small firm and the co-operatives. But there is extension downward and upward. Small expatriate firms are found operating alongside branches of large ones and also substantial West African traders, especially in the small and medium-sized towns in the areas with a traditionally marketless society. Again, it must be remembered that each category is very heterogenous. Nevertheless the classification is an aid in the understanding of the complex situation.

SMALL WEST AFRICAN TRADERS

The African trader is a vitally important link in the commercial chain since it is through his activities that most agricultural and craft products enter the exchange economy and that food and consumer goods are finally sold. The members of this category may be men or women. Most African societies have marked division of labour with clearly assigned roles for each sex. Thus amongst the Yoruba of Western Nigeria, the Adja of southern Dahomey and the Ga of southern Ghana the women are expected to engage in trade and have exclusive rights to their trading gains. Consequently a very high proportion of women are so engaged. Those not actively engaged are the old and those who have temporarily ceased because of social customs that interfere with such activity. In this area markets are the province of women and so great is their predominance that Hodder has observed that only a handful of the people in the Yoruba rural market are men.[5] Amongst the Afikpo Ibo, on the other

o

hand, both men and women engage in trade although here again there is some division of labour between the sexes. Men trade in goods requiring greater amounts of capital, mainly imports. Similarly, types of goods which required the seller's travelling considerable distances to obtain them are sold by men. But a number of products are sold by both sexes and cigarettes, matches, soap and sugar are sold exclusively by boys.[6]

Four sub-groups can be distinguished, though they are not mutually exclusive, (i) market traders, (ii) petty traders, (iii) itinerant hawkers and (iv) urban and rural shopkeepers.

MARKET TRADERS operate in the network of rural and urban markets that has evolved in West Africa. This network is closest where population densities are moderate or high. Hodder has suggested a density of 50 persons per square mile (20 per square kilometre) as being the minimum below which markets do not occur in Yorubaland.[7] Periodic and daily markets can be distinguished, each class consisting of day, morning and evening markets. Periodic markets are held at regular intervals. In Yorubaland they may be two-, four- or eight-day, in Mossiland (Haute Volta) the normal periodicity is three-day with a 21-day cycle of bigger, more important markets.[8] They may be organised on a 'ring' system, each ring being composed of an integrated sequence of markets taking place over the days of a period. The successive markets are not normally adjacent and so nowhere is far from a market for more than two or three days. Periodic markets may be sited in the bush at the junction of pathways, in hamlets and villages on the roadside or in towns and cities. In Yorubaland periodic markets attract large numbers of traders and it has been conservatively estimated that over half a million people move daily along paths and roads to and from markets.[9]

Daily markets are mainly a feature of towns, but Assessawa market in the Krobo food producing area of Ghana is not in any settlement. In traditionally marketless societies they are the creation of local authorities in the Colonial Era, or have evolved because of increasing trade. The larger the town, normally the more numerous and the larger the daily markets. At Dugbe in Ibadan as many as 30,000 people may pass through in a day. But periodic markets apparently show

little correlation with distribution and hierarchy of settlement.

Contrasts in goods offered for sale in rural periodic and
urban daily markets are in quantity, quality and choice
rather than in range. This includes (i) products collected
in the bush; (ii) staple foodstuffs; (iii) cooked foods; (iv)
locally processed and craft goods, palm oil, soap and pots;
(v) imported or locally manufactured consumer goods.
Traders specialise by commodities, but there is mobility
between classes of goods, traffic in medicinal plants is the
preserve of elderly women, cooked food mainly of younger.[10]
There is also specialisation of commodity areally within the
market, a world wide phenomenon.[11]

Market traders act as the final links in the distributional
system of either imported or locally manufactured goods,
purchasing from African or expatriate wholesalers and
retailing to petty trader or consumer in smaller bulk. Conversely they are the first links in the chain for staple foods or
export crops. They may also be craftsmen-traders who work
in the market place and sell the products of their industry.
In addition there are the wholesalers who travel from market
to market buying local products for sale in the towns. But
goods, particularly staple foodstuffs, can pass through many
more hands than is suggested here. Hodder has observed,
'In a few cases, articles have been seen to change hands as
many as five times during the course of one day, and the profits
made at each transaction have been thought to be negligible.'[12]

PETTY TRADERS differ from market traders in the place
where they conduct business. In rural areas, especially in
traditionally marketless societies, they operate from their
own home and usually sell manufactured goods. These are
obtained in the market in retail quantities—a tin of cigarettes,
a packet of cube sugar, a dozen boxes of matches—and are
broken down into smaller units for resale—a cigarette, a
few lumps of sugar, half a dozen matches. Petty traders of
this type are found amongst the Wolof of the Saloum district
of Gambia, where the range of stock varies with availability
of money in the community according to the agricultural
season.[13] Elsewhere petty traders may gather at some central
point in the hamlet or village under some suitable shady tree.

Such gatherings, called 'small markets', are not formally recognised as markets and lack the control to which the market is subject. In towns, 'small markets' are commonly located beside or at the intersection of major pedestrian flows.

ITINERANT HAWKERS are of two main kinds. The first operates within a limited area. Thus women wander from compound to compound selling cooked foodstuffs, fresh fruit or imported goods, whilst in large towns others trade fresh fruit to the expatriate and better-off African communities. The distinction between this type of African trader and the others discussed above is a very fine one and indeed an individual may trade as each successively.

The second, more distinctive, type is the long distance trader engaged in the internal and intra-continental export exchange. Itinerant Hausa traders, for instance, are found along the length of the West African coastlands selling goods ranging from patent and native medicines to craft goods. The Elder Dempster mailboats were licensed to carry deck passengers between ports east of Bathurst at very low fares. Many of the deck passengers were traders and their embarking with trade goods, food supplies for the journey, cooking pots and personal chattels was like a scene from a Conrad story. Nowadays, however, the principal long distance trade conducted by Hausa traders is with southern Nigeria. Cattle, groundnuts, cotton, locust-beans, and Hausa cloth and other craft goods are brought southwards and kola, ginger, Yoruba cloth and manufactured goods form the return traffic. Goods are moved by road, rail, and on foot to the numerous foci of this trade in the southern towns. As the volume of trade increases so does the number and scatter of agents, usually close kin because of the dependence of the trader on their integrity, and in addition a lorry fleet may be purchased.[14]

Itinerant traders are also important in the early stages of produce buying. Using money advanced to them by buying agents, they contact the individual farmer and bring in small quantities of export crops to the buying stations.

The final category of African trader consists of URBAN AND RURAL SHOPKEEPERS. Village shopkeepers and their small urban counterparts carry only small stocks, mainly of imported goods. The shop may be a ground-floor room or the verandah of the trader's house or a stall in front. In some of the towns, shanties built of packing cases, corrugated iron or woven matting serve as shops. Such structures are found on the edge of the central business district in Freetown,[15] while in 1963–64 there were still examples on Broad Street in the central business district of Lagos, lending remarkable contrast to the townscape of commercial Lagos. In traditionally market-less societies the village shopkeepers are extremely important in local commerce as they perform some of the functions of the rural market.

There is also a smaller number of African shopkeepers operating on a substantial scale. Some of these in the large towns are specialists, booksellers, stationers and chemists. Others operate general stores and in scale of operations, range of stock held, and turnover compare with the Levantine traders. Thus, there were Yoruba women in Zaria in 1950 running businesses with an average monthly turnover of $5,600 and Hausa shopkeepers operate on a similar scale.[16] From retail businesses on this scale it is but a short step to wholesaling, and Smith has demonstrated the evolution of operations of the Hausa general merchant interposed between the expatriate importers and the village shopkeepers and marketeers.[17] Similarly, Bauer has published brief case histories of successful African traders. By way of illustration one of these is quoted *in extenso*.

I met in Onitsha three African ladies who have been in partnership as traders for twenty-five years. Two of them had been at school together and had attended Y.W.C.A. sewing classes. In their spare time they sewed, sold cloth, saved their earnings and with their savings bought palm kernels which they sold to a European firm. Subsequently they bought merchandise, mainly textiles, from the same firm, thus trading both in produce and in merchandise. Later they withdrew from produce buying and began to deal exclusively in import merchandise. Today (i.e. circa 1954) their annual turnover exceeds £100,000. ($280,000).[18]

CO-OPERATIVES

Co-operation can make most impact in three fields, (i) consumer supply, (ii) produce marketing and (iii) credit provision. The last aspect will be considered later in the chapter. Consumer supply co-operatives are not as yet widespread, although government-backed attempts to establish them have been made in Ghana and in the Western Region of Nigeria. In Ghana the Co-operative Wholesale Establishment was set up in 1948 to supply the needs of retail societies, which themselves increased in numbers, in membership and in turnover until 1961. In 1962, however, the Establishment ran into financial difficulties which led to its final liquidation. In Western Nigeria the Supply Association, an organisation of cocoa marketing, thrift and loan societies, was inaugurated as a large-scale wholesaler with retail branches throughout the Region. A number of retail shops have been opened and goods have been distributed through petty traders organised into co-operative distribution groups. But progress, as far as can be judged, has been unspectacular, for three reasons. The first is keen competition from existing traders with low overheads and prepared to work on slim profit margins. The second is lack of capital, and finally there is a lack of trained personnel.

Co-operative marketing has been more successful. The marketing societies bridge the gap between the marketing board's buying point and the farmer. This gap is a field of competitive buying and selling in the hands of middlemen, mainly African traders. The individual farmer is ill-equipped in market intelligence and cash resources. The societies can replace individual weakness in the market with strength derived from numbers, and accordingly they have attracted some measure of government assistance in the form of grants and loans. The societies are amalgamated into unions and the latter commonly act as licensed buying agents for the marketing boards. In Northern Nigeria in 1963, for instance, there were 30 such unions, of which 23 were licensed buying agents, and they handled produce to the value of $4·04 million in the 1962–63 buying season. Similarly in Western Nigeria and in Ghana substantial proportions of the cocoa crop are handled by marketing societies and unions. Co-operative organisation is also a feature of francophone West Africa. In Côte d'Ivoire, for instance, to quote but two examples, COBAFRUIT is responsible for the marketing of bananas and pineapples in the export field, whilst poultry producers formed COPRAVI to market their chickens and eggs in Abidjan.

SMALL EXPATRIATE TRADERS

The most numerous group of small expatriate traders are the Levantine traders, ubiquitous in anglophone countries, less so in the francophone areas. The Lebanese, in particular, form a close-knit community and the sons of traders tend to establish their own businesses as close to their parents as possible. They are found in small colonies in West African towns both large and small, operating wholesale and retail businesses. The Levantine store is owned and operated by one family which commonly lives on the floors above the shop. While many are general stores selling a wide variety of goods, there is a tendency to concentrate on cheap cotton fabrics. In their retail activities, they serve an almost complete income range of the African population as well as the expatriate population in the larger towns. But the same business also often acts as wholesaler to African petty and market traders. In addition, a minority also import some of the goods they sell and others trade in staple export commodities, often accepting these in payment for goods wholesaled to African customers.

In addition to Levantine owned businesses, there are also in anglophone countries small Indian owned businesses operated by their owners. These are very much like their Levantine counterparts, from which they are almost indistinguishable in the variety of goods stocked. In the larger towns of francophone West Africa, there are French and Algerian shopkeepers operating their own businesses, usually of a specialist nature, and French hoteliers and restaurateurs.

LARGE EXPATRIATE FIRMS

As a result of a long period of evolution, followed by rapid change since the mid-1950s, these enterprises are diverse, but certain trends can be established. They originated mainly by amalgamations of general merchanting firms or individuals.

They were concerned with the wholesale and retail distribution of imported goods and with the buying of produce for export. The largest concern, the United Africa Company (UAC) dealt in a range of some 50,000 items bought in some 60 different countries,[19] though the bulk of the trade was in a few staples such as sugar, soap, beer, cement and roofing material. This form of enterprise was appropriate when purchasing power was limited as were indigenous capital and managerial expertise.

Before independence, there was a tendency for French firms to operate in the French territories and British firms in the British. A few British firms had branches in French territory, but two French firms, *Compagnie Française de l'Afrique Ouest* (CFAO) and *Société Commerciale de l'Ouest Africain* (SCOA) operated extensively in British territory, as did Swiss based Union Trading Company (UTC), a few Levantine mercantile houses and some Indian-owned chains of department stores.

After 1945 there was a great expansion of export trade together with very high prices for primary products and consequently incomes rose and with them demands for goods and services. These now included more sophisticated items, imported luxury foods, cosmetics, cars, radios and so on. Indigenous capital became more freely available and large scale and specialised trading became more attractive, in both retailing and in produce buying. For the expatriate firm costs have risen, since independence certain sectors of trade have been reserved by some countries for citizens, and everywhere the scale of government intervention has increased.

In the face of these changes, the firms have become more specialised and have altered their structure. Some of them, notably UAC, have withdrawn from produce buying. They have also withdrawn from selling lines of merchandise in which they have no particular advantage over their indigenous competitors. They have also sold or leased their smaller up-country wholesale-retail stores. Instead they have concentrated on five principal fields. (i) They act as large-scale wholesalers of imported and locally manufactured goods especially of a technical or specialist nature, motor vehicles, machinery, or pharmaceuticals. (ii) They retail goods requiring large amounts of capital and after-sales service, such as air-conditioners or electric cookers. (iii) They operate departmental stores in the large towns catering for the expatriate and African middle-class communities. (iv) They provide specialist service facilities such as garages, and (v) to an increasing extent they participate in manufacturing.

There is a growing trend since 1955 for subsidiary companies to be set up in each country, registered locally and with African participation in capital, direction and management. They are becoming increasingly identified with the particular country within which they operate, and outwardly at least are becoming less expatriate and more indigenous. In addition, the older firms have been supplemented by others from the metropolitan countries, from elsewhere in Western Europe and from North America.

STATE CORPORATIONS

State corporations are a feature of the Socialist States of West Africa, Guinée, Mali and Ghana, but there is considerable variation in commercial policies and structures. In Ghana the National Trading Corporation was founded in 1962. The Government bought a large expatriate firm's interests in the country and took over the Commonwealth Trust Limited, and used these to form the kernel of the Corporation which grew rapidly until 1965. Since then progress has been erratic, largely as the result of the country's economic difficulties. The Corporation is, however, the largest trading concern in Ghana. It imports and sells a complete range of consumer goods and capital equipment in competition with private exterprise, although it enjoys a monopoly of certain imports. Like its private enterprise competitors, it sells consumer goods both wholesale and retail and maintains the largest network of wholesale and retail outlets in the country. In Mali, on the other hand, the state has assumed control over the sale and distribution of certain non-perishable foodstuffs, notably rice and millet. Private trading has ceased in these commodities but continues in perishable foodstuffs such as fish.

The Produce Marketing Boards, another manifestation of state enterprise, are more widespread, but are geared exclusively to the export of major agricultural staples. As we have seen, until World War II the buying of export staples had been in the hands of expatriate companies. In the 1930s, because of low prices, there had been much agitation against the system. During the war the British Government replaced it with a centralised shipping and marketing organisation. After the war individual colonial governments continued with the concept of central control of buying and marketing. In Ghana the Cocoa Marketing Board was created and in Nigeria Produce Marketing Boards were set up in each Region for buying, the shipping and marketing being handled by the Nigerian Produce Marketing Company, owned by the regional boards. Similar organisations were set up in Sierra Leone and Gambia.

A fixed purchase price for each crop handled by the Boards is declared at the beginning of each season. This is based on the expected movement of world prices and estimated crop yields. The theory was that in time of high world prices the official price should be lower than the open world price, enabling reserves to be built up so that when world prices fell the official prices could be maintained. In fact, during the period of sustained high prices during the late 1940s and early 1950s, the accumulated balances became so large that substantial sums were loaned to the Governments for capital development. Governments came to depend on this as a major source of capital and there was an increasing reluctance to maintain the level of official prices when produce prices declined during the late 1950s and early 1960s. Since many of the projects were aimed at stimulating industrialisation and urbanisation, the farmers suffered a double deprivation, and the more backward rural areas were in fact subsidising the rapidly growing towns.

Similar arrangements were made in the francophone countries, where *Caisses de Stabilisation des Prix* were set up in each country to control the marketing of staple exports. In Togo there are four such, set up between 1955 and 1958, to control cocoa, coffee, cotton and groundnuts. Guinexport handles Guinée's agricultural and mineral exports, and the export of agricultural staples is centralised in both Dahomey and Côte d'Ivoire. Prices to the producers, however, were allowed to reflect market prices much more closely, and this led to considerable smuggling of cocoa and other commodities from anglo- to francophone countries at times of high prices.

The marketing boards do not engage in buying export produce and transporting it to ports. These functions are performed by 'Licensed Buying Agents'. At first these were mainly expatriate companies, but the pace of Africani ation quickened from 1955 onwards and those expatriate companies with diverse activities increasingly withdrew from produce buying. The Licensed Buying Agents are chiefly small African traders and local co-operatives, but there are some larger organisations such as the government owned Cocoa Purchasing Company of Ghana. Licensed Buying Agents receive a commission on tonnage handled together with transport costs from buying station to port based on the official route between the two. This official route may include mileage on dirt roads at a higher ton-mile rate than on tarred roads. In some cases, the whole route is by road, in others it is to railhead or waterway, when the rail or steamer rate is added. If the Licensed Buying Agents can find lower cost routes or means of transport they may retain the difference between the official rate and the actual cost, though naturally the official routes are continuously under review.

PATTERNS OF TRADE

We have defined internal exchange as taking place over long distances within a single country and intra-continental exchange as taking place across the international frontiers of West Africa. This is regardless of the origin or final destination of the commodities being traded. It is true, however, that the accident of frontiers means that in some areas a trade may be internal and in others intra-continental. There is considerable exchange between Forest and Sudan, kola north and cattle south. In Nigeria this is internal, but between Ghana and Haute Volta it becomes intra-continental.

A glance at Figure 8.1 shows something of the complexity of West African trade, but because of the fragmentary nature of the evidence it is difficult to build up a complete picture. The inter-continental exchange is well documented, and to a lesser extent the intra-continental. To a large extent, however, this must be considered along with the internal exchange, and here documentation is very patchy, making it impossible to estimate quantities and values of goods involved, let alone the patterns themselves. Nothing more can be attempted here, therefore, than a general statement, illustrated by reference to particular studies.

We can, however, distinguish four major strands in the pattern. The first consists of *imported goods*, landed in the ports and moved up-country through the distributional system already outlined. Hodder has shown how imported stock fish reaches the consumer in Ibadan.[20] Stockfish are cod and haddock caught in the Arctic Sea, sun-dried and shipped, mainly from Norway, in large quantities to West Africa, where it is widely preferred to locally produced competitors. In 1966 some 25,546 tons of stockfish were imported into Nigeria, accounting for 2·7 per cent. of imports by value. It is normally imported through Lagos by large expatriate firms and sent to the Ibadan depots for distribution. There it is bought by small wholesale traders, who are usually Nigerian traders with sufficient credit standing to purchase several bales of stockfish at a time. The Nigerian wholesalers sell the stockfish to the many retail traders, i.e. to the street hawkers and to the market traders in the day markets and surrounding periodic markets. It may pass through several hands before finally reaching the consumer.

The second strand is of *export produce* moving from the producing areas to the ports. The patterns of movement of crops for export in Nigeria have been recently studied.[21] The crops are taken by the farmers or small African traders in small lots, often by bicycle or donkey, to the gazetted buying stations scattered liberally throughout the producing areas. At the time of White's study, 1958–59 each of the major export crops had its individual pattern of movement. Groundnuts relied heavily on the railway, with water transport less important. All road routes converged on a limited number of railheads and river ports, of which Kano, Gusau, Bukuru and Baro were the chief. Within the region there were three main axes of evacuation, roughly parallel, the railway from Nguru through Kano and Zaria, the road from Maiduguri to the Bukuru railhead and the River Benue from Yola.

The main routes out of the region were the railways to Apapa and Port Harcourt and the Niger down to the Delta ports. Whilst groundnuts and also cotton relied heavily on rail transport, cocoa relied almost entirely on road transport, with the Benin-Akure-Ibadan-Apapa road as the axis of evacuation. The main traffic is towards Ibadan, the dominant cocoa buying centre, and onwards to Apapa. The hinterland of Apapa for cocoa, and also for palm kernels, extends beyond Ondo and is much larger than that of Sapele, which extends to the north of Owo. Palm produce from the Eastern Provinces, on the other hand, was evacuated to a greater extent by waterway and by rail, although the importance of road transport was increasing. The three major transverse axes were the Niger leading to the Delta ports of Warri, Burutu and Sapele, the railway and parallel road from Enugu and Umuahia to Port Harcourt and the Cross River with its port at Calabar. The patterns of movement of Southern export crops have recently changed with the opening of a more direct road link from Benin via Ijebu-Ode to Apapa in the Western provinces and with the Biafran war in the eastern provinces. Similar patterns have been described by Tricart in Côte d'Ivoire and Sénégal.[22]

The third strand is *long-distance trade in craft goods and in certain staples*, such as meat and fish, or in kola nuts, the producing areas of which are separated by considerable distances from important components of the market. Trade in cattle and kola nuts serve as examples of this aspect of internal trade. The kola trade is in the hands of merchants from the Sudan, mainly Hausas, who buy nuts in southern markets in the producing areas. The nuts are packed, an operation requiring skill and care, in centres such as Shagamu in Western Nigeria, Sunyani in Ghana and Agboville in Côte d'Ivoire, for transport in large lots by lorry or rail to the main northern markets and distributed from them to local rural markets.[23] The trade in cattle is conducted over even longer distances. Most of the stock is reared by nomadic Fulani herdsmen in the grasslands of the francophone and anglophone Sudan whilst major markets are to be found in the ports and towns of the Forest. Separating the two are some thousand miles or more of country most of which is tsetse-infested. The traditional way of overcoming this broad gap between producing and consuming areas is by trekking the beasts on the hoof between the two. The animals are purchased from the producer by Hausa traders and driven southwards in small herds by drovers, acting as agents. The stock is consigned to Hausa traders or sold to such traders in the larger towns, although many are sold in smaller towns along the route. Finally the beasts are sold to butchers who may be Hausa or may be southerners.

The direction of the flow of the cattle trade is the reverse of that in kola nuts and the same trader often deals in both. But the cattle trade is perhaps the more significant for our purpose as it illustrates some of the problems of development in West Africa. The organisation, methods and distances covered in the trade have been severely criticised by the Nigerian Livestock Mission as being wasteful.[24] Certainly the trekking of beasts over long distances is wasteful in that there is both an appreciable death rate and considerable loss of weight and deterioration in quality of the meat amongst stock en route. The number of transactions between first purchase and ultimate retail sale was similarly criticised as wasteful. Both these aspects of the trade are, however, a reflection of economic conditions. The producing areas are widely scattered, the market is thinly spread and the prices the market can bear are low. In these circumstances numerous transactions are necessary to build up herds of economic size for droving southwards. Trekking minimises overhead costs and transit charges and thus survives competition from rail or lorry.

Various attempts have been made to reduce such waste but any success has always been at the expense of costs and therefore of the poorer sections of the market. Thus about half of the cattle moved into southern Nigeria from the north now come by rail (Table 8.1). But transport by rail raises the cost of meat in southern markets appreciably, although the quality of rail borne stock is better. In West Cameroun, on the other hand, a meat scheme was set up in 1959, the object of which is to buy stock in prime condition, slaughter it locally and freeze it for distribution. The scheme was begun with a cold store in the Bamenda grasslands at Bali and a refrigerated lorry from which meat was sold direct to the consumer. An abbattoir at Bali and cold stores in the consuming area at Kumba, Tiko and Victoria were subsequently added. Nevertheless, fewer cattle were dealt with by the scheme in the first four years of its life to 1963 than were slaughtered in Mamfe Province in that year alone.[25] This is a particularly acute problem for the interior states, where economic development is hindered by a cruel lack of suitable products for export coupled with expensive imports from outside West Africa. Ambitious plans for abbattoir building in Mali, for example, have had to be curtailed partly because of the difficulties of assuring them satisfactory stock supplies and partly because of the high cost of refrigerated transport to the major markets of the south. Similarly a project for freezing part of the fishing catch in Abidjan for distribution in the interior has collapsed. Four depots were estabished at Bouaké, Dimbroko, Divo and Gagnoa, but the expenses involved were considerable even without taking account of amalgamation charges (Table 8.2). As P. Platin remarks, 'under these circumstances it is not hard to understand that clients in the bush were not particularly attracted to frozen fish and showed a reluctance to buy a product whose price, burdened by these expenses, was greater than their means.'[26]

The final strand consists of *shorter distance internal* and of *local trade* between neighbouring areas with differing resources and between towns and their surrounding rural areas. In this sector data are scarce and consequently analyses sometimes conflict. Akinola suggests that the farming region that supplies the bulk of Ibadan's food and the tributary area of the Ibadan markets are both nearly coincidental with Ibadan Province.[27] Conversely Hodder[28] suggests, with more reason, that Ibadan draws its food supply from the far north and southward to the coast. Westward, movement across the Dahomey frontier is limited and eastward the Mid-West Region supplies little. The area is thus elongated north-south across a variety of environments and following the main lines of communications. The extensive character of the food supply area and the influence of communications upon its shape have been demonstrated for Accra.[29] Subsequently the area from which Koforidua draws its goods and its customers has been studied.[30] Most of its lies within the Forest Zone, including a part of the Akwapim Hills, but it also includes part of the savanas of the Volta basin to the East. In lower Dahomey the Tardits[31] have demonstrated how the differing products of various geographical units, *terre de barre* cuestas and transverse valleys, coast and inland areas are exchanged.

PATTERNS OF EXTRA-CONTINENTAL TRADE

In 1966 the level of world exports was approximately seven times that of 1938, if no allowance is made for currency inflation, and about three times allowing for inflation. Since 1950 the rate of growth of world trade, at six per cent. per year, has outstripped that of population growth, so that per capita trade is increasing. Such progress in world trade is not uniformly distributed amongst nations or groups of nations. The Non-Communist developed countries continue to dominate world trade patterns, accounting for over two-thirds of all trade. The rate of growth of their exports, however, 6·4 per cent. between 1950 and 1960 at constant prices, has been lower than that of the centrally planned economies, 10·7 per cent. although, of course, calculated from a lower base. The exports of the group of less developed countries, on the other hand, rose by only 3·6 per cent. in the period. This is mainly, if not entirely, because the less developed economies export mainly primary products, the market share of which has been falling. In addition world market prices for tropical agricultural foods fluctuate markedly, with the result that a reduction in value of exports may conceal fairly substantial increases in tonnage.

EXPORT TRADE

The West African countries display certain of the trade characteristics of less developed economies, but in growth of trade deviate from the expected (Table 8.3). Only in Dahomey and Portuguese Guinea have exports grown at less than the world rate. The exports of Sénégal increased almost eight-fold between 1938 and 1966, but the 1938 figures also included exports of Mali and Mauretanie, so they may have grown at slightly below world rate. Similarly, a three-fold increase between 1953 and 1966 of exports from Haute Volta is certainly below world rate. Of the remaining West African states Gambia, Ghana and Sierra Leone each enjoyed growth of exports of about the world rate whilst Guinée, Côte d'Ivoire, Liberia, Niger and Nigeria enjoyed spectacular growth. There is no single explanation for this variety. Some of the more outstanding examples of growth took place from a very small base, the seventy-five-fold increase in Liberian exports being the prime example. But the seventeen-fold increase registered by Nigeria was based on fairly substantial exports in 1938. Similarly, being land-locked of itself apparently had little effect as Niger experienced a thirty-five-fold increase in her exports, albeit from a tiny base. The political framework seems to have had limited effect also in that Guineé, with its highly centralised export organisation enjoyed a growth well above world average if rather inferior to that of the Côte d'Ivoire with its reliance on free enterprise. The large scale exploitation of mineral resources, whether oil in Nigeria, iron ore in Liberia and Mauretanie, bauxite in Guinée or phosphates in Togo, is certainly of significance in explaining some of the more spectacular advances.

On a medium-term view agricultural prices were high in the post-war years and early 1950s, sinking progressively from the middle of the decade into the nineteen sixties, but this conceals short term variations in harvest. These points are illustrated in Tables 8.4 and 8.5 and Figure 8.2. In the face of these variations producer countries have adopted measures to stabilise prices. Among these measures are commodity agreements, such as those for coffee and for cocoa, which normally involve some form of quota system, and bilateral trade agreements, of which there were in 1966 some 125 between African and non-African countries and a further 54 between African countries. There is a tendency as prices decline for production to be increased in an effort to maintain income.

This variation in export earnings from primary products is a trade characteristic shared with most less-developed economies, as is the overwhelming reliance upon those primary products. Indeed most West African countries not only specialise on primary production for export but rely to a

P

considerable extent upon a single crop or mineral for their export earnings. Over 60 per cent. of export earnings in 1963 were derived from sales of iron ore by Mauretanie, groundnuts by Niger and Gambia, coffee by Côte d'Ivoire, alumina by Guinée, diamonds by Sierra Leone and cocoa by Ghana

Figure 8.2. Average annual prices of 'Accra well-fermented' cocoa, 1950–66
Source: Cocoa Statistics

(Table 8.5). Nigeria is apparently the exception but here the specialisation is equally strong on a provincial basis. The Western provinces depend heavily on cocoa, the Eastern provinces on palm products and increasingly on petroleum, the Northern provinces on groundnuts. Strenuous efforts have been and are being made by West African Governments to modify this state of affairs, and by 1966 significant changes had occurred (Table 8.5). These efforts take two forms, (i) the development of exports in existing but relatively unimportant products and (ii) the introduction of new crops for export. Thus the Côte d'Ivoire government has particularly encouraged expansion of cocoa and banana production, of pineapple growing and processing and of timber exploitation to reduce the dependence upon coffee exports. Further diversification is envisaged with expansion of palm products, coconuts and rubber.

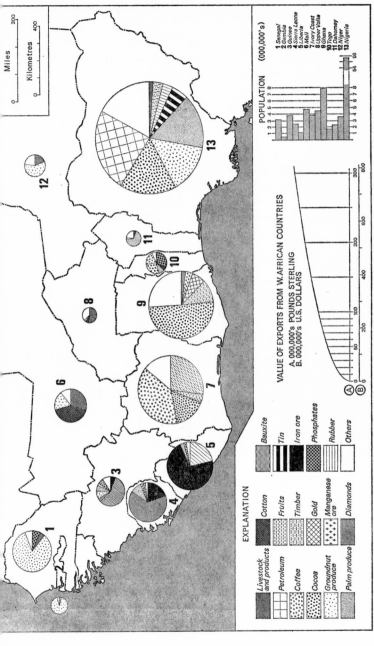

Figure 8.3. The value of exports from West African countries. *Source: Trade Statistics*

IMPORT TRADE

Imports have also grown rapidly since 1938, often at an even greater rate. Only in Côte d'Ivoire and Liberia have imports grown less rapidly than exports while rates of growth were about the same in Nigeria, Guinée and Sénégal. It is not possible, because of limitations in the data, to indicate the position of Mali, Mauretanie and Haute Volta in this respect. Again there is no simple explanation for the variations in growth rates of imports. Land-locked states have increased their imports at rates similar to those of their coastal neighbours. Countries with considerable government ownership and control of the economy have performed little worse than neighbours relying to a greater extent upon free enterprise. As with exports, some of the more spectacular increases of imports such as the forty-five-fold increase of Niger, the fifty-seven-fold increase of Liberia, took place from a tiny base, but the seventeen-fold increase in Nigeria's imports occurred from a fairly substantial one. (Table 8.6). Further there is no close correspondence between growth rates of exports and of imports.

Thus many West African countries suffer from chronic balance of payments problems even on current account. The exceptions are Guinée, Côte d'Ivoire, Liberia, Mauritanie and Nigeria. The problem is worsened when invisibles are taken into account, since most West African countries are, on balance, purchasers of services and have large foreign investments to service. In those parts of francophone West Africa which remained in the C.F.A. franc zone, the balance of payments deficit is underwritten by France so that the situation for these countries is problematical only as far as the metropolitan country may tire of underwriting the economies of its former colonies. The British Government does not adopt such a benevolent policy towards its former colonies and the situation has become critical in Ghana. The Nkrumah regime ran down reserves from $560 million to zero and ran up an external debt from zero to some $550 million. This was caused not only by deteriorating terms of trade but also by a high degree of inflexibility in the productive structure of the economy, so that diversification of the export economy did not progress; by imports sucked in by an extensive programme of import-substituting industries, which in itself created the need for imported raw materials; by an extensive programme of investment in the tertiary sector such as an airline, a shipping line and the tourist industry, which created considerable imports in the short term and debts in the long-term; and by a too rapid rate of investment in the infrastructure In the face of this rapid run-down of reserves imports have been licensed, leading to critical shortages not only of consumer and capital goods but also of spare parts necessary to maintain industries in operation, investment has been heavily cut, the currency has been devalued, long-term debt rapayment has been re-scheduled and a series of stand-by arrangements have been negotiated with I.M.F. to provide a breathing space in which to effect more lasting solutions.

The structural patterns of imports into West African countries is also typical of that of less-developed economies (Table 8.7). Manufactures, both of consumer and of capital goods, account for the bulk of imports, but the proportion varies from country to country. At one extreme only 53 per cent. of Senegalese imports consists of manufactures while, at the other, manufactured goods account for 85 per cent. of Nigeria's imports. Perhaps surprisingly, food, drink and tobacco account for significant percentages, notably in Haute Volta, Sénégal, Côte d'Ivoire, Togo and Dahomey. Imports of food into West Africa have been studied by Morgan for 1956.[32] They included not only luxuries, such as tinned and, dried fish, tinned milk and beer, but staples such as sugar wheat, flour and rice, which do nothing to remedy deficiencies in West Africa's supply of vitamins or proteins. Subsequent declines in world market prices for West African produce, have meant a rise in the costs of imported food in terms of the purchasing power of exports. Thus food imports have contributed to the unfavourable balance of payments situation discussed above and governments have taken various measures to reduce imports of food.

The structural pattern of trade is, however, changing at least in detail, and the most significant trend in imports is a relative decline in consumer goods, matched by a relative increase in capital goods as the policies of import-substitution industrialisation take place. This is illustrated by Nigeria although not all West African countries have progressed as far as Nigeria.

CHANGES IN TRADE PATTERNS

The structural pattern of inter-continental trade as described above still displays the features of the classical colonial economy (Table 8.8). So also do geographical patterns of foreign trade, but to a lesser degree. The classical colonial economy depended overwhelmingly on the metropolitan power as a source of imports and as an outlet for its exports. Whilst the former metropolitan power remains important, most West African countries have as a matter of policy endeavoured to widen their trade relationships since independence. This policy has been pursued with greater or less vigour and with variable results, so that current trade patterns fall along a continuum from most to least colonial.

But trade patterns are particularly fluid. Not only are there short term fluctuations, initiated by political decisions as well as by economic forces, but there are underlying trends of more permanent change. In analysing these trends, 1961 has been adopted as the base year, being the first year of independence of many West African countries.

By 1961, while both the former British and French colonies had the classic colonial pattern of trade, there was a fundamental difference between them. The Commonwealth countries enjoyed the normal preference for all Commonwealth members in those commodities which attracted UK tariffs. But there were no guaranteed prices, nor were there quotas for most of the commodities exported from West Africa. In return a somewhat lower tariff preference was given to UK imports, except for Nigeria, banned from doing so under the Niger Basin Treaty of 1885. This, and the dominance of British mercantile houses in the importing countries, maintained the UK as the largest trading partner, but the proportion of trade with other countries was rising throughout the 1950s.

On the other hand, very close links were maintained between France and the francophone countries, and France's trading position remained far more dominant than that of Great Britain. This resulted from a number of consistent policies. The West African countries enjoyed a guaranteed market in France for the majority of their exports. Generous quotas were arranged and guaranteed prices paid on these, prices which during the 1950s were generally higher than world levels. In return considerable tariff preferences were given on French goods. The relationship of the West African franc to the French franc was maintained at a level advantageous to the former. Finally, substantial French aid was channelled to the colonial territories.

For the rest, the Portuguese and Spanish territories were linked in much the same way to their metropolitan countries. Liberia, though politically independent, traditionally looked to the USA, and its trade patterns showed many of the characteristics of those of its neighbours.

After 1961 the trends in the relationships between the UK and France and their former colonial territories continued to diverge. The political and fiscal structures of UK—West African trade remained unaltered and British shares in the foreign trade of the Commonwealth countries continued to fall. This was the result of a policy of diversification pursued by the West African governments and of world trends such as a falling British share of international trade and rising EEC and US shares. But also important were the growth of consumption of commodities such as cocoa by the eastern bloc countries, more favourable credit terms from other countries, and imports tied to foreign aid grants and loans.

For most of the francophone countries, there was much less change and France continued, though to a slightly lesser extent than formerly, as the dominant partner. The biggest change was brought about by the creation of the European Economic Community in 1957.[33] As a condition of entry, France had insisted her colonial links should not only remain unchanged, but that the whole EEC should be open to produce from the colonies of member states and that the whole EEC should contribute to the cost of development assistance.

With the independence of the French West African colonies and the Belgian Congo, it became necessary, if these arrangements were to continue, to re-negotiate them between the

EEC and the newly independent countries. This was done under the Yaoundé Convention which came into effect in 1964 for five years. There were two, related, parts.

The first dealt with trade. States adhering to the Convention could enjoy preference quotas and tariff exemption within the EEC. Technically the guaranteed prices paid by France would have to cease, though in practice the French continued to give a measure of price support. The second dealt with aid. The overseas aid of the whole EEC would continue to be channelled to the Yaoundé countries.

In theory it was open to any former colony to become an 'Associated State'. In practice all the francophone countries except Guinée did so. Nigeria also sought some form of association, but in the end concentrated on bilateral trade agreements. In the event too, the bulk of the trade of francophone West Africa remained with France, with two exceptions, Mali and Guinée, both of which for political reasons sought to break their links with France and turn for trade and aid to the communist countries.

We may sum up by saying that in general the trend is towards greater diversification away from the former colonial pattern. The least change is showed by Portuguese Guinea. As a group, the Associated States of the Yaoundé Convention, though in varying degrees, have increased their trade with other EEC countries, particularly Togo with Federal Germany. Liberia, still with strong US links, has also increased trade with Germany. Gambia, Sierra Leone and, particularly, Nigeria have shown increasing diversification away from UK. During the Nkrumah period, Ghana sought trade links with communist countries, a trend reversed after his fall to the benefit of the USA, which increased its share of import trade to 25 per cent. in 1968, and the EEC countries who together bought more from Ghana in the first half of 1968 than did the UK. The trade with communist countries by Mali and Guinée, after very rapid post-independence growth is showing signs of decline and Mali is once again seeking closer trade and financial links with France.

Finally, the small and declining proportion of trade between West African countries must be noted. The only countries that conduct a substantial portion of their trade with their neighbours are the land locked countries. Much of this will be imports and exports in transit to and from the ports of the coastal countries. For the rest, exports from these countries to their southern neighbours are more important than are imports. Malian exports to West African countries have increased from 53 to 90 per cent. in the period 1961–66 and similar exports from Niger from 19 to 33 per cent., but those from Haute Volta fell slightly to 73 per cent. In imports Mali draws a fairly consistent 13 per cent., notably from Côte d'Ivoire, while Haute Volta has increased its imports from 26 to 36 per cent. of the total. Of the coastal countries only Dahomey (16·5 per cent.) sends more than 5 per cent. of its exports to other West African countries.

The low levels of intra-West African trade are usually accounted for by suggesting that the economies are basically similar and therefore there is little need for trade. Whilst this may be true, two comments should be made. Firstly, only trade passing through customs posts is recorded. Land frontiers are long, difficult to police and not really recognised by local inhabitants. It is probable that significant amounts of unrecorded trade take place, and smuggling also occurs, such as that of cocoa from Ghana to Togo, diamonds from Sierra Leone to Liberia and textiles and bicycles from Nigeria to Dahomey. Thus published statistics are almost certainly under-counts but it is not known to what extent. Second, this position is likley to change as industrialisation proceeds in those countries, such as Ghana, Côte d'Ivoire and Nigeria, where economic growth is proceeding most quickly. Certainly, there is an increasing number of bilateral trade agreements between West African states, though any increase in intra-continental trade is dependent on the possibility of free-trade and economic unions.

It is tempting to explain the trade described and analysed above in political terms, particularly the swing in the trade of the radicals to the eastern bloc. Whilst political factors have been relevant, it appears to be a mistake to place much emphasis upon them. There have been strong economic forces at work also. Trade patterns are currently fluid and the search for the most advantageous trade pattern is likely to continue. In these circumstances it is hazardous to predict future changes. The whole subject is one that is little worked, particularly by geographers, and would repay detailed investigation.

TABLE 8.1

CATTLE TRADE BETWEEN NORTHERN & SOUTHERN NIGERIA

Year	On Hoof	By Rail	Total
1956–57	157,275	138,819	296,094
1957–58	137,053	156,498	293,551
1958–59	141,548	157,911	199,459
1959–60	155,262	167,342	322,604
1960–61	165,769	197,429	363,198
1961–62	163,601	203,922	367,523
1962–63	171,580	199,822	371,402
1963–64	204,725	200,924	405,649

Source: Northern Nigeria Ministry of Animal and Forest Resources.

TABLE 8.2

COST OF FROZEN FISH DISTRIBUTION
COTE D'IVOIRE, 1962

(Francs CFA per kilogramme: 275 Francs CFA = $1.00)

Depot	Freezing and Storing	Agency Expenses	Transport	Total
Gagnoa	24	19	4	47
Dimbroko	24	15	5	44
Bouaké	24	8	5	37

Source: Marchés Tropicaux et Mediterranéens

TABLE 8.3

THE GROWTH OF EXPORTS
(value in mil. US $ f.o.b.)

	1938	1958	1966
Côte d'Ivoire	11	150	310
Dahomey	3	18	11
Gambia	2	12	14*
Ghana	32	263	244
Guinée	3	23	58
Haute Volta	x	5	16
Liberia	2	54	151
Mali	x	x	13
Mauretanie	x	x	46†
Niger	1	18	35
Nigeria	47	380	792
Portuguese Guinea	1	7	—
Sénégal	19	137	149
Sierra Leone	11	55	83
Togo	2	15	86

Source: United Nations, *Statistical Yearbook, 1967* New York, 1968.

Notes. 1. Trade with the countries of former French West Africa is excluded prior to 1965 by Sénégal, prior to 1959 by Dahomey and Guinée; prior to 1960 by Niger; prior to 1961 by Côte d'Ivoire, Mali, Mauretanie and Haute Volta.
2. Data for Mauretanie and Mali are included with Sénégal in 1938 and 1958.
3. Data for Upper Volta are included with Côte d'Ivoire in 1938.
* (1965)   † (1964)

TABLE 8.4

SELECTED COMMODITY PRICES, 1960–1964

Source Commodity Market	Ghana[1] Cocoa London	Côte d'Ivoire[2] Coffee Le Havre	Nigeria[1] Groundnuts European Ports	Nigeria[1] Palm oil European Ports	Sénégal[1] Groundnuts France
1960	62·2	31·8	19·4	22·4	20·6
1961	49·5	30·5	17·3	22·8	21·3
1962	46·8	30·9	17·1	21·0	21·3
1963	57·3	28·3	18·2	21·8	21·3
1964	52·4	35·9	18·7	23·3	21·3

Source: UN Economic Bulletin for Africa, Vol VI, No. 1. 1966.
1. In US units per kilo.
2. In US cents per pound.

TABLE 8.5

EXPORTS BY CATEGORY OF PRODUCT 1963 & 1966
(percentage by value)

Côte d'Ivoire	1963	Coffee 63, Cocoa 19, Bananas 6
	1966	Coffee 39, Cocoa 17, Lumber 19
Dahomey	1963	Palm Kernels 54
	1966	Palm Kernels 23·0, Palm Oil 17, Cotton 11
Gambia	1963	Groundnuts 73
	1966	Groundnuts 38, Groundnut Oil 38
Ghana	1963	Cocoa 70
	1966	Cocoa 66
Guinée	1963	Alumina 60·0, Bananas 10, Palm Kernels 7
	1966	No data
Haute Volta	1963	Live Animals 49
	1966	Live Animals 50·0
Liberia	1963	Iron Ore 48, Rubber 38
	1966	Iron Ore 71, Rubber 18
Mali	1963	Groundnuts 39
	1966	Cotton 34, Fish 23, Live Animals, 21, Groundnuts 9
Mauritanie	1963	Iron Ore 68, Fish 8
	1966	Iron Ore 93
Niger	1963	Groundnuts 66
	1966	Groundnuts 57, Live Animals 13, Groundnut, Oil 9
Nigeria	1963	Groundnuts 20, Cocoa 18, Palm Kernels 11, Petroleum 11, Rubber 6, Timber 4
	1966	Petroleum 32, Groundnuts 14, Palm Products 12, Cocoa 10
Sénégal	1963	Groundnuts 32
	1966	Groundnuts 35, Groundnut Oil 36
Sierra Leone	1963	Diamonds 64, Iron Ore 19, Palm Kernels 10
	1966	Diamonds 59, Iron Ore 18, Palm Kernels 10
Togo	1963	Cocoa 26, Phosphates 24, Coffee 18
	1966	Phosphates 43, Coffee 22, Cocoa 19

Sources: UN and national publications

TABLE 8.6

THE GROWTH OF IMPORTS
(value in mil. US $ c.i.f.)

	1938	1958	1966
Côte d'Ivoire	9	109	257
Dahomey	3	21	34
Gambia	2	11	16[a]
Ghana	38	237	352
Guinée	5	62	53
Haute Volta	x	9	28
Liberia	2	38	114
Mali	x	x	36
Mauritanie	x	x	16[b]
Niger	1	11	45
Nigeria	42	466	718
Portuguese Guinea	1	8	15[a]
Sénégal	29	208	161
Sierra Leone	7	67	100
Togo	2	18	47

Source: UN, *Statistical Yearbook 1967*, New York 1968, Table 148.
Notes. 1. Trade with the countries of former French West Africa is excluded prior to 1965 by Sénégal; prior to 1959 by Dahomey and Guinée; prior to 1960 by Niger; prior to 1961 by Côte d'Ivoire, Mali, Mauretanie and Haute Volta.
2. Data for Haute Volta are included in Côte d'Ivoire in 1938.
3. Data for Mauritanie and Mali are included with Sénégal in 1938 and 1958.
(a) 1965
(b) 1964

TABLE 8.7

IMPORTS BY CATEGORY OF PRODUCT, 1966
(percentage by value)

	Food, drink tobacco	Raw Materials	Energy Products	Machinery and Transport Equipment	Other Industrial Products
Côte d'Ivoire	19·8	2·2	5·3	27·2	45·0
Dahomey	24·2	1·8	4·5	17·9	51·6
Gambia	22·2	1·8	2·8	19·1	54·1
Ghana	16·5	0·9	4·2	32·7	45·7
Guinée (1962)	17·7	0·0	3·8	18·1	60·4
Haute Volta	27·7	11·4	5·9	17·0	38·0
Liberia	19·4	1·0	9·1	28·1	42·4
Mali	20·9	7·0	6·4	15·6	50·1
Mauritanie	13·9	1·3	5·7	47·4	31·7
Niger	14·0	4·4	8·5	21·8	48·0
Nigeria	11·0	2·8	1·5	37·5	47·2
Sénégal	35·7	5·3	6·1	15·0	37·9
Sierra Leone	22·7	1·3	7·9	23·2	44·9
Togo	22·7	2·3	4·2	22·5	48·3

TABLE 8.8
TRADE WITH FORMER METROPOLITAN POWERS
(percentage by value)

	Exports		Imports	
	1961	1966	1961	1966
Côte d'Ivoire	51·6	38·7	67·9	57·7
Dahomey	72·1	52·4	59·3	51·9
Gambia	30·7	59·8	39·2	36·0
Ghana	21·5	16·9	36·8	28·7
Haute Volta	10·3	18·0	61·0	44·1
Liberia	44·1	34·8	49·0	45·5
Mali	17·7	8·6[a]	68·1	29·6
Mauritanie	44·6[a]	20·6	72·5[b]	54·5
Niger	77·6	52·2	47·8	51·6
Nigeria	43·8	37·0	38·2	29·9
Sénégal	86·0	73·7	64·9	51·0
Sierra Leone	79·1	68·0	60·1	28·3
Togo	52·4	40·3	41·2	30·7

Notes. (a) 1967
(b) 1962

REFERENCES

1 'Pan' is the West African term used to describe corrugated iron sheet commonly used as a roofing material, particularly in areas where thatched roofs were traditional.

2 See *inter alia* Bauer, P. T., *West African Trade*, Cambridge, 1954 (re-issued London, 1963)

3 Hodder, B. W., *Economic Development in the Tropics*, London, 1968, p. 203

4 *Ibid*, p. 204

5 Hodder, B. W., '*Rural Periodic Day Markets in part of Yorubaland*', *Trans. Inst. Br. Geog. 29*, 1961, pp. 149–59

6 Ottenberg, S. and P., *Afikpo Markets: 1900–1960*, in Bohannan, P. and Dalton G. (Eds.), *Markets in Africa*, Evanston, 1962, pp. 147–8

7 Hodder, B. W., '*Distribution of Markets in Yorubaland*', *Scot. Geog. Mag., 81*, 1965, pp. 48–58

8 Skinner, E. P., *Trade and Markets Among the Mossi People*, in Bohannan and Dalton., *op cit.* p. 257

9 Hodder, *op cit*. No. 5, p. 153

10 Tardits, C. and C., *Traditional Market Economy in South Dahomey*, in Bohannan and Dalton, *op cit.*, pp. 93–4

11 Compare, for example, Koforidua market with Akinyele. *See* Hodder, B. W., *op cit.*, No. 5: McCall, D. F., *The Koforidua Market*, in Bohannan and Dalton, *op cit.*, particularly figure 3 p. 150

12 Hodder, *op cit*. No. 5

13 Ames, D. W., *The Rural Wolof of the Gambia*, in Bohannan and Dalton, *op cit*., p. 46

14 Smith, M. G., *Exchange and Marketing Among the Hausa*, in Bohannan and Dalton, *op cit*., p. 306

15 McKay, J., '*Regions within a Tropical City: Freetown, Sierra Leone*', *Regions Within Towns*, Inst. Brit. Geog., Study Group in Urban Geography, 1966 (mimeo)

16 Smith, M. G., *op cit*. p. 315–317

17 *Ibid*.

18 Bauer, *op cit*. p. 31

19 United Africa Company, '*Redeployment: An Aspect of Development in Tropical Africa*', *Statistical and Economic Review*, 28, 1963, p. 2

20 Hodder, B. W., '*The markets of Ibadan*' in Lloyd, P. C., Mabogunje, A. L. and Awe, B. (Eds.), *The City of Ibadan*, Cambridge, 1967, pp. 187–8

21 White, H. P., '*The Movement of Export Crops in Nigeria*', *Tijds. Econ. en Soc. Geog.*, 54, 1963, pp. 248–253

22 Kayser, B. and Tricart, J., '*Rail et Route au Sénégal*', *Ann. de Géog.* 66, 1957, pp. 328–350: Tricart, J., '*Le Café en Côte d'Ivoire*', *Cahiers d'Outre-Mer*, 10, 1957, p. 209

23 See *inter alia*, Onacko, E. A., '*Shagamu and its District: a Short Geographical Account*', *Nig. Geog. Jour*. 2, 1958, 14–25: Lelong, M. H., '*La Route du Kola*', *La Révue de Géographie Humaine et d'Éthnologie*, 4, 1948–9, pp. 35–44: Tricart, J. '*Les Echanges Entre la Zone Forestière de Côte d'Ivoire et les Savanes Soudaniennes*', *Cahiers d'Outre-Mer*, 9, 1956, pp. 209–238

24 *Report of Nigerian Livestock Mission*, Colonial No. 296, H.M.S.O., 1951

25 Gleave, M. B., '*The West Cameroon Meat Scheme*', *Geog.*, 50, 1965. pp. 166–8

26 '*The Ivory Coast Market*', *Marchés Tropicaux et Mediteranéens*, 15 June, 1963, p. 35

27 Akinola, R. A., '*The Ibadan Region*', *Nig. Geog. Jour.*, 6, 1963, pp. 102–115

28 Hodder, B. W., *op cit*. No. 20, p. 187

29 White, H. P., '*Internal Exchange of Staple Foods in the Gold Coast*', *Econ. Geog.*, 32, 1956, pp. 115–125

30 *Ibid*, pp. 123–124

31 Tardits, C. and C., *op cit*.

32 Morgan, W. B., 'Food Imports of West Africa', *Econ. Geog.* 39, 1963, pp. 351–362. Data in this paper relate to 1956. For 1961 *see* Morgan, W. B. and Pugh, J. C., *West Africa*, London 1969, pp. 568–571

33 Cosgrove, C. A., '*The EEC and Developing Countries*' Chapter 4 in *Economic Integration in Europe*, London 1967: Cosgrove, C. A., '*The Common Market and its Colonial Heritage*', *Journ. Contempt. History*, 4, 1969, pp. 73–87: Wells, S. J., '*The ECC and Trade with Developing Countries*', *Journal of Common Market Studies*, 4, 1965–6, pp. 150–68

CHAPTER 9

Transport & Development

It is a truism to stress the importance of communications and transport as factors in social and economic development, for the level of development is obviously controlled by the level of investment in these sectors of the infrastructure. In West Africa this connection is of particular interest. It is frequently simple and direct and can be demonstrated from first principles. In Europe transport development seldom involves the creation of an entirely new line of communication, but rather the modification of an existing line, even though the improvement may be so radical that a new dimension is introduced. In West Africa, on the other hand, the whole process may be followed from its very beginning. Even within the last twenty years entirely new lines of communication have been created by the building of a new road, and the consequences can be studied *ab initio*.

Roads have been constructed through areas hitherto devoid of any track passable by wheeled vehicles. For the first time lorries arrive with trade goods in significant quantity (previously very small amounts might have been brought in by pedlars on bicycles). For the first time there is now both an incentive to dispose of crop surpluses for cash in order to purchase these goods and also a new ability to evacuate produce hitherto unsaleable through lack of a local market. In short, a cash economy will be widely introduced for the first time and with this the possibility of economic advance.

There are, however, even more far-reaching consequences. The settlement pattern will alter as villages are re-located along the roadside to take advantage of ease of movement and possibilities of trade. There will also be radical changes in the pattern of land-use. Land near the road will be cultivated for longer periods, because access to the road makes disposal of the crops easier, while land remote from the road will go out of cultivation. New crops for cash sale will also be introduced. These may even replace the traditional food-crops, for they may give a higher return per acre, and food can now be brought in from elsewhere. Social consequences are also considerable. A new way of life is introduced. The area is brought into closer contact with the outside. More people will travel away from home and more strangers arrive, and new ideas and knowledge will be thus introduced.

In 1955 one of the authors travelled up to the advancing road-head of the new trunk road being built northward from Hohoe in the Volta Region of Ghana. On either side were new cocoa farms. Ahead of the road the forest was being cleared for further plantings, which would come into bearing by the time the road had been built up to them. The small village of Kajebi was almost visibly becoming a town as cocoa-buying stations, retail stores and garages were being hastily erected to take advantage of the cocoa boom, in which the new road had enabled the district to share.

The spread of a cash crop, up to the climatic limit, can always be traced in terms of transport development. In Ghana cocoa cultivation started in Akwapim, within reasonable head-loading distance of the port of Accra. In the 1920s it spread along the new railway, opened throughout in 1923, from Accra to Kumasi *via* Koforidua and Juaso.[1] The railway was never extended beyond Kumasi and the spread of cocoa-growing northward to the forest edge and westward to the frontier was controlled by road building and the subsequent development of road-transport. In the 1950s further expansion was made possible in Brong-Ahafo by feeder-roads, financed by the Cocoa Marketing Board.

North of the Forest, in an area of Guinea Savana denied by climate the possibility of valuable tree-crops, yams and upland rice have become important sources of cash income. This was made possible by the opening of the road from Atebubu, on the trunk road northward from Kumasi, eastward to Kete Krachi, and the provision of a feeder system of lorry tracks. These put the area into contact with the towns of the Forest and Coast with their growing demand for food.

In Northern Nigeria the development of the groundnut

Q

industry has a similar basis. Cash cropping was first intro-duced into the Kano area after the railway was opened in 1911, when cotton and not groundnuts was expected to be the chief traffic. Later groundnut cultivation spread along the line to Nguru (1930) and that from Zaria to Gusau (1929). The area of cultivation was further extended by the building of roads outward from the various railheads. Many were quite short, but others were important trunk roads, such as that from Gusau to Sokoto and that from Kano to Daura, which also allowed groundnuts to be exported from Niger. But, although Bornu had a suitable climate, developments there had to wait until the 1950s with the completion of the tarred trunk road from Bukuru railhead to Maiduguri, 383 miles (616 kilometres).

A similar story can be traced in Sénégal, where groundnut development followed the lines of communication.[2] For Côte d'Ivoire Tricart[3] has traced in detail the consequentials of transport development on the main areas of cash cropping.

In Chapter 6 we have already traced something of the close connection between the exploitation of mineral deposits and the provision of adequate transport facilities. Transport is also an important factor in industrialisation. Here, however, it works in both a positive and a negative direction. While the coastal towns are still the main concentrations of purchasing power, in order to provide a sufficient basis to establish manufacturing industry, especially of consumer goods, it is necessary to extend the market as widely as possible over the whole of a particular country. On the negative side, transport costs on imported goods may provide a natural protection which may allow industrial development in a high-cost area. This applies particularly to the inland areas of the Sudan. To manufacture cement at Sokoto in Northern Nigeria may be more costly than at Ewekoro in the south-west. But the venture would be economic if the cost of Sokoto cement in the North is less than that of Ewekoro cement *plus* the cost of the 600 mile rail haul.

So far we have considered only the physical provision of a mode of transport as an instrument in economic development. The cost of using it is also of fundamental importance. We have seen (Chapter 1) that inland areas suffer a double cost-disadvantage over the Coast, net income from exports being reduced and the cost of imports being raised, by the extra transport charges. The mere provision of transport is not enough if costs are still too high to encourage movement of produce and goods. The provision of facilities for the evacuation of cotton from the Inland Delta of the Niger to the port of Dakar was not enough to ensure the growth of cotton cultivation. On the contrary, growth was inhibited by the high transport charges.[4]

Transport costs can be minimised and the spread of facilities encouraged in proportion to the flexibility of the system. There are several ways of looking at this factor. In the first place, the capital requirements of a means of transport should be flexible to permit their adjustment to the growing intensity of the traffic flow. Ideally, in the pioneering stage, when traffic is small, investment should be kept to a minimum. As traffic builds up, investment should be increased in direct proportion, the aim being to convey the increased traffic at the lowest possible unit cost, the investment reducing operating costs, but at the same time not incurring excessive interest and redemption charges.

In this respect a road system is by far the most flexible of all transport modes. At the pioneering stage minimum investment is needed for clearing a trace, for a few culverts and for little else. As traffic builds up a gravel surface can be provided and later a 'tarmet'[5] one, while bridges replace fords and ferries. Thus the original track is converted into a first class trunk road, and in turn this will be provided with a constant addition of second class branch roads and pioneer feeder tracks. Unfortunately, in practice, road improvements tend to lag behind traffic increases. This leads to unnecessarily high unit costs by checking the use of larger lorries and by increasing vehicle maintenance costs and decreasing vehicle life.

Conversely, a railway requires a heavy initial investment, however limited the traffic expected. As traffic increases it is not only costly to increase capacity to match, but particularly expensive to undo the initial short-cuts taken to reduce investment. Thus extensive re-location of the line between Lagos and Abeokuta (opened 1901) became necessary in the 1920s to reduce curvature, while Sierra Leone became burdened with a loss-making line of impossibly narrow-guage (75 cms.) that the country could never afford to widen.

Flexibility also gives the ability to pioneer areas hitherto beyond the reach of transport, and to cope with rapid changes in direction and volume of traffic, all at the lowest possible cost. In these respects road transport is the most flexible medium anywhere. In West Africa the manner in which it is organised provides an exceptionally close adjustment to the economy and the society and at the same time provides a very low cost medium for all but the heaviest volumes and the longest distances.

ROAD TRANSPORT & ITS ORGANISATION[6]

The road net is related to three variables, the levels of economic development, of population density and of vehicle ownership. It is thus most closely meshed in those parts of the Forest which are most highly developed, in the cocoa belts of Ghana and of Western Nigeria and in south-eastern Côte d'Ivoire. It is also closely meshed in the coastal regions of Sénégal. In all these areas the economic and social development is highest, population densities well above average and vehicle numbers greatest. An apparent exception is Iboland. Here population is very dense and development is advanced, but resources are limited. The road net is moderately well developed, but vehicle numbers are low in comparison with the other areas and much reliance is placed on bicycle transport.

Road patterns are also the result of other factors. Trunk roads are provided as links between areas of high or moderate road densities across regions otherwise roadless. In contrast, the lack of bridging points over major rivers has a constricting effect. It is impossible to reach Northern Nigeria from the south without crossing either the Niger or the Benue, but in 1970 there are only three bridge points along the 1,000 miles (1,600 kilometres). International and even provincial frontiers have the same effect. There are only three motorable roads across the Nigeria-Dahomey frontier, and less than 12 across all the frontiers of Ghana. Even within Ghana, there are only four road links southward from Ashanti and Brong-Ahafo to the coastal provinces.

Most trunk roads now have a tarmet surface, though foundations may leave much to be desired. Even a bitumen strip, however, is most important, for gravel roads become badly corrugated under even moderately heavy traffic and the consequent vibration severely reduces vehicle life. The secondary roads are much more rarely tarmetted but are normally provided with a gravel surface, of varying quality according to the material available and with culverts and bridges. They are usually passable except after very bad rain. It is important that at least some main roads in an area should be all-weather ones. Closure for any length of time during the rainy season not only interrupts the economic life of the community, but increases transport costs by reducing the productivity of the lorry fleet. Finally, there is a very large mileage of unsurfaced tracks, passable only in dry weather, but fulfilling a vital pioneering role. Characteristically, the trunk roads of the francophone countries in relation to traffic density are of a higher standard, while the secondary systems tend to be best in those countries formerly British colonies.

To minimise bridging costs roads are often aligned along watersheds, while bridges over small streams are frequently single-tracked, incidentally forming accident black-spots. Over larger rivers railway bridges have been decked to allow passage for road vehicles, a practice common in Dahomey and Togo. In Nigeria dual-purpose bridges at Jebba and Makurdi provide two of the three crossings of the Niger-Benue into Northern Nigeria, the third being the top of the Kainji Dam. Elsewhere, with growing traffic volumes, ferries form intolerable bottlenecks and have led to the building of large and spectacular bridges across the Volta at Adidome and at Segankope and across the Niger at Malanville and Asaba/Onitsha.

The road net is constantly being improved and extended by new trunk roads and the upgrading of existing ones, by the building of secondary roads and the addition of large but unrecorded mileages of motorable tracks. Even so, large areas remain devoid of roads, in the remaining areas of High Forest, in parts of the Middle Belt, and in the Sahel generally.

Finance is provided from a wide variety of sources. Funds for the building and upkeep of trunk roads are the responsibility of central governments, normally from their own resources, but occasionally foreign aid funds are earmarked for road building, such as the F.I.D.E.S. (*Fond d'investments pour développement économique et sociale*) grants for the improvement of the road from Cotonou to Bohican in Dahomey. The secondary system is the responsibility of Provincial and Local Authorities. Marketing Boards have provided funds for 'feeder'[7] roads, while roads have been built by timber and mining companies and by civil engineers to enable them to reach construction sites. Individual villages also provide themselves with a link to the nearest main road on a self-help basis. It is policy in all countries to finance roads from general taxation sources and to keep licenses and fuel duty as low as possible in order to minimise transport costs.

Investment in lorries is one of the rather limited range of outlets for personal savings, and, like retail trade, road transport has always been principally the concern of Africans. Vehicles are also frequently bought on hire purchase from large importing firms. There is widespread defaulting on repayments, for the short average vehicle life due to poor roads is further shortened by a high accident rate and bad maintenance. It has, however, been shown that in some countries such as Côte d'Ivoire, since the vendors are generally importers, bad risks can be compensated for by having their goods transported at very low rates by the purchasers.[8]

For the most part lorries are owned and operated singly or in very small fleets and are driven and maintained by the owner and relatives. There are, however, regional differences in lorry types and organisation. In the former British colonies an unspecialised vehicle emerged at an early date. On an imported chasis in the three- and seven-ton range a home-built wooden body with a roof is provided, the exact form varying from country to country. Planks for passengers are placed as required across the vehicle. In this way the lorry can be speedily adapted to carry freight and passengers in any desired proportion. Each vehicle is given individuality, partly to allow its regular patrons a means of identification, by slogans in English or vernacular, ranging from the sacred, 'Save us,

O Lord' through home-spun wisdom, 'Sea never run dry' to the profane, 'Beautiful woman never stay with one man, why?'

This type of vehicle, affectionately dubbed a 'mammy-lorry', combines maximum flexibility with miminum cost, which more than outweighs lack of comfort and the dangers of a high accident rate. Their use, partly through Ghanaian enterprise, has spread to the coastal areas of neighbouring francophone countries. Hay[9] distinguishes between the 'mammy-wagon' and 'topping-up' systems according to whether passengers are the major or subsidiary source of revenue.

Throughout the francophone Sudan and Middle Belt and in Northern Nigeria, an open lorry is the rule, often with a locally made body, the few passengers riding atop the tarpaulin-covered load. But always the owner-driver or the operator is willing to go anywhere there is a motorable track and the chance of a load. As an instrument of social and economic development the importance of the lorry cannot be over-estimated and, in relation to traffic volume and poor roads, provides the most efficient service at the lowest cost.

Intense competition keeps rates and fares at very low real levels. Profit margins are probably very limited, and besides economical methods of operation, there are virtually no overheads. Costs are further reduced by undoubtedly wide-spread malpractices such as overloading and skimped mainten-ance. In 1962 the mammy-lorry fare from Ibadan to Lagos, 80 miles (129 kilometres), was 45 cents. Passenger fares tend to be maintained at a recognised level. They are frequently published at the lorry-park, an inevitable feature of all towns. Goods rates are the results of individual bargaining.

There are theoretical limits imposed by bridges and road foundations on axle weights and therefore on capacities of vehicles. But with the development of greatly improved trunk roads, specialised vehicles have emerged. The trend began in the early 1950s with the introduction of petrol-tankers. These soon penetrated to all the large towns, elimina-ting the practice of carrying petrol in 40-gallon drums on ordinary lorries. Then from 1955 onwards came a split between passenger and goods vehicles on the trunk routes.

The capacities of specialised goods-carrying lorries grew rapidly and consequently ton-mile costs were reduced, enabling them to be operated economically over long distances. Thus 20-tonners are used to evacuate groundnuts from Maradi (Niger) to railhead at Parakou (Dahomey), 630 miles (1014 kilometres). In Nigeria, partly related to a series of railway deficiencies in the years after 1964, similar lorries were carrying an increasing proportion of groundnut products all the way to Apapa.

With the spread of heavy lorries, larger haulage firms came into existence, at first European, Levantine or Algerian owned, but later, especially in Northern Nigeria, under West African ownership. Some firms are relatively small family businesses, but others are very large such as Transafricain, which covers most of francophone Sudan and Middle Belt, Tarzan Transport in Ghana and Arab Brothers in Nigeria. Before the Civil War in Nigeria a number of large Ibo-owned firms had also emerged.

Although there are some long-distance high-capacity buses, most specialised passenger vehicles are mini-buses. These first appeared in the early 1950s in the more populous and economically developed coastal regions of the francophone countries, but after 1960 they spread to the main roads of southern Ghana and Nigeria. Taxis, operated more as mini-buses than as individually hired vehicles, are also an important element in inter-urban transport. In all countries private cars are less numerous than other vehicles, for while ownership is universal among professional people, there are few owned by other classes.

The part played by the bicycle must not be overlooked. Pedlars used them to take small consumer goods beyond even the range of lorries. But even where the road system may be reasonable, if population densities are not matched by sufficient economic resources for lorries to proliferate, bicycles become the principal means of transport on feeder routes and for local journeys. Eastern Nigeria, particularly Iboland, is the best example. Here palm products are brought to buying stations on bicycles with large, strengthened carriers, consumer goods and foodstuffs, are distributed, and even passengers are conveyed by 'bicycle-taxi'. In Lower Dahomey,

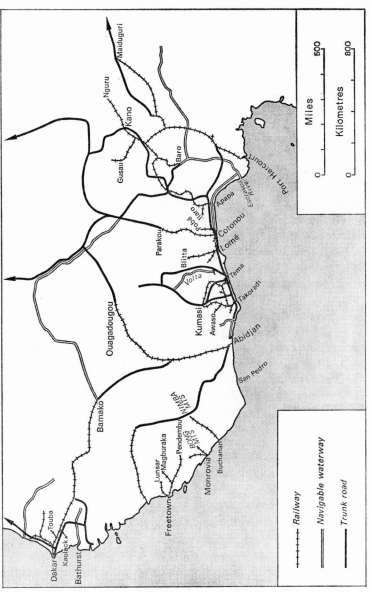

Figure 9.1. Principal transport routes

maize, the chief crop, is transported by cycle, one sack on the carrier, another thrust through the frame. In the Sudan donkeys play a similar role to the bicycle, while draught camels are still to be seen in the Sahel.

RAILWAYS[10]

Road haulage is the basic transport mode throughout West Africa, but in certain circumstances, when traffic flows are exceptionally heavy and where distances are long, rail still offers the lowest-cost means of transport. Since economic growth after 1945 has been rapid and since railway development prior to that date was so limited, there has been a constant expansion of railway facilities, including new construction, in spite of the much greater concurrent expansion of road haulage. Thus there is a contrast with conditions in Western Europe, where economic development on a broad scale pre-dated the motor age. Consequently, to ensure economic development the rail-net became so extended and close-meshed that when motor-transport became securely estabished, contraction of the rail system became inevitable.

With the possible exception of Nigeria, railway systems do not really exist. Instead, individual lines, often without branches, lead inland for varying distances from the major ports. In only two cases does a line cross an international frontier. Construction can be conveniently divided into two periods: (i) 1890–1930, and (ii) after 1950.

In the first period, there were few practicable alternatives to the railway. Lines were therefore built as an aid to general economic development and in the interests of political administration. Animal transport was precluded by trypanosomiasis infection, navigable waterways were lacking, porterage was very costly and motor transport only embryonic. In the British colonies, each government built a railway inland from the principal port and extended it for as far as they felt they could afford the investment. The French, though administering their area as separate colonies, had an overall plan. They were concerned with the establishment of their influence over the whole Sudan. The main axis of communication was the Niger, but its mouth was in Nigeria and it was divided by rapids into a number of separate navigable reaches. Accordingly all French lines were ultimately aimed at the Niger as part of a river-rail route to the sea. Not all ever got near their objective, but even the line from Cotonou, which never got beyond Parakou, 272 miles (441 kilometres) from the Niger, was called the Bénin-Niger.

During the period from 1897 to 1911 seven lines were built, leading inland from as many ports. They were of narrow gauge, metre in the French areas, 3 feet 6 inches (1·07 metres) in Ghana and Nigeria and only 2 feet 6 inches (75 cms.) in Sierra Leone. They were single-tracked, and passing places were few, while capacity was further limited by excessive curvature and gradients to keep down earthworks, and low axle-loads to save on cost of rails and bridges.

The lines were owned and operated by the Colonial administrations, because of the difficulty of attracting private capital and the need to sustain a working loss in the interest of the overall economic and social welfare. With the establishment of the Federation of French West Africa, the *Réseaux* were brought under a single administration at Dakar. With independence the lines were taken over by the countries through which they ran. The railways were constantly pushed further into the interior and branches were built to develop mines and areas of cash cropping. After 1930, however, construction virtually ceased because of the growth of road transport and the economic depression.

By 1950 the immediate effects of the war had been overcome and since then a considerable mileage of new construction has been added, where for various reasons traffic flow, actual or potential, was considered sufficient justification. Most spectacular has been the 397 mile (639 kilometre) Bornu Extension of the Nigerian Railway Corporation. Opened throughout in 1964, it was financed by the World Bank.[11] The object was to facilitate the evacuation of groundnuts from Bornu and Bauchi provinces, climatically suited to their cultivation, but remote. Figure 9.2, however, shows that the potential traffic along the new railway is very much below that available along the Zaria-Nguru line. It remains to be seen by how much crop production will expand in the future, but meanwhile traffic is far below the economic minimum to justify the investment in the line. Nor is there a basic mineral traffic and the line is something of a speculation.

In Ghana new lines have been built to link Accra with Takoradi *via* the pre-existing Central Province line and with the new port of Tema. In Liberia three railways totalling 307 miles (494 kilometres) have been built to serve the four iron mines (Figure 9.1) and in Togo a short 16 mile (25 kilometre) line serves the phosphate field. In Haute Volta the line from Abidjan was extended to Ouagadougou.

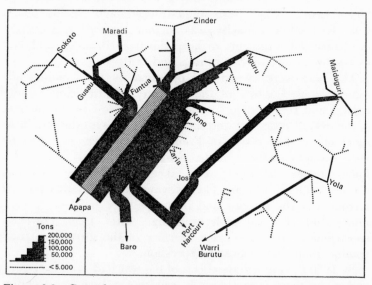

Figure 9.2. Groundnut evacuation routes in northern Nigeria, showing tonnage moved during the 1957/58 season (including groundnuts originating in Niger). *Note:* The striped band represents tonnage of groundnut products, oil and cake, moved after processing

In addition, capacity of the existing lines has been continually increased. The lines from Dakar to Thiès and from Takoradi to Nsuta have been doubled. Elsewhere new crossing-stations have been put in to break up long sections of single track, and existing passing places extended to accommodate longer trains. New and higher capacity wagons have been provided and almost everywhere steam locomotives have been replaced by diesels. These use oil instead of poor-quality Nigerian or expensive imported coal and avoid the costly provision of boiler water as well as leading to higher productivity of rolling stock through reduced journey times. In Nigeria about 10 minutes in the hour were employed in taking water and cleaning fires. In 1956 the steam-hauled express passenger train, the 'Kano Limited', was timed over the 700 miles (1,123 kilometres) from Lagos to Kano in 37 hours 10 minutes. By 1966, diesel-hauled throughout, its time had been reduced to 30 hours 30 minutes, a saving of 20 per cent. In 1956 a typical freight timing, that of No. 8 Up Through Goods from Kano to Lagos took 49 hours 50 minutes; ten years later No. 102 GX was timed at 38 hours 24 minutes.

During the period from 1945 to 1965 traffic, particularly freight, grew steadily. In Nigeria by far the largest income is from freight, but on most of the other systems passengers account for a greater proportion of the gross revenue. Traffic increases have also been accompanied by increased costs and some administrations are faced with deficits their countries can ill-afford. Many of these cost-increases, particularly in wages, are inevitable, but some administrations are not as efficient as they might be and there is much room for improving productivity of labour and of rolling-stock. Many systems are overstaffed. To quote one example, in Ghana train crews were Africanised during World War I, but European drivers were kept on much later in Nigeria (the last retired in 1954). Ever since, conditions of service have been related more to European drivers of steam locomotives when health was hazardous than to the operation of diesel locomotives by Nigerian drivers. In only a few cases is the deficit caused by lack of traffic and a high level of road competition.

The policies adopted by Governments to protect their railway investments from excessive road competition have varied. In the early days most of them gave priority to feeder roads. The construction of the Central Province line in Ghana, opened in 1927, was accompanied by the provision of a whole system of feeder roads. Ironically, these were connected to the coastal trunk road and soon diverted traffic from the railway to the small surf ports or even all the way to Takoradi. Feeder roads for groundnut evacuation were also provided to the stations along the Kano-Nguru line. In

Dahomey and Togo good roads, constantly upgraded, were provided northwards from their respective termini at Parakou and Blitta.

On the other hand roads parallel to the railways were given low priority and gaps were deliberately left in the trunk road system. In 1937 it was possible to drive from Kumasi to either Accra or Takoradi only via Prasu and Cape Coast. The Accra gap was closed a year later, but the route toTakoradi was not completed until after 1950. The trunk road southward from Kaduna was not opened until 1958, and even in 1962 the roads southward from Parakou and Blitta were execrable.

As soon after 1945 as it became possible to import motor vehicles and fuel freely, road transport increased phenomenally. Governments placed as few obstacles in the way of expansion as possible, for economic and social development depended on low cost and ubiquitous transport. In addition, the limited capacity of the Nigerian railway, and to some extent those of the other fastest growing countries, Sénégal, Côte d'Ivoire and Ghana, was overtaxed. In the 1950s this capacity was expanded and all railways began to feel the consequences of competition for general freight haulage and to a lesser extent for passengers. In Nigeria, Côte d'Ivoire and Sénégal, however, no attempt was made to limit road competition and considerable investment was made in trunk roads, which paralleled the railways. In Nigeria the large road transport firm of Arab Brothers was bought by the Northern Region Government in 1960 and operated in direct competition with the Federally owned railway. Conversely, soon after Independence, the Ghana Government took steps to protect its railway by preventing road haulage of cocoa and timber on parallel trunk roads, though with timber this was also to reduce damage to the road surfaces.

Meanwhile, however, investment in railways was everywhere continuing. It was not until the World Bank report of 1968 on Sierra Leone that there was any suggestion of eliminating railways. Even then Sierra Leone was a special case, the exceptionally narrow gauge causing particular difficulties, and here the railway is being phased out.

Traffic potential is obviously related to density of population and to the general level of economic development, especially to the availability of crop surpluses and raw materials, and to the level of consumption of such bulk items as petroleum, cement and steel. Most traffic is thus to be derived either from the Forest Zone or, though to a lesser extent, from the population 'islands' of the Sudan. The trouble is that in the Forest hauls are short and road competition particularly severe. The Middle Belt, however, is on the whole a traffic desert and if a line is to be extended beyond the Forest, unless there is a basic mineral traffic, there is no real justification unless it is extended to a populous part of the Sudan.

The Ghana railway has been among the most prosperous because, in spite of numerous proposals, it has never been extended beyond Kumasi, and has received a measure of protection on short hauls. The Northern Savana of Ghana contributes less than one per cent. to the value of exports. The principal source of revenue to the Nigerian Railway Corporation is the carriage of groundnuts and products from Northern Nigeria to the ports. The diagram (Figure 9.3) shows the nature of the traffic desert between Kaduna Junction and Ilorin, where the western line traverses the Middle Belt. In contrast with Ghana, however, very little traffic originates in the Forest Zone from Ibadan and stations to the south. This reflects very intensive road competition, exacerbated by the fact that for many years, through shortage of capacity, short-haul traffic was deliberately refused to enable the system to cater for long-distance traffic.

The diagram shows also how little traffic originates from Bobo Dioulasso on the Côte d'Ivoire–Haute Volta line. The extension to Ouagadougou, centre of the Mossi population 'island', brought a considerable increase in traffic and some justification for building beyond Bouaké. There is very little freight traffic on the Togo railway, as Blitta is in the Middle Belt and the road northward does not tap a populous part of the Sudan. Traffic to and from the more distant stations of the Guinée railway is also very limited. Conversely, the Sénégal–Mali railway, reaching the navigable Middle Niger at Bamako, has more of the characteristics of the Nigerian railway system, although it has suffered from political troubles (see page 253).

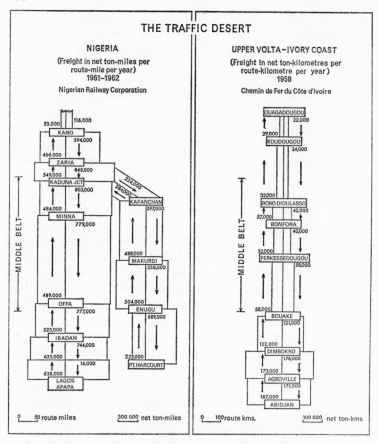

Figure 9.3. The 'Traffic Desert' of the Middle Belt

The diagram shows lack of originating traffic from the Middle Belt (Guinea, Savana, Woodland zone), in Nigeria and Côte d'Ivoire.

RIVER TRAFFIC

Only a few stretches of the major rivers are navigable by high-capacity power-craft. For the most part rivers are short and shallow and volumes vary very greatly seasonally, while not all of them tap productive regions. The Niger below Baro and the Benue up to Garoua in Cameroun have the largest volume of traffic, carried by three fleets operated by expatriate companies. But for reasons explained later (pages

251-3) traffic remains stationary in an expanding economy. While from time to time proposals are made to improve navigation,[12] the difficulty remains that these waterways serve only the unproductive Middle Belt. In the same way it was hoped that the creation of Lake Volta would lead to the development of inland navigation, but the lake shores are nowhere near the cocoa belt or the principal mineral deposits of Ghana.

For the rest, there are launch services on the Middle Niger, the lower Sénégal and the lagoons and creeks between Lagos and the Niger Delta, but the volume of goods and passengers carried is small. The Gambia river, however, remains the principal transport artery of its country. The groundnut crop, the basis of the economy, is wholly moved by river-steamers and small sea-going vessels.

The other aspect of river traffic is provided by canoes and other small craft. Their use is widespread on all rivers and lagoons. They are of considerable importance to local circulation, and communities such as those of the Niger Delta and the Rivières du Sud are entirely dependent on them. The movement of staple foods, vegetables and fruit to Freetown from villages around the Sierra Leone River is mainly by the 'Bullom Boats', modelled on early nineteenth-century ships' boats and powered by sail. Everywhere outboard engines are becoming more popular. Unfortunately, few studies of small craft traffic and circulation exist and we have no quantitative information.

PORTS[13]

Because communications across the landward limits of West Africa are either lacking or are poor and costly, and because international trade within West African remains comparatively small in volume, port development is of vital concern to all West African countries, even those which are landlocked. Port capacity is therefore a limiting factor in development. Saturation of facilities at Takoradi was considered the cause of the severe inflation experienced in Ghana between 1950 and 1952. It was just not possible to import enough goods to absorb the money created by very high cocoa prices. At

R

Abidjan throughout the 1950s increases in port capacity were constantly overtaken by increased trade so that congestion remained a serious problem. Finally, it was said of Cotonou that *'le wharf est devenue un véritable goulot d'étranglement pour les économies du Dahomey et du Niger'*[14] Costs of port operation, and especially congestion costs, must be considered in the total costs of exports to very competitive markets. Capital investment in port facilities also looms very large in overall investment in infrastructure.

The nature of the coastline as outlined on pages 32–33 is such that it operates more as a barrier than as a zone of contact between land and sea. There are only two good natural harbours along the whole 2,400 miles of coast (3,860 kilometres), Dakar Roads and the Sierra Leone River. Elsewhere there are few opportunities of penetrating dune or estuarine bar, while the lagoons are generally shallow. Unless protection can be given from the swell, therefore, ships cannot tie up to a quay to work their cargoes, but must lie offshore and transfer them to small boats. But because of the natural obstacles, the provision of artificial harbours is the more costly in relation to the traffic potential. On the credit side, however, dangerous storms are very rare and ships may anchor in safety, while tidal range is very limited and vessels can berth at any time without the aid of wet-docks.

Prior to railway building after 1900, land communications were primitive and costly. In 1898 it took 1,400 carriers at a cost of $1,950 to move some 30 tons of rubber from Kumasi to Cape Coast. The need was for numerous small ports, each with a very limited hinterland and volume of trade. Investment in facilities was therefore minimal. There were 20 such ports listed as open along the 330 miles (530 kms.) of the Ghana coastline.

Port development depended on differential expansion of hinterlands through the development of land transport. This favoured some ports at the expense of others. Any port near a navigable river would thus gain competitive advantage. During the 1890s the mail boats called at Axim in preference to any other port in western Ghana as it was near the mouth of the navigable Ankobra leading towards the goldfield, while the Delta ports handled most of the Nigerian traffic.

After 1900 the ports selected as railway terminals experienced such an increased volume of trade that they attracted increased investment. It was these ports therefore which later became the foci of local and trunk road systems during the 1920s and 1930s. Thus their competitive superiority became ever more marked.

The expanding trade was thus concentrated on progressively fewer ports, and this has been reinforced by the increased costs of ship-operation and consequently of keeping ships idle in port. It is now the object of shipowners to reduce the number of calls per voyage and the time spent in each port, which in turn creates a demand for greater sophistication in cargo handling. The increased investment to do this must be concentrated where it will achieve the maximum return, on the largest and busiest ports, where the equipment will be most fully utilised. Thus the majority of the West African trade is now concentrated on about a dozen ports. Nowhere is this tendency better seen than in Ghana, where only Tema and Takoradi are open.

Since the early pattern of port development has been dealt with elsewhere,[15] it is sufficient to say that of the major ports we can distinguish several morphological types. The 'Takoradi' type is purely artificial, long moles shelter a stretch of water from the swell and allow ships to lie alongside quays, which may be equipped as general cargo berths or as specialised berths for the export of minerals or timber or the import of petroleum. These ports, found on open and featureless coastlines of the 'Dahomey' and 'Elmina' types, are costly, and justifiable only by increasing traffic and congestion of the older ports. Takoradi, opened in 1928, was the first, and at the time of writing there are six open or under construction, the others being Tema, Cotonou, Lomé, Monrovia and Buchanan. Dakar is not strictly of this type as it lacks the moles, for there is sufficient shelter from the Cap Vert peninsula.

The other ports are variations of an estuarine type. There is natural shelter of sorts, but the main problem is the bar. At Abidjan and Lagos the lagoons are deep and the dunes have been breached. The entrance at Lagos is natural, but Abidjan is reached by the Vridi Canal. Apart from the provision of quays, the main works are to protect the entrances from the longshore drift, which would soon close them up. Freetown, on the Sierra Leone River, has the advantage of being on the Colony Peninsula, which allows access through the fringing mangrove swamps. It is an excellent example of the distinction between harbour and port and of political limitations on the latter. The Sierra Leone River is one of the world's greatest natural harbours with anchorage for 140 vessels of unrestricted draught. Because of the small size of Sierra Leone, Freetown's trade is limited and it has only two berths. Conakry on the Saloum peninsula has a similar site, though not strictly on an estuary. Of the Niger Delta ports, the only large one is Port Harcourt, with adequate road and rail connections to an extensive hinterland. It is approached over the Bonny Bar. The Escravos Bar gives access to a group of four smaller ports in the north-western part and has recently been deepened at a heavy cost (see page 253).

The function of all these ports is the handling of general cargo. The volume and nature of their trade reflects the size and production patterns of their hinterlands, which are also limited by political boundaries. In addition, Dakar functions as a bunkering port in fierce competition with Las Palmas and both its principal import and its principal export is bunker fuel.[16] Dakar's situation puts it in close proximity to the Europe–South Atlantic trade routes, and its port and its commercial airport form a port of call unique in West Africa. Freetown has attempted to develop a bunker trade, but for ships in the West Africa trade. These call at Freetown southbound to take on Kru men as extra crew for cargo handling and painting, paying them off northbound.

Of recent years there has been some development of specialised ports. The first was the pier at Pepel, $15\frac{1}{2}$ miles (25 kilometres) upstream from Freetown, which was developed during the 1930s as the terminus of the 52 mile (83·5 kilometre) railway from the Marampa iron mine. Now Buchanan in Liberia is being developed as a specialised iron ore port. At Kpémé, 22 miles (35 kilometres) east of Lomé, a pier was opened in 1961 for dealing with phosphate exports, which have now reached a million tons a year. In the Niger Delta several petroleum ports have been developed. The hulks of old tankers have been moored off the Escravos, Brass and Pennington rivers. But the largest oil port is Bonny, with six moorings connected to tank farms.

The typical vessel engaged in the West Africa trade is a modern cargo-liner of 7,000 to 10,000 tons deadweight, with refrigerated chambers and tanks for vegetable oils. They operate between Europe and North America and the West African ports between Dakar and Pointe Noire, discharging at numerous ports southbound and loading again on their northbound leg. Tramping, except in connection with cargoes of minerals and coal, is rare. Specialised vessels, tankers, and ore carriers, are being employed in increasing numbers. Nigeria and Ghana have built up their own national lines, but otherwise the liner trade is mainly in the hands of British, French, German, Dutch and Scandinavian owners. The trade is mainly inter-continental. Coasting is not well developed, the principal movement being petroleum and coal from Bonny and Port Harcourt to Lagos and other ports.

THE AIR[17]

The contribution, both actual and potential, of air transport to overcoming the essential isolation of West Africa is considerable. Immediately prior to the last war the British and the French each developed an air route to their West African colonies along the Atlantic coast. The war, bringing with it the need to supply the Middle East after the closure of the Mediterranean, led to the building of a number of major airfields, including Robertsfield (Liberia), Accra and Kano, which have maintained their importance. As Dakar and Abidjan were under Vichy control for most of the critical period, their airports, now of equal importance, did not develop until after the war. At the same time great advances were made in meteorological knowledge. After 1945 therefore aircraft were routed across the Sahara to the airports of the Guinea Coast, refuelling in North Africa until their flying range increased.

During the 1950s there was a rapid build-up of traffic, and routes were pioneered to USA via Lisbon and to Beirut (an indication of the number of Lebanese traders in West Africa). After Independence these external links multiplied, especially, though often temporarily, with Communist countries. The build-up of cargo traffic has been slower, as high value imports are limited and high value exports are lacking. Not only has new traffic been created, but passengers by sea have been diverted. The decline of passengers by sea has been accelerated by the fact that prior to Independence the Colonial Services did not count time at sea against the leave entitlement of their officers who thus created a heavy demand. By 1968 two of the three mail-boats operating between Liverpool and West Africa had been withdrawn and not replaced.

Sheer distance and poor surface transport means a considerable potential for internal air services. But in some ways operating policies have prevented this potential being realised.

Up to 1954 West African Airways were operating internal services in Nigeria and Ghana and between Lagos and Accra with Bristol Freighters, simply equipped and with high capacity seating. Fares were low, less than first class rail, while the single fare from Lagos to Accra was less than $12. These 'flying mammy wagons' were undoubtedly encouraging air travel among ordinary people. But in that year the fleet was grounded after a flying accident and was replaced by 15 seater Herons, the Lagos–Accra fare jumping to $36. Internal fares have remained high and in 1967 the return fare from Lagos to Kaduna was $103·5 (though cheaper night flights were introduced that year). Popular travel has declined and the principal users are government officers and businessmen on expense accounts.

A similar situation pertains in the francophone countries. It is also accounted for by the reluctance of governments to license aircraft of private operators wishing to pioneer new routes. State airlines are not perhaps the best pioneering instrument. During the 1960s, however, the Nigerian Government began to allow private firms to operate small aircraft on pioneer routes, especially in the north, and to start a taxi service. Privately owned aircraft, however, are rare, a notable exception being one in Sierra Leone maintained for the transport of diamonds. Another difficulty is that while light aircraft are very simple, modern aircraft of higher capacity are by and large over-sophisticated for a pioneering situation.

The most important route, with the highest traffic levels, is the international one along the coast from Lagos to Dakar. Otherwise most routes connect the coast with the more important centres of the Sudan. Obviously, the best developed system of internal routes is in Nigeria, where the largest towns are connected with Lagos and to a much less extent with one another.

In Colonial times the francophone countries were served internally and externally by Air France and U.A.T. External services from Ghana and Nigeria were provided by B.O.A.C., though they had not a complete monopoly. Internal services and an inter-colonial coastal route were provided by West African Airways, jointly owned by the four British colonies. After Independence those francophone countries which remained 'western' formed Airafrique to operate both internal and external services. On the other hand West African Airways was broken up and replaced by national air lines. During the Nkrumah regime Ghana Airways was greatly over-extended as a prestige symbol and contributed to the country's decline to bankruptcy. The progress of Nigeria Airways was much more realistic. Even so, in 1968 moves were being made towards the re-establishment of an international consortium by the anglophone countries.

CASE STUDIES

It is obvious that only a brief and generalised outline of West African transport can be given. In addition there are some factors which are important, but which have received only passing mention. These include the policies of governments, a number of which have sought for political reasons to divert traffic from lower to higher cost routes, attempts to integrate the various modes of transport, and the development of inter-modal routes. To illustrate these and also some of the generalisations made previously, the chapter concludes with some case studies of particular situations.

1. THE PROBLEM OF THE NIGER AND THE DELTA PORTS.[18] The railway from Apapa to Kano has a dual historical origin, reflecting Nigeria's political development. The first was the Lagos Government Railway, opened between Lagos and

Ibadan in 1901 and gradually extended to the Niger at Jebba (303 miles (488 kilometres) from Lagos) by 1909. The second was derived from the combined river-rail route developed by Lord Lugard between the Delta ports of Forcados and Burutu and the Northern Protectorate. The railway portion (348 miles (570 kilometres)) was from the river port of Baro to Kano and was opened in 1911. The next year the two railways were amalgamated and connected by a 160 mile (257 kilometre) extension from Jebba to reach the northern line at Minna, a reflection of the new unity of Nigeria. The 111 mile (179 kilometres) line to Baro thus sank to branch status.

After the improvements to Lagos the original Delta ports declined and many were closed, leaving only the group in the north-western part with any significant traffic. Of these Sapele and Warri were the outlets for the limited exports of the Mid-West, but this trade has always been small and only in 1967 was the inefficient ferry leading to them replaced by bridges. Burutu still has no road access. The group thus depends on river-borne traffic. But apart from the important trading centre of Onitsha, neither the Niger nor the Benue directly serves any important area of production or dense population. Contact with the Kano region is possible only through Baro.

The branch from Minna to Baro has never been improved, its capacity is limited to one or two trains a day each way, the road is very poor and cannot accommodate heavy lorries, and port facilities are primitive. As an alternative route from the North, this exists on the map rather than in reality. Nor is it in the interests of the Railway Corporation to develop the route. Freight originates south of Minna only in small quantities and traffic diverted onto the branch at Minna would leave the main line with spare capacity. Accordingly Kano–Apapa rates have a pronounced taper. In 1966 the rate for groundnuts for the 1,123 kilometres to Apapa was $21·7 per ton (1·93 cents per ton kilometre) as against one of $15·2 for the 570 kilometres to Baro (2·67 cents per ton kilometre). Since the combined rail-river rates cannot exceed those to Apapa, the river operators cannot theoretically charge more than $6·5. While they will accept traffic, they maintain that it is not worth their while to invest further capital. In 1963–64 only 76,337 tons of freight were railed southbound to Baro and 10,876 tons northbound from the port.

This severely affects the Delta ports and casts doubt on the advisability of the $36·4 million Escravos Bar Project, recently completed to increase the depth of water on the Bar, or of related proposals to improve river navigation. The port records reveal that even before the bar was deepened ships were not inconvenienced. It is the authors' view that an equivalent investment in the Apapa route would be more economic.

2. 'OPERATION HIRONDELLE'.[19] Maradi is the main centre of groundnut production in Niger. The nearest port is Apapa, 894 miles, (1,435 kilometres) 194 miles (312 kilometres) by road to Kano and thence 700 miles (1,123 kilometres) by rail. This compares with 939 (1,511 kilometres) miles to Cotonou, 665 miles (1,070 kilometres) by road to Parakou and 272 miles (441 kilometres) thence by rail. During the 1950s the French authorities however, strove to divert as much traffic as possible through Cotonou. Their aims were to make the fullest use of their investment in the port, railway and trunk road, and to reduce the cost of imports to Niger.

This was done by heavy investment by F.I.D.E.S. in the trunk road northward from Parakou and by the launching of 'Operation Hirondelle'. By this, rates on groundnut exports and basic imports such as petroleum and cement were subsidised by the Governments of Dahomey and Niger. Rates were agreed annually with the transporters providing the pool of lorries, while the railway offered special rates. With the break up of the Federation of French West Africa the *Organisation Commune Dahomey-Niger des Transports* (OCDN) was set up in 1959. At first the majority of groundnut exports used this route, but financial difficulties arose in Dahomey after Independence, while even the subsidised rates were higher than those through Nigeria. In 1965–66 118,186 tons of Niger groundnuts passed through Apapa against 27,832 through Cotonou.

3. THE POLITICAL ELEMENT—SÉNÉGAL AND MALI. Prior to Independence the Federation of French West Africa was in most ways organised as a single economic unit. Within the

Federation movement was free and there was an overall policy of investment in inter-territorial routes. One of these was the main and virtually the sole outlet of the landlocked Soudan Française, the railway from the river port and road centre of Bamako to Dakar in Sénégal. The original intention at Independence was that Sénégal and Soudan should form the Federation of Mali. This foundered a year later in 1960 through the different political complexions of the two new states, Sénégal continued to look to France and the West, while Soudan, which took on the name of Mali, tried to sever ties with France and to turn to the Eastern Bloc.

The result of this quarrel was that Mali stopped all traffic over the railway at the frontier, which was closed, and tried to divert all its imports and exports through Côte d'Ivoire, which incidentally remained Western oriented politically. Both Sénégal and Mali suffered badly from this attempt to set up new lines of communications for purely political motives. In the former, much revenue was lost to the railway and the port of Dakar. The latter suffered more. The roads to railhead at Bobo Dioulasso were very poor and needed a considerable investment, while a lorry fleet of 400 had to be ordered and paid for. The new route speedily proved more costly than the old.

Soon the frontier was unofficially open again. No through trains ran, but passengers walked across the border from one to another. This was not possible for bulk freight, and in 1963 through services were restored. Côte d'Ivoire, however, by offering special rates has endeavoured to retain some of the Mali traffic, and probably about 25 per cent. still passes through Bobo Dioulasso.

4. LOCAL CIRCULATION PATTERNS. A number of studies, already referred to, has been made of transport systems on a national scale. Fewer quantitative studies exist of local feeder flows, among them that of Hay in Nigeria. Gould worked in Ghana in 1958 and has built up a picture of commodity flow over the whole country.[20] His study includes local patterns at Bawku and Dormaa-Ahenkro.

Bawku is the market centre for Kusasi in north-east Ghana. This is the southerly edge of the Sudan and has a dense population dispersed in scattered compounds and mainly engaged in subsistence agriculture. The staple foods are guinea corn and millet, but rice and groundnuts are raised for cash. The rhythm of life is geared to the three-day market cycle. That at Bawku is held every third day and is linked with neighbouring Pusiga and Widana, not only by roads but in people's minds, as the three markets are held on successive days. They are all connected by moderately good roads to the south.

On one Bawku market day Gould found that 66·25 tons of local produce came in, 81 per cent. headloaded, 11 per cent. by lorry, 5 per cent. by bicycle and 3 per cent. by donkey, 88 per cent. originating within four miles (6·4 kilometres). It came in along ten routes converging on the town, four gravel roads and six footpaths. The lorry movement was on the roads from the east and south-west, while half the donkeys came in from Haute Volta bringing cloth and grain to be exchanged for kola from the south. Rice accounted for 27·9 per cent. of the flow and groundnuts 19·5 per cent. Guinea corn and millet provided 26·5 per cent. mainly for brewing local beer. Firewood accounted for a further 12·6 per cent.

On the second day flows were transferred to other markets and that to Bawku cut to 22·32 tons coming from less than two miles (3·2 kilometres). The traffic was almost solely for local exchange. The third day had a similar pattern but a slight increase in volume.

Dormaa Ahenkro is in the western part of the cocoa belt near the Côte d'Ivoire frontier. It is connected with Kumasi by an excellent road and is the centre of a large number of feeder roads. The people live in small villages surrounded by their food and cocoa farms. The population was increasing fast through immigration and at least eight such villages were established between 1948 and 1958. Cocoa is the principal cash crop, but not only is the area self-supporting in food, there is also a surplus.

The daily flow was much more even than at Bawku, local produce other than cocoa coming in steadily, though nominally there are only three market days a week. Over a four-day sample period 71·69 tons came, 53 per cent. by headloading, 41 per cent. by lorry and 6 per cent. by bicycle. The tributary area was wider than Bawku's, 85 per cent. coming up to 8·5

256 AN ECONOMIC GEOGRAPHY OF WEST AFRICA

miles (13·7 kilometres). Foodstuffs accounted for 69·3 per cent. of local commodities marketed. Plantain and bananas amounted to 23·2 per cent. of the total, cocoyam 18·6 and vegetables 11·0. Of non-foodstuffs palm wine accounted for 10·9 per cent. and firewood 8·3.

The pattern of cocoa movement differed radically from that of foodstuffs. Virtually all the cocoa reaches the buying stations in Dormaa from outlying villages by mammy-wagon and it comes a longer distance. Shipments from nearby settlements are small. They are much larger from villages beyond six miles, and largest of all from the areas planted since 1946. The catchment area is limited to the west by the frontier (though there are considerable illegal movements across it), by the limits of lorry transport to north and south, and to the east by competition from neighbouring buying centres. After grading the cocoa is despatched by the lorry load to railhead at Kumasi.

REFERENCES

1 Dickson, K. B., *A Historical Geography of Ghana*, Cambridge, 1969, Chapter 10

2 Péhaut, Y., *'L'Arachide au Sénégal'*, Cashiers d'Outre Mer, *14*, 1961, pp. 5–25: Pelissier, P., *'L'Arachide au Sénégal'*, Études Sénégalaises, *2*, 1952, pp. 49–80

3 Tricart, J., *'Les Échanges entre la Zone Forestière du Côte d'Ivoire et les Savanes Soudaniennes'*, Cahiers d'Outre Mer, *9*, 1956, pp. 209–238: also his *Étude Géographique des Problèmes de Transports en Côte d'Ivoire*, Paris, 1963

4 Harrison Church, R. J., *Environment and policies in West Africa*, Princeton, 1963

5 'tarmet'—a thin bitumen seal over a gravel road as opposed to 'tarmac' an impacted surface of bitumen-coated road metal.

6 Hogg, V. W. and Roelandts, C. M., *Nigerian Motor Vehicle Traffic*, Nigerian Soc. & Econ. Studies No. 2, London, 1962: Hawkins, E. K., *Road Transport in Nigeria*, London, 1958: Tricart, J., *op cit* 3: Kayser, B. and Tricart, J., *'Rail et route au Sénégal'*, Annales de Geog., *66*, 1957, pp. 328–350

7 'feeder' roads are difficult to define. Normally they are single, relatively short, branches from a trunk road, used only by local traffic, and financed from sources other than the usual Road Authorities, Central or Local

8 Tricart, J., *Étude Géographique des Problèmes de Transport, op cit*. No. 3

9 Hay, A., *'The importance of Passenger Transport in Nigeria'*, Nigerian Journal of Econ. & Soc. Studies, 1969

10 The best historical account is by Harrison Church, R. J., *The Evolution of Railways in French and British West Africa*, Proc. 16th Congress, Int. Geog. Union, Lisbon, 1949. There is no good general account of existing traffic flows and operating methods

11 Emerson, Sir R., *A Project for extending the Nigerian Railway into Bornu Province*, Proc. Inst. Civil Eng., *12*, 1959, pp. 353–366: Barbour, K. M., *A Survey of the Bornu Railway Extension in Nigeria*, Nigerian Geographical Journal, 10, 1967, pp. 11–28

12 Netherlands Engineering Consultants (NEDECO), *River Studies and Recommendations on Improvements of the Niger and Benue*, Amsterdam, 1959

13 White, H. P., *The Ports of West Africa—a morphological study*, Chapter 2 in Hoyle, B. S. and Hilling, D. (Edts.), *Seaports and Development in Tropical Africa*, London, 1970

14 Sharlet, M., *Le Bénin-Niger*, Vie du rail d'Outre Mer, Dec. 1960, pp. 3–8

15 White, H. P., *op cit*, No. 13

16 Nicolas, J. P., *Les Hydrocarbures de Soute à Dakar*, Dakar, Inst. Française d'Afrique Noire, 1960 (mimeo)

17 There is no good account of air transport other than Reichman, S., *Air Transport in Tropical Africa—a geographical approach* (2 vols.), Inst. de Transport Aerien, Paris, 1965 (mimeo)

18 Hogg, V. W., *An Estimate of the Tonnages likely to Move through the West Delta Ports of Nigeria*, Ibadan, Nigerian Inst. of Soc. & Econ. Research, 1961 (mimeo): Economic Associates—*Report on the Ports of Nigeria*, London, 1967 (mimeo)

19 For this and the following section see Hilling, D., *Politics and Transportation—The Problems of West Africa's Land-locked States*, Chapter 14 in Fisher, C. A. (Edt.), Essays in Political Geography, London, 1968

20 Gould, P. R., *Transportation in Ghana*, Evanston, Northwestern University Studies in Geography, No. 5, 1960

CHAPTER 10

Urbanisation

As we have tried to show, West Africa is undergoing rapid transition from a quasi-subsistence and mainly agricultural economy to a cash economy based on commercial agriculture, mining, industry, trade and commerce. This is linked with social change from a village-oriented rural society to a more urbanised one. Thus the focus of the economy is gradually switching from the village to the town. Towns are growing in number and increasing in size, absorbing an increasing proportion of the population and becoming more dominant in the economy. These are accelerating trends as the pace of economic development, particularly of industrialisation, quickens. These trends are commonly described by the term 'urbanisation'.

But the term means different things to different disciplines and a variety of measures is used to indicate levels of urbanisation. Sociologically, urbanisation has been defined as the force in society leading to cultural change and to the spread of behaviour and value patterns classified as 'urban'. Geographically, it is seen, in the narrow sense at least, as the extension of urban land-uses at the expense of others. Demographically, it is defined either as the growth of population in urban areas or, more commonly, as the increasing proportion of urban to total population. There is, thus, a fundamental distinction between the urbanisation of people and of land. The word is also used to depict both a state and a process of change.

There are grave data problems in attempting to assess levels of urbanisation in West Africa, whichever of these definitions is adopted. Sociologists have built up a considerable volume of theory based on studies in the area, but most of these are of only peripheral interest to the economic geographer.

Geographers are hampered by the lack of urban land-use data. Demographic data are more widely available, although uneven both in quality and in time. Many workers therefore use demographically based definitions and this approach will be adopted here.

Each of the meanings of urbanisation and the methods of measuring it depends upon the meaning of 'urban', and in the midst of the confusion from the various meanings of 'urbanisation' there is the related problem of satisfactorily defining 'urban' in the West African context. Unfortunately there is no lower figure generally accepted by West African census authorities for indicating urban status. Many re-searchers and ECA have adopted a figure of 20,000 for this purpose. This is both arbitrary and open to criticism, as some urban Africans, notably the Yoruba, spend long periods in farm settlements. But we have adopted this figure for this preliminary study.

Levels of urbanisation in West Africa are, by world standards, low. In the early 1960s, the latest time for which statistics are widely available, about 10·6 million people of a total population of 85·6 million lived in the 96 towns with over 20,000 inhabitants. Only an estimated 12·4 per cent. of the population was, therefore, urbanised and only in Sénégal does more than 20 per cent. of the population live in towns. Further, only in Sénégal and Nigeria are levels significantly above the average for West Africa (table 10.1). About 6·5 million people live in cities with more than 100,000 inhabitants, the proportion being estimated as 7·6 per cent. Thus 61 per cent. of the urban population in the early 1960s was concentrated in cities of over 100,000 inhabitants, of which there were 31 in West Africa. 23 are located in Nigeria, three in Ghana, one each in Mali, Sierra Leone, Côte d'Ivoire, Sénégal and Guinée. Only Lagos and Ibadan have populations in excess of 500,000, and no other city has a population greater than 400,000 (table 10.2). This table conflicts with that compiled by B. E. Thomas[1] for the same date, particularly with regard to Nigerian cities. This arises mainly from the difference between Thomas' estimates and the results of the 1963 census. Subsequent growth means that certain cities have moved from one size category into another between the early 1960s and the present. Abidjan, for instance, is growing extremely rapidly and had an estimated population in 1968 of 350,000. Urban population is, then, markedly concentrated in a few large cities, which are relatively restricted in their distribution. (Figure 10.4).

TABLE 10.1

PERCENTAGE OF TOTAL POPULATION IN URBAN AREAS
(towns with over 20,000 inhabitants)

Country	Year	Percentage of total population in towns of over 20,000 inhabitants	Population in cities of over 100,000 as percentage of:	
			(i) total population	(ii) population in towns over 20,000 inhabitants
Sénégal	1960–61	22·5	12·6	55·9
Nigeria	1963	14·0	8·7	61·8
Ghana	1960	12·3	9·5	77·7
Gambia	1964	8·9	—	—
Dahomey	1961	8·3	—	—
Liberia	1960	7·9	—	—
Sierra Leone	1962	7·1	5·9	82·3
Côte d'Ivoire	1960	7·0	5·6	79·3
Guinée	1960	6·6	5·7	86·6
Togo	1961	5·9	—	—
Mali	1962	4·7	2·3	70·5
Haute Volta	1960	3·1	—	—
Niger	1963	1·3	—	—
TOTAL WEST AFRICA	1962	12·4	7·6	61·3

Source: Economic Bulletin for Africa, Vol VI, No. 2, July 1966.

The primate city is, therefore, a characteristic of West Africa, even in Nigeria, and table 10.1 indicates the extent of primacy in the area. A primate city is very large compared with other towns and cities in the country. B. J. L. Berry[2] has indicated that primate cities are likely to be characteristic of countries which either are, or were until recently, politically and economically dependent on other countries, or are small countries which once had extensive areas, or are countries where the economies of scale are such as not to require cities of intermediate sizes. It has been claimed that primate cities swallow up investment and absorb manpower at the expense of other areas and places and in doing so restrict the development of other cities, that they dominate the cultural pattern and finally that they tend to have a high consumption rate compared with production rate. This is a problem to which we return.

TABLE 10.2

POPULATION OF MAJOR CITIES CIRCA 1963
(in thousands)

Country	Over 500	400–500	300–400	200–300	100–200
NIGERIA	Lagos		Ogbomosho	Ilorin	Aba
	Ibadan			Kano	Abeokuta
				Oshogbo	Ado
					Benin
					Ede
					Enugu
					Ife
					Ikere
					Ilesha
					Iwo
					Kaduna
					Maiduguri
					Mushin (Gtr. Lagos)
					Onitsha
					Oyo
					Port Harcourt
					Zaria
GHANA			Accra		Kumasi
SÉNÉGAL			Dakar		
MALI					Bamako
GUINÉE					Conakry
SIERRA LEONE					Freetown
CÔTE D'IVOIRE					Abidjan
DAHOMEY					Cotonou

Source: Economic Bulletin for Africa, Vol VI, No. 2, 1966.

Urban expansion has been most rapid since about 1935, and continued throughout the 1939–45 war. The movement of war supplies together with the development of import-substitution industries stimulated and encouraged urban growth in strategically located ports. Currently urbanisation of the population is proceeding rapidly, much more rapidly

S

than growth of total population (Table 10.3). The great variation from country to country in the rate of urbanisation is a notable feature which is difficult to account for satisfactorily. The low rate for Gambia is perhaps not surprising in view of the small size and peculiar shape of the country. But some of the economically weaker states, Mali and Dahomey for example, show the highest rates of urbanisation, whereas the four more developed states show more modest rates, although

TABLE 10.3

RATES OF GROWTH OF URBAN AND TOTAL POPULATION
(annual compound rates in percentage)

Country	Period	Total Population	Towns with over 20,000 inhabitants	Cities with over 10,000 inhabitants
Mali[1]	1955–60	2·4	23·0	—
Sénégal	1955–60	6·0	10·8	15·1
Gambia	1951–64	1·1	3·0	—
Guinée	1958–60	0·5	8·4	—
Sierra Leone	1956–63	0·5	10·4	6·3[2]
Liberia	1956–60	—	18·3	—
Côte d'Ivoire	1955–61	2·3	12·2	6·9
Haute Volta	1955–60	4·7	15·5[3]	—
Ghana	1948–60	4·1	11·5	9·1
Togo	1955–62	5·0	13·1	—
Dahomey	1956–61	4·2	24·4	—
Niger	1955–62	3·6	12·1	—
Nigeria	1952–63	5·8	16·5	13·88

Source: Economic Bulletin for Africa, Vol VI, No. 2, 1966.
Note. 1. African population only.
2. For 1959–63.
3. For 1959–61.

the increases in numbers are greater. In West Africa rates of growth of smaller towns are greater than for the large, except in Sénégal, where towns of over 100,000 inhabitants are growing at a faster rate. In Nigeria the large towns are growing only marginally more slowly than all towns. This suggests an urbanisation pattern of rapid growth of small town in the early stages of economic development, superseded by more rapid growth of fewer large towns. This is a pattern experienced in other parts of the developing world and can be expected to itensify in the next few decades. This geneial picture, however, obscures great variation in the experience of individual towns and cities.

Thus far we have considered urbanisation using a cut-off population of 20,000 as the criterion of urban status. Although

TABLE 10.4

POPULATION GROWTH OF SELECTED PORTS

DAKAR		ABIDJAN		LAGOS		ACCRA	
1891	8,737	1910	723	1856	20,000	1891	16,000
1921	32,400	1929	5,370	1890	86,559	1911	29,000
1931	53,982	1936	24,143	1911	73,766	1921	43,000
1945	123,000	1946	46,000	1921	99,690	1938	60,000
1955	230,887	1956	127,585	1931	126,108	1948	140,000
1961	298,280	1960	180,000	1952	276,407	1960	337,828
1968	c 400,000	1968	c 350,000	1963	665,246	1965	500,000

TABLE 10.5

YORUBA CITIES WITH POPULATIONS OVER 100,000

	1963 Census	1952 Census	1931 Census	1921 Census	1911 Census	1856 Bowen
Lagos	665,246	267,407	126,108	99,690	73,766	20,000
Ibadan	627,379	459,196	387,133	238,094	175,000	70,000
Ogbomosho	319,881	139,535	86,744	84,860	80,000	25,000
Oshogbo	210,384	122,698	49,599	51,418	59,821	—
Ilorin	208,546	41,000	47,412	38,668	36,342	70,000
Mushin	189,755	32,079	—	—	—	—
Abeokuta	187,292	84,451	45,763	28,941	51,255	60,000
Ilesha	165,822	72,029	21,892	—	—	—
Iwo	158,583	100,006	57,191	53,588	60,000	20,000
Ado-Ekiti	157,519	24,646	—	—	—	—
Ede	134,550	44,808	52,392	48,360	26,577	20,000
Ife	130,050	110,790	24,170	22,184	36,231	—
Oyo	112,349	72,133	48,733	40,356	45,438	25,000
Ikere	107,216	35,584	—	—	—	—

Sources: Economic Bulletin for Africa, A. L. Mabogunje, *Yoruba Towns*, Ibadan, 1962, Table 1, p. 1.

widely adopted, this limit is much higher than that used in many West African countries for official purposes. In both Ghana and Nigeria, for instance, the Census definition of a town is a settlement of over 5,000 people whilst for Sierra Leone a figure of 1,000 has recently been used. The universal applicability of the former figure is problematical. E. A.

Boateng[3] has argued convincingly that it is the proper threshold size for Ghana and although it may also be suitable for the Nigerian Middle Belt and much of francophone West Africa, its use in Yorubaland and Iboland would be misleading.[4] It would, however, be useful to consider urbanisation in Ghana using 5,000 inhabitants as the criterion of an urban place, for West Africa is characteristically an area of small towns.

TABLE 10.6

GROWTH OF FOREST ZONE TOWNS

ENUGU		KUMASI		KOFORIDUA	
Date	Population	Date	Population	Date	Population
1921	10,000	1850	12–15,000		
1939	15,000	1874	Destroyed	1921	5,000
1945	35,000	1901	c 3,000	1931	10,500
1952	62,700	1906	c 6,000	1948	25,000
1963	138,000	1911	c 19,000	1961	35,000
		1931	35,829		
		1948	53,829		
		1960	180,600		
		1968	250,000		

TABLE 10.7

GROWTH OF TOWNS IN THE SAVANA

KANO		MAIDUGURI		SOKOTO		KADUNA	
Date	Population	Date	Population	Date	Population	Date	Population
1853	35,000			1886	8,000		
1911	39,368	1911	2,400	1911	21,676		
1921	49,938	1921	16,274	1921	19,335	1921	5,438
1931	89,162	1931	24,359	1931	20,084	1931	10,628
1952	130,173	1952	54,646	1952	47,643	1952	38,794
1963	295,432	1963	139,969	1963	89,817	1963	149,910

On the criterion of 5,000, the percentage of urban population in Ghana in 1960 increases from 12·3 (Table 10.1) to 23·1 of the total. J. M. Hunter[5] has compared the growth of urban, rural and total population in the inter-censal period 1948–1960. Based on the 98 places which qualified as urban in 1960, the urban growth rate was more than double the rural: 116 per cent. compared with 52 per cent., i.e. 6·6 per cent. per year compared with 3·6 per cent. per year. During the inter-censal period the proportion of urban to total population rose from 17 per cent. to 23 per cent. Considering the expansion of those places which qualified as urban in 1948, an alternative way of assessing urbanisation, the proportion of urban to total population, increased during the inter-censal period from 14·1 per cent. to 18·8 per cent. Again urban population so defined increased at more than twice the rural rate: 118 per cent. compared with 54 per cent. Total population increased through the period by 63·3 per cent.

Before considering the distribution and growth of towns and cities it is necessary to distinguish between traditional towns (Chapter 2) and modern towns which have developed during the Colonial Era. This is an important distinction to make because of the implications for growth experience and for the internal arrangement of economic functions within the city. Consequently the structure of the two types is markedly different.

Traditional towns differ in their detailed morphological characteristics among cultural groups. But in spite of this diversity, traditional towns have several features in common which set them apart, morphologically, from their planted European counterparts. Many are or were formerly walled, but considerable areas of cultivated land were usually kept within the walls. One consequence is that the built-up area was congested and, in spite of the impact of the Colonial influence, remains so at the present time. Coastal sites and those on hill-top defensive positions were also restricted and therefore congested. The palace of the ruler commonly occupied a focal point at the centre with the town's main market outside the main gate. Trade routes focused on these and were often broad thoroughfares, but other streets were often only alleyways between high compound walls, and highly irregular in their direction. There was no zoning of land uses, all urban functions being intermingled. The larger towns also had distinctive sections or quarters occupied by people from other communities, who brought with them their techniques of housebuilding and other cultural traits, lending variety to the townscape and town life.

During the Colonial Era those traditional towns that developed with the changing economy changed in two ways.

First, new portions were added which owed much to European ideas of town planning. Low density residential areas were laid out for government officers and for other expatriates. More recently low and medium density residential areas, often laid out on a grid-plan, have been developed for the emerging African middle class, whilst Africanisation of government, commerce and industry has opened the earlier, more spacious 'European' areas to Africans. With the expansion of trade and commerce 'stranger quarters' are more numerous and larger. New urban cells have been added outside the traditional town. In some cases this has led to the development of twin towns such as Yerwa-Maiduguri (traditional-modern).

Secondly, the existing portions were modified, especially in the larger towns most affected by economic changes. New building techniques allowed the building of 'storeyed-houses' and, associated with changes in society, compounds have been broken up into a hotch-potch of single family dwellings; housing densities, already high, have increased by building in the central courtyard; additional roads have been cut through the built-up area; markets have been improved by the concentration of concrete based stalls with corrugated iron roofs and along main thoroughfares houses have been converted into shops. In the smaller towns, away from the main arteries of the new economy, development has expanded the built-up area at low densities along roads leading to the nearby, more economically developed towns. Such development results from the outward movement from the old core of younger, more progressive men, and takes the form of lower density bungalow and storeyed-houses.

The 'planted' towns clearly display European influence in their layout. The grid-plan has been widely adopted not only in new towns, such as Abidjan and Takoradi, but also in those, such as Lokoja, moved from an earlier site. Broad avenues and tree-lined boulevards are common in the larger cities especially of the francophone countries. Land is zoned according to function, industrial areas, commercial areas and residential areas being kept distinct, and in the latter case, separate areas are devoted to high, medium and low quality residences. The administrative, commercial industrial and port cities of the coast owe much to recent

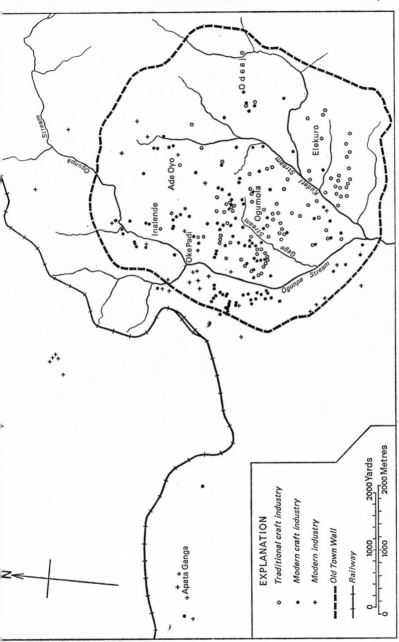

Figure 10.1. The industrial pattern in Ibadan (based on Akinola)

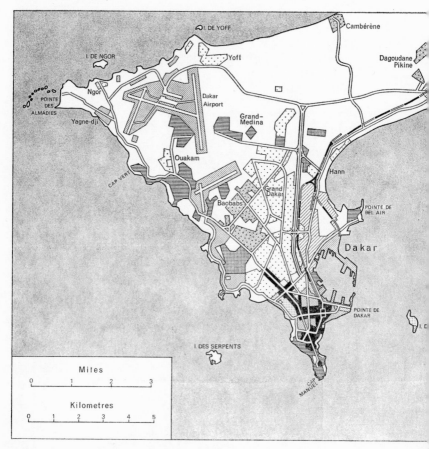

Fi

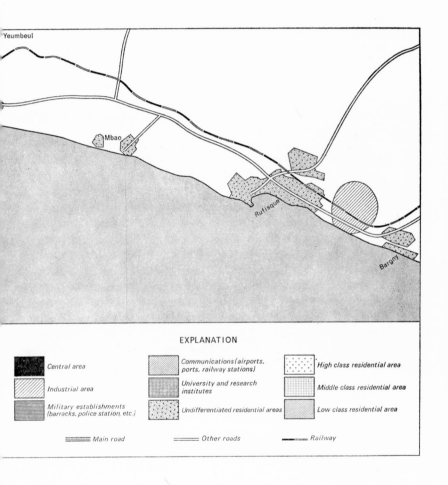

EXPLANATION

Central area

Industrial area

Military establishments
(barracks, police station, etc.)

Communications (airports,
ports, railway stations)

University and research
institutes

Undifferentiated residential areas

High class residential area

Middle class residential area

Low class residential area

Main road   Other roads   Railway

world-wide architectural trends not only in their office and factory buildings but also in some of their residential areas. Less important contrasts result from the colonial heritage, which lends a marked French, British or Portuguese atmosphere. Cities in francophone West Africa have tree-lined boulevards, pavement cafes, French pastry shops and shuttered windows. In anglophone West Africa they have cricket fields, golf courses, and a few have race-courses, whilst the hotels tend to serve morning coffee and afternoon tea.

FACTORS INFLUENCING THE GROWTH OF TOWNS

The colonial socio-economic and political systems imposed upon the traditional ones were constantly evolving, and the growth or decline of an individual town depended upon its ability to adjust to the changing situation. Three sets of factors were significant, administration, transport and mining.[6]

Administration led not only to the growth of traditional but also to the development of modern towns. Because of the hierarchieal structuring of administration in both francophone and anglophone West Africa, many centres assumed an administrative role as centres of the lowest administrative unit; the District, Division or *Subdivision*. Growth potential was greater when the town became the centre of the Province or *Cercle*. But, with the growth of the bureaucracy particularly since Independence, it is the national capitals and in Nigeria, the regional capitals, that benefited most from administration as an urban growth stimulus.

The changing emphasis of transport has led to changes in the importance of towns. Tombouctou, the great early Sudanese metropolis, is now a town of less than 5,000 inhabitants, its trans-Saharan trade having declined with the rise of maritime trade, whilst the area around it, unlike that of its early trading rival, Kano, is too poor in resources to have attracted railways connecting it with the coast. Kano, on the other hand, became the chief railhead for groundnut production, on the favourable soils of what is now the close-settled zone and the city serves as the administrative and commercial centre of this relatively prosperous area. The building of railways also led to the decline of many river ports which were important in the early development of the export trade and resulted in the gradual concentration of export traffic in a few ports. They also led to the creation of new towns to serve junctions and depots, such as Kafanchan and Minna in Nigeria or Kindia in Guinée.

The railways were the main means of developing mining, trade and, through trade, both commercial production and urban growth, until about 1930. After that date road transport began to be important and new towns developed at key points in the evolving road system, whereas older ones remote from roads declined. Many towns which had been invigorated by the railways received an even greater stimulus from road transport. Nsawam in southern Ghana is a good example of a small town which owes its importance as a collecting point in a cash crop area to rail and road transport and has many analogues in West Africa. The ports, considered later, are, as a group, a special case of town influenced by transport and include the largest, most important towns in West Africa.

Mining has tended to bring smaller towns, i.e. with less than 20,000 inhabitants, into being although there are instances such as Jos in Nigeria, Obuasi in Ghana and Bo in Sierra Leone where such towns are larger, because of the influence of other factors. In Jos and Bo administration was important, the latter being the administrative centre of the Protectorate as well as the centre of the diamond mining industry. It can still be said with Harrison Church[7] that in spite of recent considerable progress, no town can yet be described as an industrial town, but industry has been a factor in urban growth of the ports and capital cities, where most of the modern industry is located. The influence of industrialisation is much less marked in the interior towns. The reasons have been discussed in Chapter 7, where it was suggested that this difference in levels of industrialisation between coastal and interior areas and towns is likely to persist.

These factors, considered individually merely for the sake of convenience, operate as a factor complex, in certain cases each reinforcing the others. Thus Kaduna owes its origin and early development to its choice by Lugard as the administrative centre of the northern provinces of Nigeria. As such it became a rail and road centre which, in turn, led to the development of industry. Similarly Kumasi and Ibadan became administrative and later commercial centres for prosperous cash cropping areas because of their local position in the evolving transportation network. Thus rail and road centres, particularly those that are ports, are subject to the influence of each of the factors and accordingly have shown the greatest population increases in recent years. Further they are likely to continue their rapid growth in future years. This functional specialisation leads to areal specialisation and sets off town against country and also town against town. Urbanisation in West Africa is a development spread over a local spectrum from pre-industrial to industrial. In the former, functional and with it areal specialisation has progressed little, whereas in the latter it has made considerable progress. It seems appropriate therefore to treat industry and commerce in towns by case studies of cities at each end of the spectrum.

INDUSTRY IN TOWNS—*Ibadan & Dakar*

Ibadan[8] has representatives of all types of industry—traditional crafts, modern crafts and large and small scale modern industry. The traditional crafts can be divided into the compound-industries, carried on in compounds or other open spaces or on the verandahs of houses, and those, such as pottery, located near raw material sources. They are confined to the older parts of the city and are therefore found entirely within the line of the former walls and display a marked concentration in the southern and western portions (Figure 10.1). The modern crafts are more widely scattered in the area formerly enclosed by walls, and a few establishments are found outside the walls. The distribution of individual crafts varies. Corn-mills grinding maize, beans, dried yam and melon are located near markets. The clothing industry on the other hand is widely scattered. Both these groups are found in the congested area of mixed land uses. Modern industries are mainly market oriented and use electric power to drive machinery. The main factors influencing the siting of these relatively large-scale enterprises is road communications. They, therefore, occupy sites in the newer portions of the city even when within the former walls and have a peripheral distribution pattern. As Ibadan is at the pre-industrial end of the spectrum these large-scale industries are very recent in origin, their impact has not so far been great and functional, areal specialisation within the city is not yet well developed.

In the major cities on the coast, on the other hand, functional specialisation is much further developed and with it areal specialisation within the city. The industries of Dakar are (i) primary processing, (ii) market oriented, using local raw materials, (iii) similar industries using imported raw materials and (iv) industries using imported semi-finished products.[9] They are located in clearly defined zones, the oldest zone being located between the Plateau and Medina and concentrated around two groundnut oil extraction plants (Figure 10.2). This zone is close to the port and within it are industries such as fish canning and processing, flour-milling, ship repairing and heavy engineering geared to the civil engineering industry, groundnut oil plants, a brewery and soft drinks manufacturing. The second zone, an extension of the first, has developed between the railway and the roads to Rufisque and Bel-Air. The industries located in this zone include flour-milling, sugar refining, chemicals and metal fabrication. There is a small outlier of the zone in Grand Dakar in which biscuit making is found. A third zone is found along the Rufisque road between 10 and 13 kilometres from the centre of the city inland of Tiaroye-sur-Mer. Textiles, matches, packaging and metal goods are concentrated here. A fourth zone, close to the road from Rufisque to the interior and to the railway, is found at Bargny and in it there are cement works, textiles and footwear industries. A smaller zone is also developing at M'Bao, where an oil refinery has recently been established. Important factors in the evolution of this industrial pattern have been the port, giving connections with overseas and creating its own demand for certain industries, the railway and latterly roads, giving access to interior raw materials and markets, and the influence of urban planning, which has concentrated factories and workshops in areas set aside for industrial development.

A similar pattern, evolved in similar circumstances, is found in other capital-port cities such as Abidjan and Lagos.

In the latter large-scale modern industries have been grouped in Apapa, close to the port, in Ijora and Iddo, and on the industrial estates at Mushin and Ikeja, but crafts and small scale industries are widely scattered particularly in the older portions of the city (Figure 10.3). This concentration of industry by zoning is a continuing policy. In Abidjan, for instance, large scale industrial development is forbidden outside areas set aside for industry. New industrial areas are selected on the basis of several criteria. These include situation relative to existing areas of development and communications, proximity to residential areas that are planned or in the course of occupation, and availability of sufficient level land both for current needs and for anticipated expansion.[10]

COMMERCE IN TOWNS—*Ibadan & Lagos*[11]

In the traditional cities, i.e. those at the pre-industrial end of the development spectrum, commercial activities are more clearly defined functionally and spatially than are industrial as they are the more important. Thus commercial areas are more readily recognisable. In Ibadan there are twin commercial centres, the Iba market representing the traditional focus, and the Gbagi business district, the focus of modern commercialism. The Iba market, the oldest in the city, is centrally placed within the traditional city. It is a daily market which meets through the day but is busiest in the evening. Almost any type of goods except expensive imported hardware is traded in the market. Lorries bring in goods— foodstuffs, small livestock, craft goods—from a wide hinterland, others take away goods such as kola nuts. This traffic together with pedestrian and vehicular customer traffic makes the market an important focus of intra-city vehicle and pedestrian movements. In addition to the Iba market there are others which serve either as general neighbourhood centres, fulfilling the role of neighbourhood shopping centres in Western cities, or fulfilling specialised functions.

Gbagi is the modern central business district. It post-dates the arrival of the railway from Lagos which was an important factor in its early growth. It is, therefore, located eccentrically to the city centre. European-owned firms

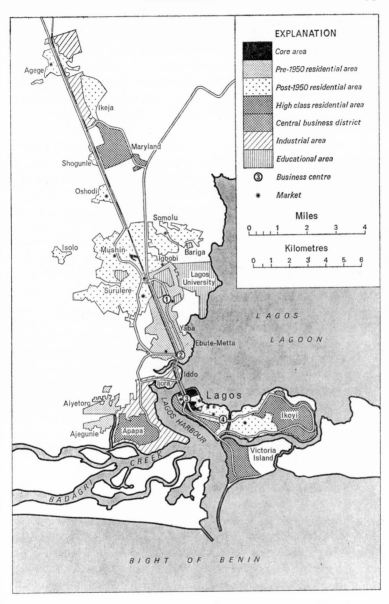

EXPLANATION

Core area
Pre-1950 residential area
Post-1950 residential area
High class residential area
Central business district
Industrial area
Educational area
③ Business centre
* Market

Miles
0 1 2 3 4

Kilometres
0 1 2 3 4 5 6

Agege
Ikeja
Maryland
Shogunle
Oshodi
Somolu
Isolo
Mushin
Bariga
Igbobi
Lagos University
Surulere
Yaba
Ebute-Metta
Iddo
Ijora
Aiyetoro
Lagos
Ikoyi
Ajegunle
Apapa
Victoria Island
LAGOS LAGOON
LAGOS HARBOUR
CREEK
BADAGRI
BIGHT OF BENIN

Figure 10.3. Lagos

located close to the railway station in the early development of the area before rent-paying capacity influenced the structure of the area. Now that it does, they are best able to pay the higher rents demanded for prime sites by virtue of the large scale of their operations. The scarcity value of land in the district is now being reflected in the upward growth of department stores and office buildings. Four almost parallel roads which converge at the eastern end make the axes of the district and the European owned enterprises, often in multi-storey premises, are found along these closest to the railway station but separated from it by a government owned area not yet fully developed. With increasing distance from the station, European firms are superseded by Levantine and Indian firms. These occupy small two-storey premises, the ground floor of which is a specialised shop dealing in textiles or clothing or occasionally jewellery, the upper floor being the residence of the owner. On the north the district is flanked by Dugbe market, a large daily market, and by motor sales-rooms and garages, found also on the southern edge.

Whereas areal differentiation by ownership is readily apparent, it is only embryonic by function. Retailing tends to occupy the frontage of the inner streets but behind the shops and stores there are wholesale and light manufacturing premises. These functions are also found intermingled with retailing along the outer two streets. Less important functions such as banking and insurance, business offices, and the various services are scattered through the districts. Thus areal specialisation has not proceeded far enough for the recognition of functional sub-districts.

In the Lagos central business district, on the other hand, which has developed on Lagos Island along the Marina and Broad Street, functional sub-districts have been identified. The warehouse and wholesale sub-district is located at the northern end of the central business district. To the east of it is the retail sub-district, the heart of the C.B.D., where Department stores are characteristic and where multi-storeyed buildings are common. Eastwards again is the financial sub-district which consists of British, American and Nigerian banks clustered loosely around the Central Bank of Nigeria, together with insurance offices. Land use is particularly intensive in this sub-district with tall office blocks replacing earlier buildings. Adjacent is the educational sub-district which owes its origin to the establishment of schools here in the 1850s. In this area there are still several schools associated with the various missions, which also have their administrative headquarters here. Finally, there is the administrative sub-district in which both municipal and federal government departments are located. This area of imposing modern buildings has developed rapidly with constitutional evolution since 1950.

The C.B.D. of Lagos is obviously better developed than that of Ibadan and this is also true of the commercial structure outside the C.B.D. Outlying business centres are developing at Sabo in Yaba, Oyingbo in Ebute Metta, and Idumota, where two business thoroughfares in Lagos, Victoria Street and Balogun-Ereko Street, specialise in textiles and haberdashery sold from small two-storeyed shops owned by Syrians and Africans (Figure 10.3). In Ibadan the road from Gbagi to Bere, lined by small African owned shops selling imported hardware and enamel-ware, leather and plastic goods and other convenience goods, is the only example. Lagos, also has representatives of the lower orders of commercial structure, the neighbourhood business street and the isolated store cluster, whereas Ibadan has only the former. In Lagos, as in both traditional and modern Ibadan, the daily markets serve as neighbourhood business centres.

The contrasts noted in the commercial structure also reflect the contrasts in the purchasing power of the population. Indeed the contrast between traditional Ibadan with its skeletal development and the modern part of the city with its more evolved structure does so too. Credence is lent to this suggestion when the C.B.D. of Lagos and Freetown are compared. Mabogunje modified the Murphy and Vance technique in his study of Lagos. McKay[12] applied it in its pure form to Freetown unsuccessfully and had to use a radically altered version to identify a C.B.D. Thus land use in Central Freetown is not as intensive as in Lagos and this probably reflects the lower purchasing power of the city and hinterland population. The study of commercial structure in the West African setting will repay much further attention.

T

THE DISTRIBUTION & GROWTH OF TOWNS

R. W. Steel[13] in describing the location of towns in anglo-phone West Africa adopted a threefold division: (i) the towns of the coast, (ii) the towns of the forest country and (iii) the towns of the savana interior. This classification has much to commend it for a discussion of both distribution and growth of towns throughout West Africa.

THE TOWNS OF THE COAST. Twenty of the 96 towns with populations over 20,000 are on the coast, twelve in anglophone West Africa. Furthermore, eight of the towns of over 100,000 inhabitants are coastal and include all the capital cities of coastal countries except Monrovia (pop. 80,992), Bathurst (28,896) and Nouakchott (12,500), which are excluded on grounds of size, not of position, and Porto Novo, a lagoon-side rather than a coastal settlement. As Steel observes, 'this coastal location of so many of the key settlements of West Africa is a reminder of the manner in which the region was opened up from the coast towards the interior, and also of the very recent political and economic development of the hinterland'.

The coastal towns were formed under European influence, with few exceptions, during the Proto-Colonial Era. The concentration of fewer but larger and well-equipped ports, which are foci in the transport networks and into which considerable capital has been invested, has been discussed in Chapter 9. The growth of the towns associated with the port activities reflects, in part at least, this trend. The large general cargo ports have grown quickly as towns. The population of Sekondi-Takoradi, for instance, has increased from 43,700 in 1948 to 75,450 in 1960. The new port of Takoradi has grown particularly rapidly from 5,478 in 1931 to 17,327 in 1948 and 40,937 in 1960. Whilst Sekondi, the old port and railway terminus is growing more slowly, from 26,416 in 1948 to 34,531 in 1960. Growth is, however, particularly rapid when such ports are also the political and administrative centres of the more developed West African countries. (Table 10.4). Whilst the growth of the port and the bureaucracy are important factors in the growth of these centres, development of manufacturing and service industries and of commerce have also been important contributory factors in recent years.

But a distinction must be made between Dakar, Abidjan, Accra and Lagos on the one hand and the remaining port-capital cities on the other. The former are experiencing metropolitan growth. The central city has burst its bounds and both employment centres and residential areas are located beyond the city margin. The population of communities such as Mushin outside the Lagos city limit, for instance, is now in excess of half-a-million and raises that of the metropolitan area to more than one million inhabitants. There are also important industrial areas, such as the Ikeja industrial estate, outside the city boundary. Similarly the Dakar metropolitan area extends outwards to engulf older centres, such as Bargny and Rufisque, and villages, such as Tiaroye-sur-Mer. It also includes a new satellite, Dagoudané Pikiné, developed to rehouse displaced Dakarois. Thus the journey to work is increasingly becoming a feature of the inhabitants' lives and a complex pattern of such journeys is emerging. This is equally true of the other emerging metropolitan areas. Whereas in the anglophone cities commuting is carried on by road, in metropolitan Dakar the railway is important for commuting from places as far from the centre as Bargny and Rufisque.

The other port-capital cities, whilst growing rapidly are much smaller (Table 10.2). This doubtless reflects the smaller, poorer population of their hinterlands and the less developed nature of the national economies that they serve. Those towns which have lost their port function have either grown very slowly or declined in population. St. Louis, which lost most of its trade to Dakar, grew only from 30,000 in 1937 to 50,000 in 1966, while Grand Bassam, which was superseded by Port Bouët and then Abidjan, grew from 4,500 in 1937 to 12,000 in 1968. Mumford and Ada, both small open-roadstead ports in Ghana, declined in population between 1931 and 1948, following closure of their ports.

THE TOWNS OF THE FOREST COUNTRY. There are three important groups of towns in the Forest country, the Ashani, Yoruba and Ibo. Of these the Yoruba are unique in antiquity, size and concentrated nature of their grouping. Although considered as forest towns, it should be remembered that they are mainly located along the transitional zone between grassland and forest, a zone that became extremely significant during the wars of the nineteenth century, when the settlement pattern was radically altered. Old towns and cities in the grasslands, Old Oyo (or Katunga) is the best example, were destroyed and new cities were founded by warrior groups (Ibadan) or by fleeing refugees (Abeokuta). Other towns, favourably located from a defensive point of view, became very large. Ogbomosho, Oshogbo, Iwo and Ile-Ife are prominent examples. Thus some Yoruba towns were already large before the Colonial Era (Table 10.5). They were based on a largely subsistence economy, although there was some division of labour, and the cowrie shell served as a medium of exchange in both local and long distance trade.

During the Colonial Era the cowrie shell was replaced by internationally acceptable currency, and new cash crops, particularly cocoa and kola, were introduced. Thus the existing money-based economy was intensified and embraced a larger proportion of the populace, who engaged in the new export trade. Those towns in key situations grew rapidly and attracted migrants from smaller, less favourably situated towns. Such migration was also stimulated by the decline of traditional craft industries. The migrant craftsmen took up new occupations such as tailoring, hair-dressing, motor or bicycle repairing, goldsmithing or even retailing. But in many towns agriculture still remains an important occupation. According to the 1952 Census, between 60 and 70 per cent. of the working males in the large towns of Ogbomosho, Oshogbo and Iwo were employed in agriculture. Even in Ibadan the figure was 35 per cent. But in Abeokuta it was only 15 per cent., with 27 per cent. in trading and clerical occupations. Ijebu-Ode had 28 per cent. in trading and 20 per cent. each in crafts and agriculture. The impact of the modern economy varies from town to town, but only Ibadan with its university, teaching hospital, department stores, office blocks and hotel has modern international-style buildings in its townscape. Thus the Yoruba town has adapted in varying degrees to modern conditions and few new towns have resulted from economic and associated social change.

In eastern Nigeria, on the other hand, towns founded under European influence are much more important. Thus Enugu owes its origins to the discovery of coal along the Udi Escarpment and its early growth to the building of the railway to Port Harcourt in 1916. Later growth followed its selection in 1929 as headquarters of the Southern Provinces. After the split into Eastern and Western Provinces in 1939 it continued its role for the smaller area. With the division of Nigeria into three Regions in 1951 it became the seat of the legislature, regional ministries, statutory corporations and other government agencies. Industrialisation took place after Independence with small enterprises located in the town and larger on an industrial estate at Emene some seven miles (10·5 kilometres) to the east. Similarly Aba is a European creation on a site formerly occupied by several village communities and in an area of commercial importance in precolonial times. Its location on the railway resulted in its early growth as a commercial centre with a variety of small industries. More recently large modern industries have been located in the town, attracted by its position on the railway and its focal position in the road system serving a densely populated area and giving good access throughout the country. Smaller towns in the area have developed from large villages, which have increasingly become oriented to the road system and developed trading activities, small scale service and manufacturing industries.

Many indigenous towns in the Forest Zone of Ashanti[14] were largely destroyed in the Anglo-Ashanti war of 1873–74 or in the civil wars that rent Ashanti in its aftermath. Only Bekwai, Mampong and Kumasi made substantial progress, and this was because of their situation for trade in rubber and cocoa in the former cases and, in the latter, because of its focal position on trade routes between northern and southern Ghana and its role as a major collecting and distributing centre for the surrounding cocoa producing area. Elsewhere in the forest towns have grown, many from villages, as a result of cocoa trading, mining or both and to their position in the transport system. Thus, in the newly developing cocoa areas of the Western Region and Brong Ahafo no town has yet achieved a population of 20,000 inhabitants. In Ashanti, Obuasi, a mining town and cocoa-buying centre, has grown to a population of 23,000, whereas Tarkwa in the Western

Region, dependent solely on mining, has a population of only 19,000, The devastation of cocoa by swollen shoot in the older producing areas led to decay of towns such as Somanya in Krobo and checked the growth of others. Koforidua and Nsawam, for instance, were large and economically broadly based, so that, though growth was probably curtailed, it continued to a reduced extent by momentum. In the rest of Ghana, towns of over 20,000 inhabitants in the forest are few, widely scattered and are all of European origin.

TOWNS OF THE SAVANA INTERIOR. These towns form part of the line of indigenous settlements close to the desert edge which owe their origin and early growth to the trans-Saharan trade routes. The Hausa towns of Northern Nigeria are important as a group because they have become integrated into the export economy through the transport links with the coast. Some, such as Kano, are of great age, others, such as Sokoto, are of more recent origin. Kano, the largest at the time of colonial intervention, with its markets, merchants and far-flung trading connections and with well-developed craft industries, has grown quickly. It assumed a wider administrative role than formerly as a provincial centre and it became the market and commercial centre for the surrounding cash crop area. Additionally, processing of primary products and secondary manufacturing industries have more recently been established. Similarly, Zaria and Maiduguri became provincial administrative centres with both traditional and modern small-scale service and manufacturing industries, whilst the former was chosen as the site for a university, an important agricultural research institute and an air-training centre. Sokoto, like Maiduguri, has enjoyed less spectacular growth as it is not on the railway, although the recent completion of the Bornu railway extension is likely to lead to more rapid growth of the latter.

New towns, particularly Kaduna and Jos, have also been founded but in the Guinea Savana and Montane vegetation types respectively. Close to the northern margin of the Middle Belt, Kaduna was selected in virgin bush as the site for the administrative centre for the northern provinces and later became the capital of the Northern Region. As such it became the seat of the legislature and government departments and it has also become an important centre of the textile industry in the last two decades. Jos owes its growth to its selection as the administrative centre for Plateau Province and also the development of the Plateau tinfields. Other towns in the Middle Belt are mainly European creations, such as Minna, a railway town, and Makurdi, an administrative centre and bridging point across the Benue. Bida is an exception, being a traditional town with a strategic location along trade routes from Hausaland to both Yoruba and Ibo country.

Although towns are fewer in number and smaller in the Middle Belt than in the Sudan, they apparently grew rapidly in the period between the Census of 1952–53 and that of 1963. Thus Bida, for example, has grown from 19,346 to 55,007, Keffi from 6,367 to 31,711, Minna from 12,870 to 59,988, Bauchi from 13,440 to 37,778 and Kontagora from 5,665 to 15,633. Thus urban growth in the Nigerian Middle Belt partially reflects the spread of cash cropping, particularly of cotton, into the area coupled with the demands for goods and services associated with such commercialisation of the local economy.

In the Sudan Zone west of Nigeria, as also in the Guinea Savana Zone, towns are more widely scattered than in Nigeria. Like those in the latter country some of the larger ones have traditional origins, and growth has resulted from their integration in the expanding commercial economy. In Sénégal the Sudanic towns are markedly coastal in their distribution and have affinities, therefore, with those of the forest in other parts of West Africa in their location. Thiès, for example, owes its development partly to its connections with the cash cropping of groundnuts in the surrounding area and partly to the exploitation and processing of phosphates, both facilitated by proximity to the coast.

SMALL TOWNS

It would be useful to consider the distribution and growth of towns in Ghana using the lower criterion of urban status, i.e. 5,000 inhabitants.[15] (Figure 10.5.)

The period since the end of the First World War has been one of rapid increase in the number of towns in Ghana from

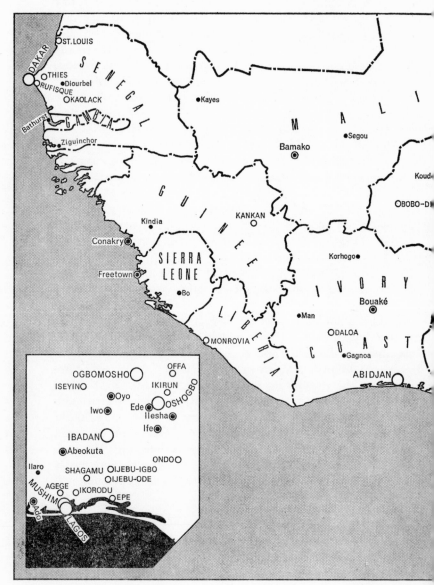

Figure 10.4. To

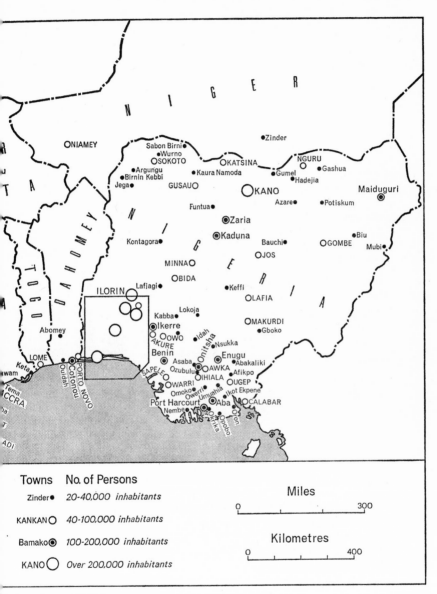

Towns   No. of Persons

Zinder●   *20-40,000 inhabitants*

KANKAN○   *40-100,000 inhabitants*

Bamako◉   *100-200,000 inhabitants*

KANO○   *Over 200,000 inhabitants*

lation of over 20,000

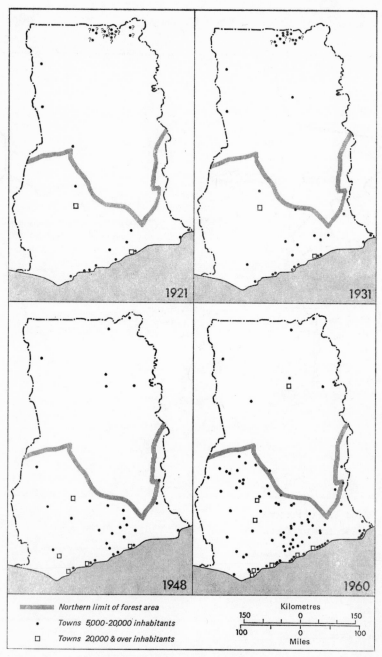

Figure 10.5. The growth of towns in Ghana (after Dickson, Steel, Hunter)

17 in 1921 to 26 in 1931, 38 in 1948, and 98 in 1960. The distribution of these towns reflected the resources of the countryside and their growth that of changing economic circumstances. In 1921 towns were markedly coastal. Some, cocoa oriented, had grown up in the Forest inland of Accra with few outside the cocoa area. By 1931 cocoa farming had begun to spread westwards and with it urban development. Mining led to the growth of centres such as Tarkwa and Obuasi. Expansion of cash cropping and therefore exports led to the growth of many of the coastal towns which served as surf ports. Outside the more developed areas, however, towns were still few in number and very widely scattered.

By 1948 further towns had emerged, again mainly in the Forest, where mining and cash cropping were carried on, and this trend has continued to the present. Thus there are only seven towns in the north, closely related to the skeletal road network, and four along the forested ranges of Volta Province. Another 30 line the coast and lagoons, all of which engage in fishing, while some, such as Keta, are important local centres of commerce. Takoradi and Tema are ports and with Accra are also developing industrial centres. 61 of the total of 98 towns are in the Forest. They include major commercial and administrative centres, such as Koforidua and Kumasi, but also small market centres closely associated with commercial food farming and the cocoa industry. Hunter recognises three groups of Forest towns west of the Volta. First is a group of 25 towns lying in the south-eastern Forest. Here cocoa farming is less important than formerly, although commercial food farming has become important. This is the older urbanised area and growth between 1948 and 1960 was slower than in the second group. This group of some 23 towns lies in the Forest of Brong Ahafo and in north-west Ashanti. Many are new towns, having grown up in the period between 1949 and 1960, reflecting the more recent spread of the cocoa industry into the area. The third group consists of nine towns widely scattered in the western Forest. Each has a special economic function such as gold mining (Tarkwa) or timber extraction (Asangkrangwa).

The small towns of Ghana have their counterparts elsewhere in West Africa which have developed in association with mining (Lunsar, Sierra Leone), with plantations and cash cropping (Abengourou, Côte d'Ivoire), with railways (Kafanchan), with rail-road interchange (Parakou, Dahomey) or with administration (Buea, West Cameroun). Reducing the threshold of urban status to 5,000 inhabitants increases the number of towns, the percentage of urban population and the rate of growth of urban population, but it does not materially affect their distribution. Towns are most numerous and growing most rapidly in the coastal belt of country between 100 and 150 miles. Particular areas of concentration within this belt are found in the 'islands' of high population density where export cash cropping is most significant and advancement of the economy has proceeded farthest. Outside these islands but within the coastal belt, towns are related to utilisation of particular resources or other local considerations. Outside the coastal belt, towns are widely scattered and usually related to the transport network except in the population islands of the Sudan Zone. Here urbanisation is more intense in the Hausa area than farther west.

REASONS FOR URBAN GROWTH

West African towns are growing quickly for many reasons, some of which have been implied in this and earlier chapters. Demographically, natural increase, considered earlier in this chapter, is one factor accounting for rapid growth of urban populations, migration from rural areas is another, whilst migration from small to larger towns is a third. But the relative importance of each is difficult to assess in view of the serious data limitations. It appears, however, that rural-urban migration is developing at an ever-increasing rate.

Prothero[16] recognises four forms of rural-urban migration:

(i) daily movements from peri-urban fringes to centrally located commercial and industrial areas. These have not yet reached the proportions known elsewhere but already cause problems, particularly in large cities such as Lagos and Abidjan, by straining inadequate transport and road systems.

(ii) seasonal movements, predominantly of young adult males, occurring during the agricultural close season.

Absences may be for periods of up to five or six months and the distances travelled may amount to hundreds of kilometres. Thus important source areas for such migrants are found in Mali, Haute Volta, Niger and in the northern parts of Côte d'Ivoire, Ghana and Nigeria. The migrants seek work in the major commercial and administrative centres and in the ports as well as in the cash crop areas of the Forest. They return home to cultivate their farms with the onset of the next wet season. In Yorubaland a reverse movement from the towns to the rural areas occurs during maximum periods of agricultural activity, when urban cocoa farmers take the harvest from their farms.

(iii) short-term movements, where migrants stay in the towns for periods of up to two years. Again migrants are predominantly adult males, commonly 'target' workers whose aim is to earn a specific sum of money for the aquisition of a wife, a radio set, a bicycle or some other durable good.

(iv) Definitive movements resulting in the severance of migrant's links with the rural area. This may occur initially or may follow several periods of urban employment. Migrants in this group, unlike those in the last two, are often accompanied by wives and families.

Such migration is influenced by both 'push' and 'pull' factors which may be grouped into economic and socio-psychological, of which the former have been shown to be more important. In rural areas there are circumstances which encourage, or even force, people off the land and into the towns. Increasing population densities in areas poorly endowed agriculturally, as in the Sokoto Province, encouraged migration. The prospect of paid labour and a regular money income is preferred by younger more ambitious men to subsistence and a small but fluctuating money income from peasant agriculture. Latterly, compulsory full-time primary education introduced into many West African countries is producing large numbers of 'educated' young men who consider themselves to be too well qualified for a career in traditional agriculture. Others migrate to the towns for full-time secondary education. The socio-psychological factors do not concern us in this work but it should be pointed out, because it is closely related to economic ambitions, that the desire to break away from traditional obligations and forms of social organisation is a significant factor in this group.

Regular wages, higher than expected incomes from agriculture, in money if not in real terms, or, alternatively, the opportunity of making money is undoubtedly an important attraction of urban areas. The opportunities for paid employment are much greater in the towns than in the countryside not only for the educated but also for the unskilled. The educated seek employment in secondary and tertiary economic activities, in manufacturing, commerce and the professions. The uneducated seek employment as labourers, messengers, domestic servants, garden-boys, night-watchmen, night-soil collectors, or set up in petty trading, or even take to begging. But the prospect of employment is often more apparent than real. West African cities are crowded with unemployed and under-employed rural immigrants, sources of many social problems in the urban areas.

But in considering the impact of migration from rural to urban areas it is a mistake to overlook its influence on rural areas. This varies from case to case. Seasonal migration, even when in large numbers, (i.e. 25–50 per cent. of adult males), does not necessarily impair the rural economy if absences occur in the agricultural close season. Indeed it may be beneficial because it reduces demands on scarce food resources, and migrants return with money and goods which bring some benefit to rural economies. But short-term migration in similar proportions tends to disrupt the rural economy, in turn stimulating further migration.[17] The source areas of migration do, however, receive benefits in the form of cash remitted by migrants to relatives, and donations, the result of 'social identification', from urban-based improvement leagues, Progressive Associations and Descendant Unions, towards the cost of rural development projects, clinics, schools or roads.

The extremely rapid growth of towns and the attendant loss of young, ambitious, able-bodied men from rural areas raises a fundamental problem in development planning, the growing imbalance between town and country and, in many countries, between one city and the remainder of the country.

The crux of the problem lies in the fact that most government revenue is derived from export taxes, the operation of Marketing Boards and import duties on basic consumer goods, and it accrues from the rural areas, but much of it is devoted to urban projects aimed either at alleviating urban problems resulting from too rapid growth or at economic development in the non-agricultural sector. Thus between one-third and one-half of the money income earned by the farmer is being invested in projects such as industrialisation, hotels, slum clearance and improved urban transport. These, together with the establishment of minimum wages and rising wage levels in towns, are making cities even more attractive *vis-a-vis* rural areas. Several possibilities are open to governments and planners. They may persist with present policies, which are devoted primarily to developing the infrastructure and the secondary and tertiary sectors and therefore favour urban areas. Kilby[18] argues that this re-distribution of wealth is harmful to economic development, both in the short- and in the long-term, and that the growing imbalance between town and country should be reduced. He suggests diverting a major part of the investment programme to rural areas, holding levels of urban amenities and wages. He considers that the agricultural sector should be developed, together with supporting investment in prestige rural projects, such as agricultural schools, highly mechanised farm settlements, the agricultural research centres, fertiliser plants and bulk handling and storage facilities.

There are assumptions to be challenged and steps in the logic to be questioned in Kilby's argument. There is, first, the questionable assumption that a formerly existing balance in favour of rural areas is preferable to the present state. Secondly, many of the rural development projects suggested would reduce the manpower requirements of the agricultural sector, particularly in areas where under-employment is currently characteristic, thus encouraging the drift from agricultural occupations to the towns. Third, there are sound economic arguments for developing both primary processing industries and secondary industries. These include keeping within the producing country some or all of the profits accruing from manufacture, reducing the reliance on exports of primary products with marked fluctuation in demand and price, and reducing the amount of scarce foreign exchange used for goods which could be produced within West Africa. Fourth, the problem is probably a regional rather than a sectoral one, in that the opportunities associated with urban areas are beneficial not only to the towns but also to the surrounding rural populations. Over much of West Africa, however, towns are too far apart to affect much of the rural areas.

This suggests an alternative based on a more balanced growth of primary and secondary sectors, coupled with decentralisation of urban functions to regional centres. In view of the locational requirements of large-scale modern industries the industry to be developed in these small regional centres would have to be small-scale and labour-intensive. Such centres would serve as markets for agricultural products from the surrounding areas and as centres for diffusion of knowledge and new ideas. A programme of this kind could be embarked upon only by lowering the overall rate of economic development, as the type of industry suggested is not as efficient as its larger, technologically based counterpart. A policy of this type was introduced into the then Eastern Region of Nigeria, but its effectiveness was difficult to assess because it was curtailed by the civil war.

If there is one universal answer to this problem[19], it has not yet been found by any West African Government. Closely related to this problem is the issue of over-urbanisation, a concept which relates the proportion of a country's population living in urban areas to the level of that country's economic development. Mabogunje argues that Nigeria is over-urbanised, firstly, because the country has numerous urban centres of pre-industrial origin with many inhabitants for whom no modern employment is available, and, secondly, because the influx into towns from rural areas results in under-employment. Thus many towns are not functioning efficiently in the sense that they are not making positive contributions in return for the capital invested in their social amenities. These towns are 'parasitic', are a drag on economic develop-ment and yet, through social 'identification' by absentee residents and by politicians currying favour with the electorate, they attract scarce capital. A few towns, the 'generative cities', are making positive contributions to economic development. Mabogunje identifies about 50 out of 329 towns in Nigeria and argues that attention should be focused upon them. There are, however, serious problems involved in developing such centres, particularly Lagos. These are associated mainly with the finance of improvements to urban areas and with urban management to raise their economic performance.

Mabogunje, assuming that policies to stimulate economic development by industrialisation will continue, suggests that further urbanisation will take place in coming decades.[20] This will take the form of uncontrolled growth and of further concentration into a few spectacularly large urban agglomerations. Obvious candidates in Nigeria are belts extending from Lagos to Ibadan, Aba to Port Harcourt and Kaduna to Kano. He argues for an urbanisation policy as part of the general economic development programme in order to prevent the regional imbalance. The four large Regions, however, were replaced in 1968 by 12 States. Like the Regions before them, the States have considerable autonomy in internal economic affairs, so that this reorganisation may retard the development of such belts.

The question of the relationship between levels of urbanisation and economic development and the possibility of over-urbanisation in other West African countries is worthy of further study. Certainly the mushroom growth of metropolitan Dakar, Abidjan and Accra-Tema is widening the development gap between their immediate environs and the less favoured interiors of their countries. It therefore appears that the need for development of regional as well as national development policies is becoming more pressing in these countries. Governments and scholars are beginning to turn their attention to it, at least in Côte d'Ivoire and Ghana.[21]

REFERENCES

1 Thomas, B. E., *The location and nature of West African Cities*, in Kuper, H (Ed.), *Urbanization and Migration in West Africa*, 1965

2 Berry, B. J. L., 'City Size Distribution and Economic Development', *Econ. Dev. Cult. Change*, 9, 1961, pp. 573–88

3 Boateng, E. A., 'Recent Changes in Settlement in south-east Gold Coast', *Trans. Inst. Br. Geog.*, 21, 1955, pp. 157–169

U

4   *See inter-alia*, Mitchell, N. C., *Yoruba Towns* in Barbour, K. M. and
     Prothero, R. M. (Eds.), *Essays on African Population*, London, 1961; and
     Morgan, W. B., '*The Grassland Towns of the Eastern Region of Nigeria*',
     Trans. Inst. Br. Geog., 23, 1957, pp. 213–24

5   Hunter, J. M., '*Population Growth in Ghana*', in Whittow, J. B. and Wood,
     P. D. (Eds.), *Essays in Geography for Austin Miller*, Reading, 1965

6   Harrison Church, R. J., '*West African Urbanization: a Geographical View*',
     Soc. Rev., 7, 1959, pp. 15–27

7   *ibid*

8   Akinola, R. A., '*The Industrial Structure of Ibadan*', *Nig. Geog. Jour.*, 7,
     1964, pp. 115–130: Callaway, A., '*From Traditional Crafts to Modern
     Industry*' in Lloyd, P. C., Mabogunje, A. L. and Awe, B. (Eds.), *The
     City of Ibadan*, Cambridge, 1967

9   Hauser, A., '*Les Industries de Transformation de la Région de Dakar*',
     Études Sénégalaises, 5, 1954, pp. 69–83

10 *Urbanisme*, 111–112, 1969, p. 46

11 *See inter alia*, Mabogunje, A. L., *Urbanization in Nigeria*, London, 1968,
     Chapters 9 and 11, idem., '*The Evolution and Analysis of the Retail
     Structure of Lagos*', *Econ. Geog.*, 1964, pp. 304–23

12 McKay, J., '*Regions in a Tropical City: Freetown, Sierra Leone*', *Regions
     Within Towns*, Institute of British Geographers, Study Group in Urban
     Geography, 1966, *mimeo*

13 Steel, R. W., '*Some Problems of Population in British West Africa*', in Steel,
     R. W. and Fisher, C. A. (Eds.), *Geographical Essays on British Tropical
     Lands*, London, 1956

14 Dickson, K. B., *An Historical Geography of Ghana*, London, 1969, Chapter
     11

15 Hunter, J. M., *op cit.*, and Dickson, K. B., *op cit.*, Chapter 12

16 Prothero, R. M., '*Socio-Economic Aspects of Rural-Urban Migration in
     Africa South of the Sahara*', *Scientia*, 59, 1965, pp. 1–7

17 *See inter alia*, Finnegan, R., *Survey of the Limba People of Northern Sierra
     Leone*, H.M.S.O., 1965, pp. 133–136
     Prothero, R. M., '*Migrant labour from north-western Nigeria*', *Africa*, 27,
     pp. 251–61
     idem., *Migrant labour from Sokoto Province, Northern Nigeria*, Kaduna, 1959
     See also idem., '*Migrant labour in West Africa*', *Jour. Local Admin. Overseas*,
     1, pp. 149–55 and for a general account of population mobility *see*, idem.,
     '*Continuity and Change in African Population Mobility*', in Steel, R. W. and
     Prothero, R. M. (Eds.), *Geographers and the Tropics:* Liverpool Essays,
     London, 1964

18 Kilby, P., '*Balancing Town and Country*', *West Africa*, August 29, 1964

19 A general account of urban problems of Tropical Africa forms part of
     Steel, R. W., *The Towns of Tropical Africa* in Barbour, K. M., and
     Prothero, R. M., *op cit.*

20 Mabogunje *op cit.*, Chapter 12

21 *Urbanisme*, 111–112, 1969, and Grove, D. and Huszar, L., *The Towns of
     Ghana*, Accra, 1964

CHAPTER 11

A Conclusion

The economy of West Africa, and with it the society, has been changing very rapidly and at an increasing rate during the Independence Era since 1945. This book has attempted a brief record of those changes from a geographical viewpoint. That is, the main emphasis has been on the spatial distribution of those changes and of the causative factors of change and also on the areal differentiation in the rate of change. To this end, certain themes have been emphasised throughout the book and it is appropriate to summarise them.

The first of these themes is the continuing importance of the residual traditional economy. The central areas of the principal cities differ little in form and function from their counterparts in any part of the world and in every part of West Africa the traveller who returns after a few years' absence will notice great changes. Nevertheless, the traditional sector remains overall the basis of the economy as it does of the society, though regionally its significance varies on a continuum from almost nil in the larger towns to its complete predominance in the remoter rural areas.

Agriculture remains the basic economic activity and this activity shows most traces of the traditional. The bulk of the unmeasured over-all output (as opposed to that for export) is for subsistence. That part sold for cash, whether it be food crops or crops grown specifically for export or local processing, is, with few exceptions particularly that of cocoa, the marginal surplus of production from a multitude of small-sized holdings. The vast majority of farmers are peasants who pursue, more or less unaltered, traditional methods of husbandry based on rotational bush fallowing and supported by a traditional way of life.

By contrast, the traditional hand-craft industries show much greater change, but a considerable residuum of the traditional remains in methods of production and marketing. Again, the traditional commercial structure still remains, operating mainly through women and, over large areas, the periodic market rings.

The second theme is the modernisation of the economy, and it is on this that most of the literature concentrates. While granting its present importance, and particularly its potential importance, we have tried hard to put it in its true perspective. The rate of modernisation and the degree so far achieved vary greatly among the various sectors of the economy. It also takes two distinct forms, though there may be some blurring along the boundary between the two. The first operates through the evolution of the traditional economy, which therefore forms the base from which modernisation begins, and emphasises the need for study of the traditional. The second is the direct importing of modern methods of production and economic organisation, resulting in a clear break with the traditional. The relative importance of these two processes varies among the various sectors of the economy.

Agriculture, the most important sector, is the least affected by modernisation, and this is the fundamental problem facing West Africa. What modernisation has taken place in agriculture is mainly through evolution of the traditional economy. This has been principally the now universal spread of cash cropping, though the proportion of the total production sold will vary very greatly from area to area. It will also vary from harvest to harvest, especially if cash sales are the marginal surplus of subsistence crops. Consequently, food prices in large towns fluctuate considerably and this is one of the problems of urbanisation.

There is also increasing use of exotic crops, such as cocoa, and to a lesser extent of selected seeds, such as those of oil-palms. Otherwise the peasant sector is characterised by very limited investment in land improvements and in modern tools. The few examples of capital accumulation are in the planting of tree-crops, and some government inspired attempts at land improvement. The livestock sector is even less affected by modernisation.

The influence of direct importation is also limited. It is virtually confined to the plantation system, for the success of the farm settlement remains unproven. Though tending to increase in significance, and, though individual plantations may be large, their contribution to overall agricultural production is limited.

In the fields of other primary production, sea-fishing shows both modernisation of the traditional through the use of outboard engines on canoes and the introduction of imported systems, large power vessels and rationalised distribution of their catch. The modernisation of forestry and mining has been virtually wholly through external and large scale organisations, financed either by foreign firms or by West African governments.

The industrial sector shows a greater advance than does the agricultural but chiefly through the external method of the factory system. Traditional crafts have evolved through the adoption of modern tools, potters may now use the wheel and tailors sewing machines. Modern crafts, baking, car repairing, metal working, have also been introduced. The output of small craftsmen is thus large in total and growing in range and production, but the more spectacular advance has been in the establishment of modern factory industries. These are financed mainly by foreign firms and by central or provincial governments, often in partnership. The rate of growth is limited by the size of the market in both population and purchasing power *per capita*, for the easy first stage of import-substitution has already gone a long way.

The commercial sector shows the same blend of evolution and of importation, but the influence of the small scale indigenous operator is much greater, and this is the main field for capital formation by the ordinary people. The universal spread of currency and availability of consumer goods has completely modified the traditional sector and of course greatly extended it. The main trend is towards greater specialisation into retailing and into wholesaling and produce buying, though much of the original lack of specialisation remains.

Except in towns, retail trade is wholly in the hands of West African traders and has been greatly modified by the proliferation of markets and shops. In the larger town centres, retail trade, organised by individual West African or expatriate merchants or by expatriate firms tends to become more specialised and to approach the standards of advanced economies, the larger the town the nearer being this approach. Wholesaling is performed by smaller merchants and by large firms, but the former tend to specialise in the products of agriculture and crafts and the latter in factory produced and imported goods. Co-operation has a very limited part, but a bigger one in produce marketing.

Modernisation of the infrastructure is almost wholly through large scale organisation, normally by government finance or foreign aid and by foreign contractors, except perhaps in road works. The one exception is that investment in lorries and mini-buses is mainly by small scale private individuals, and this together with retail trade and town-housing for rent form the main outlets for small savings. Unfortunately, however, most of the profits from agriculture are put into these activities with their higher rate of return rather than being ploughed back into the land.

The third theme is the differential rate of modernisation between areas. There is great variation in such indices of economic development as *per capita* income, gross national product and, important in West Africa, overseas trade per head of population. In general it is the larger countries and the coastal countries which show up best. Using these indices, Côte d'Ivoire, Ghana, Sénégal and Nigeria are the most modernised. The inland countries show a much lesser development, as do the smaller coastal countries.

But within each of these countries there is a wide gap between the various parts, the towns are more modernised than the rural areas, the coastlands than the interiors and so on. It is possible to trace a pattern of differentiation, which is general and irrespective of national boundaries.

Everywhere modernisation has proceeded faster in the towns than in the rural areas and in the larger rather than in the smaller towns. The coastal towns are the more favoured, but of the interior towns, political capitals have received a greater share of capital investment. Outside the towns, where they have not given rise directly to town development, areas of mineral extraction are the ones of greatest development. Of the agricultural areas it is those which produce the highest proportion of cash crops in the total output.

There is, however, differential development between the Zones. In general the Forest is most highly modernised, especially in the cocoa belts of Ghana, Nigeria and in southeast Côte d'Ivoire. Conversely, where the Forest has been little developed, in the East Cross River Basin and in southwest Côte d'Ivoire, there has been little attempt at modernisation. In general, however, the greater the proportion of Forest in the area of a country, the greater the degree of modernisation in that country. This explains the comparative lack of modernisation in Dahomey. The exception is Sénégal, which has a long history of economic development.

The Sudan shows much less evidence of modernisation, both in towns and in the country. In the rural areas there is less contrast between the main concentration of cash cropping and other areas. The former are, however, characterised by more towns and better roads. In addition Northern Nigeria has more traditional towns than have other parts of the Sudan.

The Middle Belt, away from the trunk roads, shows least evidence of modernisation, as its resources are least. Northern Ghana and Côte d'Ivoire, virtually all within the Middle Belt, are very much less developed than are the southern parts of those countries. These latter areas, together with the western provinces of Nigeria and the Dakar-Thiès area of Sénégal, are the most modernised in West Africa.

The fourth theme concerns the conflicts between the traditional and the modernising elements in the economy. These are bound to arise during a period of rapid change, but the situation is rendered the more difficult because West Africa is emerging directly from simple, unevolved economies and societies into the modern world-wide ones without intermediate stages of mercantilism and capital formation such as were experienced in western Europe after 1500.

These conflicts can be seen in labour and capital supply, utilisation of natural resources, and the interaction between society and economy. A few actual examples may be summarised. The extended family system is of great value in the almost complete absence of social security in a period of rapid urbanisation and industrialisation. It can, however, act as an economic and social disincentive, for any individual who makes good becomes financially responsible for numerous distant relatives.

Again, there is the difficulty of the application of capital to the traditional agricultural systems, which we have dealt with in some detail. Because of this, much of the government capital available for agriculture goes into plantations, and there is thus an increased cleavage between the two sectors of the agricultural economy. This is exacerbated by the draining of profits from the land into higher yielding investments. Governments passively assist in this by not encouraging through tax structure the ploughing back of agricultural profits, but also, in the Commonwealth countries, the governments set a bad example by partially withholding from the farmers money raised by the produce marketing boards. Some of this has been diverted to investment in urban projects, thus doubly penalising the rural areas. In addition the rural way of life carries a much lower social prestige. This encourages the drift to the towns, which is faster than the creation of jobs there, resulting in unemployment and underemployment.

Fifthly, perhaps the most important of these recurrent themes is the importance of the supply of capital. Time and time again it emerges that capital supply is the limiting factor in economic development. It is mainly lack of capital that is the cause of the slower rate of development in the basic agricultural sector than in the other sectors of the economy, though some of the difficulties involved in agricultural investment have been stressed. It is lack of capital that holds back expansion of the infrastructure. Conversely, because of the higher returns, adequate supplies of foreign capital are available for mining and manufacture, while for the latter there is also government capital available for prestige projects. In these sectors there are also other limiting factors, notably lack of transport facilities, lack of managerial expertise, and the extent to which government policies attract or inhibit foreign investment.

The second important limiting factor is the inadequacy of the infrastructure. Over large areas the road system is inadequate or even non-existent, and though the organisation of road transport is favourable to pioneering the small-scale traffic flows, low unit-cost bulk transport is almost absent

other than for a few purpose-built mineral railways. In spite
of considerable investment, power supplies are inadequate and
costly.

The third limiting factor is the lack of skills, labour and
managerial.

There is however one important factor which has been
touched on only incidentally, and this may be termed the
political factor. One of the difficulties of the Independence
Era has been the trend towards political fragmentation. For
the francophone countries, Independence was accompanied
by the break up of the French West African Federation,
while even the federation of Sénégal and Mali lasted less
than a year. As a result of this, Mali forced itself to depend
for a time on the high-cost route to Abidjan. For several
years before the end of the Nkrumah regime the frontier
between Ghana and Togo was closed.

Apart from Nigeria, no West African country exceeds
six million in population, and even in Nigeria centrifugal
tendencies are strong, as evidenced by the tragic civil war.
Even more than during the Colonial Era markets were regarded as being defined by national, and in Nigeria, regional
boundaries. Thus they are limited by small areas and low
total potential purchasing power.

To obtain the maximum results from limited capital investment it is logical that some form of regional groupings should
evolve, free trade areas or economic communities, so that
economies of scale can be achieved, and wider economic
planning made possible. The difficulties in the way of such
development must not be underestimated, but conversely
there are examples of co-operation.

These include Airafrique, the air line jointly owned by most
of the francophone countries. These countries have also
joined in the *Banque Centrale des États de l'Afrique de l'Ouest*,
which is the issuing bank for their common currency, and
which also has important functions in the administration
of foreign aid funds. The *Organisation Commune du Dahomey
et du Niger* (OCDN) deals with the transit trade through
Dahomey to and from the landlocked Niger, and this has a
much happier history than the relations between Sénégal
and Mali within this field. Unfortunately there are no similar

examples from the anglophone countries. In these, Independence resulted in the break-up of any common services, the West African Currency Board, the West African Inter-Territorial Secretariat (which co-ordinated scientific research) and the West African Airways Corporation. Instead, each country strove to develop a national air-line, a national shipping line and so on.

It is true that in both social and economic planning estimations have almost invariably fallen short of the actual, but regional planning would at least establish an order of priorities, so that a given level of capital investment could be concentrated where it would achieve maximum effect. Thus the Franks Commission of 1944 made the (with hindsight) astonishing recommendation that only one university institution was needed for the four Commonwealth Countries. Conversely, it was equally true that in 1969, with ten such institutions supply had for the time being outrun demand.

On a purely national basis, no country, with the possible exception of the over-regionalised Nigeria, has a large enough market for even an uneconomically small steel plant. On the other hand, the West African market as a whole could probably support a large scale, viable plant now and another one in the not too distant future. It would, however, require some form of regional association and a common market to establish priorities for location and the timing for establishing the plants.

Again, there was certainly a case for a 'Takoradi' type harbour and port to be shared by Togo, Dahomey and the Niger transit traffic. In the event, however, both Togo and Dahomey have acquired one. Neither is economically viable, being built with foreign aid at artificially low interest rates. The funds for the second port could with more return, economic and social, be invested elsewhere in the deficient infrastructure.

There is also need for regional association for the purpose of economic planning in agriculture. It is seldom the practice to look at West Africa as a whole, in the way it has become customary to examine the EEC. Looking at each country separately we may applaud individual efforts to diversify away from the undoubted over-specialisation in export crops. Looking at the sub-continent as a whole we see the less satisfactory spectacle of each country diversifying into its neighbour's specialities. Yet economic and geographic theory tells us that in communities of any size, specialisation of the parts is the key to the advance of the whole.

But in spite of all its problems, the pace of development in West Africa has been very fast indeed. It remains to assess the prospects, immediate and long term. In the short term, economic expansion, and with it social advance, is most likely to continue at least at its present rapid pace. For it must be remembered that the rate of advance is, if anything, increasing in recent years as past investment decisions begin to bear fruit. Experience has shown that expansion has almost invariably exceeded the forecasts, even in the agricultural sector. Certain countries, however, are starting from a higher base level and their potential resources are greater. There is thus a gap, which tends to increase, between on the one hand the coastlands and the Forest, and those countries which embrace within their bounds a large proportion of these, and on the other hand the Middle Belt and Sudan, together with the landlocked countries, which contain a high proportion of these zones.

In the longer term, however, forecasting becomes more difficult and estimates show much divergence. The main question is the relationship between economic expansion and population growth. So far, in spite of the spectacular progress, the former has at best only equalled population growth, and in some areas has failed to keep pace. Gross Domestic Product *per capita* has thus remained stationary or even fallen. This will unquestionably delay the date of economic 'take-off', which in any case must vary greatly among countries. What no one can forecast with any accuracy is the date when any West African country, even Côte d'Ivoire, presently the most advanced and the most stable and with the greatest potential resources, can achieve a satisfactory growth rate that will free it from dependence on foreign aid.

The precise model for economic expansion is also a matter on which a wide divergence of views has been expressed. Many are agreed that the agricultural sector is a key to economic advance. But there is no agreement on the means by which productivity per acre and per worker can be increased. In the peasant sector increased output is mainly from more land being taken into cultivation and from increased population.

Industrialisation is even more widely seen as a key, almost as a universal panacea, but there is a division of opinion as to whether industrialisation policy should be principally aimed at small scale enterprises, dispersed with relatively low capital intensity and high labour intensity to 'mop up' the large pool of unemployed, underemployed and persons released from the land by intensification of agriculture, or whether it should be aimed at concentration in a smaller number of large capital intensive plants with low unit-costs.

Those advocating the first mentioned approach point to India as an example, but there are unrecognised differences in the situation. West Africa nowhere has such a pressing population problem. There is not, in sheer numbers, such a huge potential labour force. Nor would even the most radical agricultural reform release large numbers from the land. On the contrary, much of the sub-continent could be said to be underpopulated in many ways. Secondly, rates of pay in West Africa, related to skills and productivity, are not exceptionally low. Indeed in industries such as construction there is a case for considerably more mechanisation. Finally, there is not, as in India, the same widespread tradition of small-scale craft industry and modest capital accumulation. Attempts at over-rapid fostering of small scale industry with government funds have by no means been invariably successful.

On the other hand, many large scale projects have been embarked on for prestige reasons. But scale and capital intensity are needed if the products of manufacturing industry are to compete with imports and not to be permanently high-cost protected by penal import duties. Large scale, modern industry also acts as a training ground for skills at all levels, manual, technical and managerial, as well as creating a climate in which smaller scale industry can flourish.

One is forced to the conclusion that there is no single answer and that, within the framework of regional association which we have suggested is vital, each country must work out a policy most suited to the needs of the regions within its borders.

About the infrastructure there is far less controversy. All are agreed that it is inadequate and that it is a limiting factor in progress. More investment is needed in roads and vehicles, in railways, in ports and their handling equipment and in power plants.

But whatever the long-term future of West Africa, economic advance has been spectacular. This rapid progress, however, must not obscure the two fundamental facts. Firstly, now and for some time yet, the indigenous economies, modified to a lesser or greater extent, form and will form the basis of human activity and endeavour. Secondly, rates of change in the modification of these indigenous economies and of the introduction of methods from abroad vary greatly from region to region.

A geographical approach to the study of the West African economy is thus an essential in the fuller understanding of West African development, and provides the justification for this book among the increasing volume and excellence not only of the economic literature on West Africa, but of geographical literature providing general regional analysis or the economic geography of single aspects of the economy or of single countries.

We have therefore taken the geographical approach to the study of the economy as a whole as our starting point and have sought to outline the geographical factors affecting the distribution of economic activity. We have also sought to identify and analyse the various factors in the economic development of West Africa and to examine the differential rates of their progress.

In addition the time for this book would seem appropriate as the position of economic geography in West Africa has reached something of a watershed. The highly sophisticated techniques that have been developed in recent years within the field of economic geography have been available, but hitherto the supply of data on which they depend has been too limited in scope and accuracy. In certain sectors of the economy and in certain countries the stage is being reached when the supply of data is becoming a sufficient basis for the profitable employment of the new techniques. It is therefore time for stock-taking in the form of geographical analysis of existing knowledge, gathered through traditional studies, and for pointing to some of the gaps in that knowledge that can be filled by applying the new techniques. To cite three such gaps as examples: a fuller knowledge of the processes and consequences of urbanisation is needed; not enough is known about possible regional economic grouping; and we need to know more of the internal structure, development, and functioning of the 'islands' of socio-economic advance.

Our motive in writing this book is our deep interest in and concern for West Africa and our wish to increase understanding of the area, its problems, its difficulties and its successes.

A Select Bibliography

This is intended as a guide to further reading on the geography and the economic theory of under-developed countries, of course with special reference to West Africa. Works referred to in the text are not included. Most books include a good bibliography.

Anyane, S. L., *Ghana Agriculture*, London, 1963.
Amin, S., *Le développement du capitalisme en Côte d'Ivoire*, Paris, 1967.
Badouen, R., *Les banques de développement en Afrique*, Paris, 1964.
Bauer, P. T., *The Study of underdeveloped economies*, London, 1963.
Biebuyck, D. (Edt.), *African agrarian systems*, London, 1960.
Birmingham, W., Naustadt, I. and Omaboe, E. N., *A Study of contemporary Ghana*, (2 vols.) Accra, 1966.
Boserup, E., *The conditions of agricultural growth*, London, 1965.
Buchanan, K. M. and Pugh, J. C., *Land and people in Nigeria*, London, 1955.
Chambers, R. J., *Settlement schemes in tropical Africa*, London, 1969.
Deschamps, H., *Le Sénégal et la Gambie*, Paris, 1964.
Dumont, R., *False start in Africa*, London, 1966.
Fage, J. D., *An Atlas of African history*, London, 1958.
Fage, J. D., *Introduction to the history of West Africa*, Cambridge, 1955.
Gourou, P., *The Tropical World*, London (4th edition), 1966.
Hance, W. A., *African economic development*, London (2nd edition), 1967.
Hailey, Lord, *African Survey, Revised, 1956*, London, 1957.
Harrison Church, R. J., *West Africa*, London (5th edition), 1966.
Kilby, P., *Industrialization in an open economy: Nigeria 1945–1966*, Cambridge, 1969.
Kindleberger, C. P., *Economic Development*, New York, 1966.
Lacoste, Y., *Une géographie du sous-développment*, Paris, 1965.
Lacoste, Y., *Les pays sous développés*, Paris, 1960.
Lacoste, Y., *Perspectives de la géographie active en pays sous développés*, Paris, 1964
Laroch, H., *La Nigeria*, Paris, 1962.
Little, K., *West African Urbanisation*, Cambridge, 1965.
McIlroy, R. J., *An introduction to tropical cash crops*, Ibadan, 1963.
Moss, R. P. (Ed.), *The Soil Resources of Tropical Africa*, Cambridge, 1969.

Mountjoy, A., *Industrialisation and Underdeveloped Countries*, London, 1963.

Myint, H., *The economies of the Developing Countries*, London, 1964

Myrdal, G., *Economic theory and underdeveloped regions*, London, 1957.

Munnich, H., *Fragen der Industrialisierung in Tropish Afrika*. Leipziger Geographische Beiträge, 1965.

Naval Intelligence Division, *French West Africa*. Volume 1. *The Federation*, London, 1943. Volume II. *The Colonies*, London, 1944.

Peterec, R. J., *Dakar and the West African economic development*, New York, 1967.

Richard-Molard, J., *Afrique Occidentale Française*, Paris, 1952.

Rostow, W. W., *The process of economic growth*, Oxford, 1953.

Rostow, W. W., *The stages of economic growth*, Cambridge, 1960.

Rougerie, G., *La Côte d'Ivoire*, Paris, 1964.

Seck, A. and Mondjannagni, A., *L'Afrique Occidentale*, Paris, 1967.

Skinner, S. W., *The agricultural economy of the Ivory Coast*, Washington, 1964.

Stapleton, G. B., *The Wealth of Nigeria*, London, 1958.

Thompson, V. and Adloff, R., *French West Africa*, London, 1958.

Udo, R. K., *The geographical regions of Nigeria*, London, 1969.

Varley, W. J. and White, H. P., *The Geography of Ghana*, London, 1956.

Whetham, E. H. and Currie, J. I., (Eds.), *Readings in the applied economics of Africa*, Cambridge, 1967.

Index